Landing Zones

Landing Zones

Southern Veterans Remember Vietnam

•

James R. Wilson

Duke University Press   *Durham and London 1990*

Library of Congress Cataloging-in-Publication Data
can be found on the last page of this book.

Dedicated to

Carol Ann Elizabeth Drazba, ANC

Her name is on the Wall

Contents

•

Acknowledgments

•

Many men and women throughout the South, veterans and nonveterans alike, contributed freely and generously to the making of this book. To those veterans whose stories do not appear in these pages for varying reasons, I wish to express my sincere appreciation for taking time to talk to me. Thanks are also due Mary J. Abernethy, John H. Adams, William T. Brown, Spencer J. Campbell, Ph.D., Ethel J. Cofer, Chuck Davidson, Harvey D. Fletcher (for permission to quote from *Gather Round Strangers*), David Gillis, William Kirkland, Michael A. Kukler, Maggie Godson, Marilyn Hartman, Bobby Lee Hayes, Patricia Hill, Loren and Libby Levson, the late Wingate H. Lucas, John Pippen, Judith Ruderman, Ph.D., J. David Simpson, Claude and Norma Smith, Larry Spence, Emily Strange, Jean and Goodloe Sutton, Peter Tattersall, Gene Tester, William Thomason, James L. Riggs, Philip Shiman, Lovelea Usack, Kenneth R. Watson, Richard White, Linda Jean Wilson, Gen. Louis H. Wilson, USMC (Ret.), and Aaron Yielding.

To Wanda Lindley, who transcribed the interviews, I am most grateful for consistently accurate and timely work. I am also grateful to William R. Finger, Carol Krucoff, and R. C. Smith, who so ably critiqued the narratives written from those interviews.

And not the least, I extend special thanks to Joanne Ferguson, editor-in-chief of Duke University Press, and to my wife, Betty Leona Krimminger. Joanne is a transplanted Arkansan with a deep interest in the South and its people. I benefited greatly from her gentle encouragement and endless patience. Betty, who accompanied me on more than a few of my interview trips, was throughout the life of this project a source of much wise criticism and many profitable suggestions. I could not have written the book without her.

CHINA

Hanoi

Haiphong

LAOS

Vinh

Vientiane

South China Sea

Udon

DMZ

Quang Tri

Hue

Da Nang

THAILAND

I CORPS

Chu
Lai

Quang Ngai

Kontum

Pleiku

Qui Nhon

II CORPS

CAMBODIA

Ban Me
Thuot

Nha Trang

Phnom Penh

III CORPS

Saigon

IV CORPS

Vung Tau

Can
Tho

Vietnam circa 1969

Introduction

•

If I may take some liberty with the words of Marcel Proust, this oral history is both a remembrance of things past and an evocation of things present. It is a view of the Vietnam War and how that tragic conflict continues to shape the lives of twenty-four southern men and women. Each was a player on the vast stage of the war in Southeast Asia. They range from the best-known commander of the American ground forces in Vietnam, Gen. William C. Westmoreland, a South Carolinian who spent four and a half years in the combat zone, to Danny Riels, a fellow Mississippian who was in-country less than six weeks before suffering a paralyzing wound in his first battle. Whether general or private, all speak honestly and forthrightly about what has become known to a generation of Americans as the Vietnam Experience.

The genesis of this book dates from the mid-1980s, when I was working on a master's degree in the Liberal Studies program at Duke University. In readings for a course taught by Dr. Alex Roland, a history professor who served as a marine officer in Vietnam, I came across undocumented claims that southerners went to Vietnam in larger numbers than their comrades from other regions of the United States. In fact, they did.

If the South may be defined as the eleven states of the Confederacy, as it is for the purposes of this book, these states were home to almost one of every three soldiers, sailors, marines, and airmen who served in Vietnam from January 1, 1965, to March 31, 1973. In terms of numbers, the South provided 825,000 of the 2,594,200 Americans who went to Vietnam, or 31 percent at a time when the region had less than 25 percent of the U.S. population.[1] Southerners also died in disproportionate numbers. The war

1. In 1981 the Veterans Administration estimated the number of veterans with service in

cost the South 15,437 dead, about 28 percent of the 55,622 American servicemen and women who died in Vietnam. (A total of 58,479 Americans died in South Vietnam, North Vietnam, Laos, Cambodia, and China.)[2] Without in any way denigrating the sacrifices made by other regions of the United States, it may be fairly said the South shouldered more than its share of the human cost of Vietnam.

The key to understanding the South's contribution to the war, notes Owen W. Gilman, Jr., in the *Encyclopedia of Southern Culture*, can be found in the region's fundamental belief that a cause must be served with honor. Beginning with the American Revolution and continuing through the wars that followed, southerners have been among the first to take up arms for their country. The Mexican War was fought largely by southerners under the command of Gen. Winfield Scott, a Virginian. The Civil War led to the creation of the South's own army and navy, as well as a flag and an anthem that still evoke the romance of the Lost Cause. Most of the great captains of that era, Generals Robert E. Lee and Thomas J. "Stonewall" Jackson foremost among them, were southerners. In World War I, Sgt. Alvin York, a sharpshooting Tennessee mountaineer, earned immortality for his self-effacing bravery, and in the much larger conflict that followed twenty years later, Lt. Audie Murphy, a Texan, won more medals for valor than any other American soldier. Vietnam was no exception when it came to southern courage on the battlefield: 29 percent of the Medals of Honor went to soldiers from Dixie.[3]

Southerners inducted into the armed forces during the war usually stayed in the region for their basic and advanced training. Major combat and combat-support training bases were in Alabama, Georgia, Florida, Louisiana, Texas, and the Carolinas. Swollen with trainees destined for

---

Vietnam by their home states as follows: Alabama, 59,000; Arkansas, 30,000; Florida, 117,000; Georgia, 60,000; Louisiana, 59,000; Mississippi, 30,000; North Carolina, 89,000; South Carolina, 58,000; Tennessee, 58,000; Texas, 205,000; Virginia, 60,000. See *Data on Vietnam Era Veterans* (Washington, D.C.: Veterans Administration, Office of Reports and Statistics, 1981), 7. The figure for the total number of U.S. troops who served in Vietnam appears in *Selected Manpower Statistics* (Washington, D.C.: Department of Defense, Directorate for Information Operations and Control, 1976), 60.

2. Deaths by state: Alabama, 1,216; Arkansas, 591; Florida, 1,619; Georgia, 1,585; Louisiana, 887; Mississippi, 643; North Carolina, 1,614; South Carolina, 902; Tennessee, 1,302; Texas, 3,427; Virginia, 1,309. These figures, current to 1985, were compiled from Defense Department records by Michael A. Kukler. Author's interview with Michael A. Kukler, publisher, *The Vietnam Veteran*, Gastonia, N.C., April 23, 1989.

3. Owen W. Gilman, Jr., "Vietnam War," in *Encyclopedia of Southern Culture* (Chapel Hill: University of North Carolina Press, 1989).

Vietnam, these bases fed a war-induced prosperity; by 1967, 42 percent of the stateside military payroll was going to soldiers stationed throughout the southern states.[4] Twenty years later, the region was still home to many Defense Department bases. Georgia alone, for example, had twelve major installations.

While patriotism undoubtedly led many southerners into the military in the 1960s, another, more coercive force also had an impact on them: the draft. Poor whites and blacks who could not gain the deferments offered by college or marriage found themselves particularly exposed to conscription. For more than a few of these men necessity assumed the mantle of virtue, for they saw in military service a way out of the poverty they had known all their lives. Eventually the draft reached into all social and economic classes. When his letter came from the draft board, Atlanta mortgage banker Jack Candler, a member of one of that city's First Families, reported for service, as the vast majority of southerners did. He went not with fervor for a war he knew little about or had any personal stake in, but because he believed it was his duty to go.

Candler and most other southerners went to Vietnam when the South nurtured a strong vision of itself as a place deliberately apart from and suspicious of mainstream America. By the late 1960s the rest of the country had come to regard the South as little more than a sullen redneck bastion hostile to social and political change, a view that grew out of the region's sometimes violent resistance to the black struggle for civil and voting rights. The struggle for equality went on throughout the war years, becoming in effect if not name a revolution that changed the social and political landscape of the South. Ironically, it was on the killing fields of Vietnam that many southerners, white and black, at last saw through the wall separating them. They realized that enemy bullets offered equal opportunity for death, as Charlie Earl Bodiford, who grew up in racially troubled Selma, Alabama, makes clear in his account.

Because southerners sensed they were outsiders twice over in Vietnam, it was not unusual for them to seek each other out and coalesce into informal groups within their units. Some even carried the most vivid and controversial icon of the South, the Confederate battle flag, into combat on tanks and armored personnel carriers. A Viet Cong guerrilla or a North Vietnamese soldier seeing the Stars and Bars whipping back and forth on a radio antenna for the first time no doubt feared the Americans had picked up a new ally. Unfortunately, the battle flag took on a more onerous

4. Ibid.

meaning in the relatively secure rear areas, where racial tension sometimes sparked confrontations between whites and blacks in the latter years of the war. While the flag undoubtedly was a symbol of white supremacy to some soldiers, for others it may have had a more profound meaning. Spencer J. Campbell, a Louisiana psychologist who fought in Vietnam as a marine, has suggested that to these soldiers, the battle flag was an old symbol pressed into the service of a new Lost Cause.

Southerners also took another provincial hallmark to Vietnam: their music. From the Demilitarized Zone to the Mekong Delta, Armed Forces Radio blanketed Vietnam with the lonesome, often propagandistic wail of country music. Songs such as Loretta Lynn's "Dear Uncle Sam" and Stonewall Jackson's "The Minute Men Are Turning in Their Graves" tried, with varying success, to explain why America was fighting in Vietnam. As late as 1970, Merle Haggard's "Okie from Muskogee," a pro-war song first performed at Fort Bragg, North Carolina, quickly climbed to number one on the country music charts. By expressing the South's support for Vietnam even as the rest of America wrote it off as a national debacle, such songs helped create a social and political milieu that generally made it easier for southern veterans to come home than their comrades from other parts of the country.[5]

However history finally judges Vietnam, the war likely will continue to defy easy analysis or categorization. At its most basic level, Vietnam was both a guerrilla war of small, violent firefights and a conventional war of large pitched battles. It can be divided roughly into three main periods: 1961 to 1965, when the American effort was small and mainly advisory; 1965 to 1969, the period of the military buildup, the Tet Offensive, and the beginning of withdrawal; and 1969 to 1972, Vietnamization and the departure of the last American ground combat units. The order of the twenty-four narratives in the book generally follows this chronology.

Edited from interview transcripts, each narrative consists of three divisions: what the veteran was doing before entering the armed forces (or if already in the military, his or her circumstances before going to Vietnam), what happened in the war zone, and how the Vietnam experience affected life in the years afterward. The narratives were selected from fifty-three interviews I conducted from July 1988 to February 1989. Almost half of the interviews were made in August 1988 during a 5,000-mile journey through nine southern states.

5. Melton McLaurin, "Country Music and the Vietnam War," *Perspectives on the American South* (New York: Gordon and Breach, 1985), 3:153.

In the course of my travels, which eventually took me some twelve thousand miles throughout the South, I was heartened to see how much Vietnam veterans are doing for themselves, both collectively and individually. In Lafayette, Louisiana, State Representative Odon L. Bacque, a former Green Beret officer who served in Vietnam, told me how he organized a "welcome home" celebration for fellow veterans in the bayou country, then went on to sponsor a series of self-help programs for veterans. In Birmingham, I joined thirteen members of the Alabama State Council of the Vietnam Veterans of America on a Saturday afternoon as they debated ways to gain a seat on the board of the state Department of Veterans Affairs. Their chairman was Park Barton, a respected Tuscaloosa attorney who flew helicopters in Vietnam in 1969–70. Representation on the state board was vital, Barton told me, because "by 1992 Vietnam veterans will be the largest group of veterans in Alabama." On the east coast of Florida, Chuck Davidson, badly shot up when the Viet Cong attacked his river patrol boat in the Mekong Delta in 1967, contributes three hundred dollars a month of his disability pension to help homeless Vietnam veterans in Melbourne. "A lot of these veterans are tumbling in and out of marriage and family breakups," Davidson said one night as we visited a homeless veteran and his family camping in a city park. "They are also enduring long firefights with the bureaucrats of the Veterans Administration."

These examples, which can be multiplied many times, reminded me that wherever or however a Vietnam veteran may live, the war continues to have a long reach. Among the southern men and women whose stories appear here, that reach spans almost thirty years. For most, the war entered their lives in the mid-1960s, shortly after graduation from high school or college. It is no exaggeration to say that Vietnam became a war of the young after 1965; the average age of the Americans who fought there was nineteen, compared to twenty-six in World War II. Vietnam evolved into a war of teenagers, not only for the Americans but also for the Vietnamese who fought against them.

The Vietnam I knew lasted for sixteen months during 1966–67, when I was an army press officer with Headquarters, U.S. Army Vietnam, in Saigon; with the Third Brigade of the Fourth Division, at the Michelin rubber plantation northwest of the city; and with the forward headquarters of the First Cavalry Division, in coastal Binh Dinh province. Unlike most soldiers and marines who stayed in one area during their tour of duty—and for whom that area became Vietnam—I had a military job that allowed me to travel throughout much of the country. Accordingly, I was able to see the full sweep of a war that may well be, as General Westmoreland notes in this book, a crossroads in American military history.

Like most Vietnam veterans, I went to the war alone and I came home alone. And like most others, in the years afterward I rarely talked about what I saw and experienced in the combat zone—I sealed the war in a compartment, a place of safekeeping for which only I had the key. As I conducted the interviews for this book, interviews that not infrequently called forth spirits from the vasty deep for both my subjects and myself, I began to understand that Vietnam has at last become a shared experience for all whose lives were touched by its fire.

Along the way to these words, I learned much about Vietnam, about what went wrong and what went right. But more than anything else, I came away from writing this book with enormous admiration and compassion for the men and women of the South who went to the war, who on the whole performed so well, and who ultimately gave so much of themselves for so little. May each find a safe landing zone.

Chapel Hill, North Carolina
March 12, 1990

Gather round strangers
and take heed
what I have to tell you
is not for the squeamish
come I shall enlighten you
to things that will
make you laugh
that will amaze you
and cause you to cry
and after all is said
I desire not
your sympathy
nor want rejection
I ask not
for your judgment
just understanding.
—*Harvey D. Fletcher, USMC (Ret.)*
Raleigh, North Carolina
Vietnam 1967–68, 1970–71

Edward E. Bridges

Alexandria, Virginia

Army Special Forces, 1962–63

●

Ed Bridges and I spent the better part of a Saturday in a Chinese restaurant in Petersburg, Virginia, as we talked about the early days of the war. A polite, stocky man dressed in a gray sleeveless sweater and slacks, Ed was a member of Special Forces Detachment A-113, an Okinawa-based Green Beret unit ordered to South Vietnam late in 1961. Under the aegis of the CIA, the detachment established the first of many Civilian Irregular Defense Group (CIDG) programs, beginning at a small Montagnard village in the Central Highlands. CIDG soon spread the length of Vietnam as it sought to combine village defense with social and political measures designed to win the "hearts and minds" of the people.

Ed went to Vietnam at a time when it was no more than a name on the map to most Americans. In a sense, our meeting in an oriental restaurant in Petersburg to talk about Vietnam seemed oddly appropriate, for it was from Petersburg that Robert E. Lee's Army of Northern Virginia retreated to Appomattox in April 1865. Now Ed and I had met to talk about another divisive conflict a hundred years later that also ended as a lost cause.

As he spread a collection of Vietnam snapshots on the table, Ed told me he left college to enlist in the army in 1958. "I had finished my junior year in mechanical engineering at Mississippi State University, but I didn't go back to school in the fall because I was undecided about what I wanted to do," he said. "I thought going into the army would give me time to mature and gain a better understanding of what I wanted out of life." After earning the gold bars of a second lieutenant at officers' candidate school in 1960, a series of assignments led him into Special Forces.

"During my training at Fort Bragg," Ed said, "I went through a longer and more thorough training program than did many people who came along later. This is only speculation on my part, of course, but I think we had more time for training before Vietnam got into full swing." Among the techniques he learned was how to make explosives and chemical agents from off-the-shelf ingredients such as household bleach, agricultural fertilizer, and aluminum filings.

Today, the young Special Forces lieutenant who went to Vietnam with a sense of high adventure twenty-eight years ago is the chief executive officer of Sea Farm Group, Ltd., a shrimp aquaculture project in Guatemala. Ed Bridges's CIA-directed war had come before the big-unit, high-casualty conflict that I went into in 1966: only 246 Americans died from hostile action in South Vietnam between 1960 and 1964. The Vietnam War he knew may have been different and less lethal than the war that burst forth in 1965, but it nonetheless demanded as full a measure of courage.

I was at Fort Bragg in 1961 when President Kennedy came down to officially give Special Forces the Green Beret. One of the demonstrations we put on for him and the press during his visit included catching, cooking, and eating snakes. That's how Special Forces picked up the nickname "snake eaters." That didn't help our image with a lot of old-line army officers. They considered Special Forces types unruly and undisciplined. In their opinion, we appeared to break unit tactics and commit a host of other operational sins. Outwardly, we probably did come across that way, but in fact we exercised a lot of internal self-discipline. We were individuals who had to act in concert for the common good of our units. We were, in a way, the entrepreneurs of the army—very flexible but totally committed to our mission.

We felt we were unique in the army. During the 1961–62 era, there weren't many of us because most Special Forces groups, which were authorized 1,250 officers and men, weren't at full strength.

I had applied to be released from active duty in 1961, but was kept on extended duty after the Bay of Pigs affair in April of that year. As a result, I found myself with an assignment to the First Special Forces Group on Okinawa, which already had a B-Team in the Danang area of South Vietnam. This unit of twenty-four officers and men was providing counterinsurgency training for the Nung Chinese who lived around Danang.

I took a couple of weeks' leave at home before going to Okinawa in early November of 1961. My father, who had a cotton plantation near Greenville, Mississippi, was ill at the time, and I wanted to be with him. He told me he was very proud that I was in the army and was going to Okinawa. My mother, on the other hand, never said much about it.

A few days before Christmas, I was promoted to first lieutenant and assigned to Detachment A-113 as its executive officer. I also got my orders for Vietnam. A-113 consisted of two officers and ten enlisted men, all sergeants and above. My commanding officer, Captain Ron Shackleton, and half of the team left Okinawa for Vietnam at the end of 1961; I followed in January with the rest of the men. We knew our team would be one of two under the operational command of the Combined Studies and Observation Group, a CIA operation in Vietnam.

I looked forward to going to Vietnam. In the fall of 1961, the United States had about thirty-two hundred highly professional military people in South Vietnam, most of them in some kind of advisory role. Few of them were outside Saigon and the other big cities. I had started thinking about making the army a career, and I remembered a popular saying among young officers: "Long wars make young majors." Maybe I was both naive and gung-ho enough to think I could get the gain without the pain.

When I left Okinawa with my half of the team, we went to the Philippines for a three-day stopover that included getting visas for entry into South Vietnam. It was a fairly formal process that later seemed something of a joke, at least when you take into account what our mission was. In addition, I had already turned in most of my army-issue clothing. I walked off the airplane in Saigon in khakis that had no insignia of rank on them. I and the other members of my team spent our first few days in Vietnam at a CIA safe house near Tan Son Nhut Airport. The safe house was a two-story villa used by Special Forces people passing through Saigon. It had a yard big enough to park several vehicles and was enclosed by a high wall for security. I remember it as a comfortable place with a living room, dining room, and central stairway that spiraled up to a balconied second floor, where the bedrooms and bathrooms were located. It had belonged to a French colonial planter of some means.

We didn't have time to see much of Saigon. We spent most of our time getting briefings from the Combined Studies people and preparing to move north to link up with the rest of A-113. In early 1962, Combined Studies was pretty optimistic about the progress of the war. Our job was to "win the hearts and minds of the people," in this case the Montagnards, to keep them from going over to the Viet Cong. Unfortunately, the Vietnamese had created a lot of resentment among the "Yards" by resettling refugees from North Vietnam on tribal lands. The French, for the most part, had kept the Vietnamese out of the highlands.

On our third day in-country, we boarded an old World War II–era C-46 transport at Tan Son Nhut and flew up to Ban Me Thuot airport, which was near a small village of thatch-roof huts called Boun Enao. That's where our advance party had set up shop. Since the whole countryside was under the control of the Viet Cong, we had to move fast to arm and train the Montagnards for self-defense. We also finished the fortification of Boun Enao, work that had been started by the villagers before my team's arrival. We built elephant traps, berms, punji stake pits, and bamboo fences. We also burned or cut all the vegetation around the village to clear fields of fire. By the time we finished it, the camp resembled forts built by the army during the Indian Wars.

Boun Enao was the model for the Civilian Irregular Defense Group or "Sidgee" concept. The village got to be a popular tour stop for people like Defense Secretary Robert McNamara and General Maxwell Taylor, as well as some other Kennedy administration figures. McNamara, incidentally, struck me as a very headstrong, impatient man who rarely let other people get a word in edgewise.

When we first got to Boun Enao, we knew very little about Montagnard culture, and what we did know was very general. A-113 was assigned to work with the Rhade, Jarai, and Mnong tribes. Of the three, the Rhade and the Jarai were the largest tribal groups in the highlands. We soon got to know a lot about all three tribes, not only from the people themselves, but also from missionaries in the area. The missionaries, who represented most major religious denominations, helped us learn the languages and different customs of each tribe. We learned enough about the languages, in fact, to compile a dictionary for our group headquarters in Okinawa. Some of the missionaries, who had no interest in the political situation in Vietnam and wanted only to help the Montagnards, were killed by the VC. I could only admire the way the survivors went on with their work in the face of that kind of danger.

Our Combined Studies case officer was David Nuttle, an agricultural adviser from Kansas who had worked for the International Voluntary Service. He had been recruited by Combined Studies because of his impressive knowledge of the Montagnards and the Central Highlands. Nuttle made sure Combined Studies supplied us with weapons, ammunition, and money to pay the irregular troops we were training. Our weapons included German, Danish, American, and Swedish submachine guns, as well as .30-caliber carbines and other World War II equipment. We even had some bolt-action Springfield rifles. Most of our problems were not with the weapons themselves, but in trying to hold down the types of ammunition. We had .30-caliber, .45-caliber, and 9mm, but some weapons of the same caliber used different ammunition, such as the 9mm short round. For heavy weapons, we later got some 60mm mortars and 75mm pack howitzers.

Combined Studies never told us the nuts and bolts of how to accomplish our mission. We would be told, "This is the objective in this area and we need it done within this period of time." We then got an outline of the resources the agency thought we would need to accomplish the mission. Our weapons, ammunition, money, and sometimes uniforms would be brought in by airplane or dropped to us by parachute if necessary. After a while, though, we found it easier to buy most of our supplies, except for weapons and ammunition, at the local markets. While this policy helped create good relations with the villagers, it also turned one of my NCOs into quite a supply artist. I didn't care where he got what we needed, so long as he came back with the right number of "tiger suit" uniforms or whatever he went off for.

At first, we didn't run combat operations out of Buon Enao. Our job was to train the Montagnards to fight the VC and keep an eye on infiltration along the Cambodian and Laotian borders. After four months, though, we had enough trained Montagnards to begin running patrols. We used them because we had so few Vietnamese to work with; most Special Forces camps had only one or two Vietnamese assigned to them. The Montagnards made excellent soldiers, in my opinion. Many of them had been fighting since they were eleven or twelve years old. They were very good at small unit tactics and seemed to know instinctively how to protect their flanks. In a way, combat was almost like a family situation with them: you protect your brother and your brother protects you. There were no heroes among them, either. Everybody worked together as a team. I found them very brave under fire. They wouldn't hesitate to run out and help a team member who was in trouble.

Yet, in another sense, the Montagnards were like children. They took a very simplistic approach to almost everything. For instance, they practiced an animistic religion in which the issues of life and death held a meaning quite different from our way of thinking. Life to them was a series of stages, and death was nothing more than the means of moving from one stage to another. They were also a very competitive people who basically saw the world in terms of good guys and bad guys. If you were one of the good guys, then you got their total support. If you were one of the bad guys, they wouldn't work with you. In fact, they might even work against you. The Vietnamese government learned that in 1964 during the so-called Montagnard Uprising.

On our first patrols, we carried C- and K-rations and a lot of rice. The longer we stayed in-country, the less inclined we were to carry canned rations. Their weight began to mount up on ten-day or two-week patrols, when our feet had to carry us the whole way. We finally started using improvised rice bags—two GI socks filled with rice. We supplemented our "rice diet" with powdered vegetables and dried shrimp that we bought in the markets.

We had to do a lot of improvisation. We learned how to make our own early versions of the jungle boot because regular leather boots were too heavy and promoted some nasty fungal infections. We experimented with everything from L. L. Bean moccasins in the beginning to an invention of one of my team members, who made jungle boots by putting a piece of sheet metal between the rubber sole and innersole of high-top canvas sneakers. Later, we refined his design with old tire treads sewn to the soles for better traction. The metal plate provided some protection against punji stakes.

We also learned how to make stationary bazookas for the defense of Buon Enao. We could get plenty of 3.5-inch bazooka rounds, but the launchers themselves were hard to come by. They were also easy to bend or break. We made our rocket launchers by nailing two boards together at right angles and anchoring them in the ground at a thirty-degree angle. Then, after taking the rocket motors off high-explosive bazooka rounds, we attached them to a length of split bamboo big enough to hold two grenades. We took the pins out of the grenades and, with the safety handles still in place, put the bamboo around them. We bound the bamboo with rubber strips to hold the whole package together. Sure, it didn't have very good flight characteristics, but it was a nice little piece of defensive destruction out to fifty yards or so.

Homemade napalm was another specialty. We made it from GI soap and gasoline with a little Composition-4 thrown in for good measure. A little dicey to make, but very effective.

Four Special Forces people died in Vietnam during my first three months there. They didn't die while advising, nor did they die from an overdose of small talk. People can say what they will, but Combined Studies and Special Forces were basically running the tactical part of the war in early 1962. I think the MAAG people were either envious of our role or resented what we were doing—I never could decide which.

I didn't have any direct contact with the VC until March or April of 1962, when I was on a patrol that went into a village controlled by them. The villagers were being used much like slave laborers to grow food for the

VC. Our job was to round up the people and move them out of the area, then burn the crops in the fields. While we were doing all this, we suddenly heard gunshots. The VC had been out of the village when we got there, but they came back in a hurry when they spotted the smoke from the burning fields. Although our main responsibility was to remove the villagers, we returned the VC fire and chased them for a short distance. They didn't seem very inclined to press the issue.

In April of 1962, Combined Studies temporarily split A-113 and I moved with several of my men to Phoc Tinh, near Cam Rahn Bay. Our objective, at least as I understood it, was to set up village defense forces in the area, start recruiting an intelligence-gathering network, and run limited patrols. We stayed there two months until an A-Team came in from Okinawa to take over what we had started.

With A-113 at full strength again in the highlands, we moved to a different area to help open Highway 14, the main north-south link between Ban Me Thuot and Loc Tien. We set up a Montagnard training camp halfway between the two towns. As we trained more and more people, we began to leapfrog our way to Loc Tien with temporary camps. Loc Tien was where Bao Dai, the last emperor of Vietnam, had his summer palace. When we got there in August, we were confident we had accomplished something strategically important on the Darlac Plateau.

August was also the month A-113 finished its temporary duty in Vietnam. At the time, our reason for being there was still not very clear to me. But that wasn't much of an issue for me. I was in an elite outfit and saw Vietnam as more high adventure than anything else. I wasn't looking for the big picture. My team went back to Okinawa for three weeks of debriefings that also included very thorough medical examinations. We passed on whatever pearls of wisdom we had picked up about the nature of the conflict in Vietnam and then took some leave before training began for a new assignment. I was one of those fortunate enough to go down to Malaysia to attend the British Jungle Warfare School operated by the SAS, the Special Air Service. The British told us a lot about the Malaysian Communist insurgency in the 1950s, which they were successful in putting down, and we shared information about our experiences in Vietnam.

I went back to Vietnam with A-113 in January of 1963. This time, I knew a lot more about the political situation, why we were there, and what we were supposed to accomplish. The U.S. now had twenty-two thousand men in-country and a military effort that was better organized than it had been a year earlier.

I went back to a hotter war. The VC were clearly getting substantial logistical support not only from North Vietnam, but also from China and the Soviet Union. In 1962, the VC were served by a primitive supply system. They relied on booby traps made from bamboo and other local materials that didn't use a grain of gunpowder. A year later, the VC were shouldering AK-47s and 82mm Chinese mortars, and they were soon to get RPGs. I considered them good fighters to begin with, but now they were getting better. They knew their home ground and how to take tactical advantage of it. They knew how to terrorize and intimidate. And they were tough to get information out of. Very few of the VC captives that I saw ever broke down under interrogation.

The North Vietnamese were moving down the Ho Chi Minh Trail in considerable numbers. My team became part of the Trailwatcher program, responsible for keeping an eye on various sectors of the trail from the Laotian border down to the French leprosarium at Di Linh. Using small cameras equipped with heat sensors, we were able to get some idea of how heavily the trail was being used. The trail itself was described by one of my team members as "about four bicycles wide," but some stretches of it were big enough for trucks. This was especially true in areas of high jungle. Over the years, the North Vietnamese had tied tree branches together in these areas to hide the trail from aircraft.

By mid-1963, our Special Forces operations began to feel the first effects of the Regular Army mentality. We could see that the war was evolving away from an unconventional conflict into one of large-unit battles. Moreover, we were being pressured to dress and act more like regular soldiers. We didn't understand this interference in our way of doing things; there seemed to be no rhyme or reason to these changes. Maybe it all went back to the belief in the army that you don't have to tell junior officers why, just what to do, but I think a lot of us resented being reined in because we believed we were winning against the Viet Cong.

In my opinion, 1963 was a decisive year for the United States in Vietnam. I was in Nha Trang in November when the coup against President Ngo Dinh Diem took place. Security was very tight—nobody went in or out of our compound. The ARVN brought in an airborne battalion to secure the airfield and other military installations. No matter who was in the presidential palace, security had to be maintained. To make matters worse, President Kennedy was killed about three weeks later. It was a very hard time for all of us Americans, of course. But from the standpoint of the war, I've come to feel that Kennedy let us down to some degree, and I'm certain many other Special Forces people feel the same way. Kennedy had promised a lot to us when we got the Green Beret at Fort Bragg, but when the "old guard" army began to press him for a bigger role in the war, his support for Special Forces began to fade. I know this is a rather simplistic view of a very complicated situation, but it's the way I felt then and the way I feel today.

The high spot of the Vietnam War for me was meeting the woman who would become my wife. Jacqueline was living in Saigon with her parents. Her father was a retired army lieutenant colonel who worked for the U.S. Information Agency. I met her at an old French club called the Cercle Sportif during a short leave in the city, and I couldn't get her out of my mind. We were married three years later.

Saigon was full of interesting people in 1963. One of them was Col. Arthur "Bull" Simon, who led the helicopter raid in 1970 on the Son Tay Prison Camp in North Vietnam. He spent several days at the safe house, which gave me a chance to get to know him. Simon had spent World War II in the Philippines as a guerrilla, and he believed that had kept him from the rank and recognition that he deserved. He said he would have been better off if he'd thrown in the towel with the army and joined the CIA after the war. Although Simon was a man who thought out one problem at a time, he had a clear understanding of the enemy in Vietnam. I thought he possessed a superb tactical mind.

I had decided by late 1963 to get out of the army and go back to college. Even though I was on the promotion list for captain, I knew that there wasn't much chance of advancement in the army without a degree, and I didn't want to stay in without that basic qualification for getting a general's star. Beyond that, Special Forces officers were perceived by the promotion boards as outside the mainstream of the army, a view that led to its own problems with advancement.

At the end of the year, I left the army and resumed my studies at Mississippi State University. I received a bachelor of arts degree in history and mathematics, with a minor in languages, in August of 1964. But I wasn't through with the army. When I went back to college, I joined a Special Forces detachment of the Mississippi National Guard in Jackson. In the fall of 1964, I was at Fort Bragg for a parachute jumpmaster course when the Montagnard Uprising occurred. I managed to make several jumps, but most of my time was spent writing biographies of the Montagnard leaders. I had known most of them.

As I look back over almost thirty years, I think we made a serious mistake when we converted the Vietnam conflict into a high-stakes game. So long as it was small stakes, nobody—especially the Soviets—was going to pay much attention to it. But when Vietnam became a matter of national prestige, it also became a very different war. I believe we were fighting a winnable war as late as 1964, but then it got out of control: every time we raised the ante, the other side put even more chips on the table. The Soviets have now learned the same lesson in Afghanistan.

If we intended to win in Vietnam, we should have kept the objective in mind and been prepared to pay the price to achieve it. And what was the objective? To destroy the enemy's capability to make war—and that we didn't do. We never faced up to that most basic principle of war. If you stop to think about it, the same thing happened in the Civil War. The South didn't want to conquer the North; it just wanted to make the North stop fighting. The North, on the other hand, set out to destroy the South's capability to wage war.

And like the Civil War, Vietnam basically tore the fabric of this country apart. I can never truly sympathize with those who went to Canada and other countries, who packed up and ran away from their obligation to the society in which they lived. I have no argument, though, with those who gained legal deferments to stay out of the war. They don't bother me. Nor do I have a problem with Jane Fonda. Sure, she did a lot of things that I oppose and even condemn, but I do respect her right to say and do what she did. That was her right as a citizen of the United States.

Vietnam was not without some personal value to me. I learned how to survive, and that lesson has had an indelible imprint on my life ever since. I learned that it's important not only to accomplish your mission or goal, but to stay alive to accomplish it. If you stay alive but only partially accomplish your goal, you can come back the next day and try again.

I think of myself very much as a Vietnam veteran, even though I was in a different war from the one that began in 1965. As a member of the Special Forces, my war was a very personal one because I worked so closely with the people of South Vietnam. I felt very ashamed when we pulled out in 1975. Maybe being a southerner has something to do with it, but I deeply believe in honoring a commitment. We didn't do that. Whatever price we paid, the Vietnamese people paid far more than we will ever know.

Gen. William C. Westmoreland

Charleston, South Carolina

COMUSMACV, 1964–68

•

I parked my car on Tradd Street, a couple of blocks from the Battery in Charleston's Historic District, moments before my two o'clock appointment on a Friday afternoon with the South Carolinian who commanded the American ground war in South Vietnam from June 1964 until July 1968. A few butterflies whirred in my stomach at the prospect of interviewing General Westmoreland, whom I remembered from my months in Saigon as COMUSMACV, an inaccessible, austere figure of near-Olympian power. Suddenly, a blue Buick sedan wheeled into a parking space as I walked up to the house where Westmoreland and his wife have lived since his retirement in 1972 as army chief of staff. A large bumper sticker on the rear of the Buick caught my eye: "I am a Vietnam Veteran."

Westmoreland stepped out of the car and greeted me warmly. "Have you been waiting?" he asked. I assured him I had not. Still trim and ramrod-straight in his mid-seventies, he retains the habits born of four decades in the army. "Westy" doesn't believe in keeping people waiting, and by the same token he doesn't expect to be kept waiting by them.

In an elegant drawing room dominated by an oil portrait of Katherine "Kitsy" Westmoreland, his wife of forty-two years, we took our places on a small sofa and talked about the war. Through a pair of French doors, I could see a spacious, brick-walled garden and a small building that houses Westmoreland's office. There, he spends about twenty hours a week on Vietnam and related matters.

As the interview unfolded, a Westmoreland quite different from the one known to most Americans during the Vietnam era began to emerge. His may be a face that belongs on Mount Rushmore, as someone once said, but the private Westmoreland is quite a different man, possessed of a warmth and wit that would disarm many of his critics. Several times during our conversation, the general paused to purse his lips and gaze through the French doors as he thought about an answer to one of my questions. The war is never very far away from the nation's "number one Vietnam veteran," as he sometimes calls himself. Sitting there with him, I realized that I was not only with the Westmoreland of the big battles and the celebrated libel suit against CBS, but also with the only American general who, as the journalist Laura Palmer noted, fought first for his country, and then for the reputation of his soldiers.

After the Korean War, I was on the General Staff at a time when a lot of correspondence was going back and forth within the government on what to do, if anything, about the French predicament in Indochina. This was before the fall of Dien Bien Phu in 1954 and the Geneva Accords that led to the partition of Vietnam. I knew what was going on in Indochina, and I was convinced that the logistical support we were giving the French was akin to trying to stop a juggernaut with a T-model Ford. It was a feeling that we were just pecking away at the problem of Indochina, that anything we could do to affect the situation there was not going to be very significant.

Also during this time I attended a very vivid doom-and-gloom briefing given to General Matthew Ridgway by the surgeon general of the army. He had studied the health and disease problems of the French in Southeast Asia and was very pessimistic about the ability of Americans to survive in that climate. I didn't buy that kind of thinking at all; the French had been in Indochina for almost a hundred years. But I have long believed Ridgway's thinking was deeply influenced by that briefing because he took a strong stand not long afterward against sending troops to rescue the French. To what extent his recommendation influenced the Eisenhower administration's overall decision not to send troops, I have no idea.

From the Pentagon, I moved to take command of the 101st Airborne Division at Fort Campbell, Kentucky, in 1958. While there, I started what I called the Recondo School, which emphasized small-unit combat against guerrillas. The name Recondo is a contraction of "reconnaissance-commando" and I insisted that everything the troops learned in that school be put to good use in training. To do that, the staff always cranked a counterinsurgency scenario into the 101st's maneuvers. So what I am really saying is that I and my officers were aware of the nature of revolutionary warfare well before Vietnam. We knew Chairman Mao's three-phase doctrine of war, and I for one later kept his Little Red Book near my bedside. I also made it a point to learn the theories of Sun Tzu, the ancient Chinese philosopher, who placed great emphasis on the psychological elements of battle.

During this time, too, the Special Warfare School was established at Fort Bragg. Special warfare and the Green Berets got a lot of attention in the Kennedy administration. I was the superintendent at West Point when President Kennedy came up to give the commencement address to the class of 1962. He said the army of the future would be fighting guerrillas, and it took special training to be able to do that successfully. Even before I became commander of MACV two years later, I could see Mao's three-phase doctrine of revolutionary war at work in South Vietnam. Phase One had started out with guerrillas and political cadres at the local level; Phase Two had involved recruiting forces for hit-and-run warfare against the government to weaken it at all levels; and Phase Three, the direction in which the insurgency was clearly moving, called for conventional war undertaken to defeat regular army units and seize and hold terrain.

Hanoi's propaganda machine, which had its psychological warfare headquarters in Paris, as well as a substantial satellite operation later in Stockholm, claimed that the guerrilla war in South Vietnam was home-grown. Anybody who took the trouble to investigate that claim could see that the war in South Vietnam was being directed from Hanoi. There was little homegrown about it. By 1963, North Vietnamese regulars were streaming down the Ho Chi Minh Trail into South Vietnam—Phase Three of Mao's doctrine. Of course, the image that Hanoi wanted to convey to the rest of the world—and in this it was very successful—was one of a bunch of rag-tag guerrillas supported by the peasants. The Phase Three part of the insurgency was conveniently left out of that propaganda. Those of us on the ground in South Vietnam didn't fall for Hanoi's propaganda at all. And how was the war eventually won after American troops were withdrawn? By North Vietnamese troops, well-equipped and well-disciplined, coming down from the North to the South.

In fact, if we had been militarily organized in Vietnam according to the propaganda perceptions of the Communist insurgency when the Tet Of-fensive took place in 1968, we'd have been wiped off the map. Tet would have been a total disaster for us instead of the victory it was. You don't de-feat well-organized platoons, companies, and battalions of the enemy, sup-ported by rockets and artillery, with small groups of counterguerrilla troops. The North Vietnamese and the Viet Cong had begun moving boldly into Phase Three in 1964, and by the summer of 1965 they were so strong that an average of one ARVN battalion a week was being rendered ineffective.

I was not naive about the nature of the Vietnam War. I knew that the support of the American people was essential if we were to achieve success in Vietnam. I spent my first six weeks in-country traveling around and talking to hundreds of people to get a good feel for the situation. Just before I was appointed COMUSMACV, I had a one-on-one meeting with Defense Secretary McNamara at the old U.S. embassy in Saigon—I think he wanted to size me up and see if I was the right man to replace General Harkins—and I told him how I felt about the war at that point.

"Mr. Secretary," I said, "I've come to the strong conclusion that this is going to be a long war. It is a herculean task that we face and unless something is done to keep the American people aboard, we will not succeed."

McNamara listened quietly.

"The only thing that comes to mind," I continued, "is some kind of people-to-people program, maybe having American cities such as Savannah, Georgia, adopt a Vietnamese town such as Vung Tau. The American people will have to feel a sense of broad involvement."

McNamara said nothing. I later talked to one of his aides and learned that my idea had been discussed in the White House, but President Johnson by then had decided to play the war low-key. A major part of Johnson's strategy to keep the war from becoming a political liability was his refusal to mobilize the reserves and National Guard. I don't necessarily agree, incidentally, with critics of his policy who claim the reserves would have made a big difference in the way the war turned out. When you're on the battlefield, any prudent commander, whether on the attack or defense, has a reserve. And one of the most difficult decisions a commander has to make is when to commit that reserve. If he commits it to battle too soon, it will be dissipated before he can launch the *coup de grâce*. If he commits the reserve too late, it won't have the desired impact on the outcome of the battle. Calling up the reserves in the United States was the counterpart to that battlefield analogy.

If the reserves had been called up in 1965 or even in 1966, there would have been a hue and a cry to bring the boys home before even a third of them had reached Vietnam. Then, when all of them had been called up and deployed, two years would have gone by and the American people would be anticipating the end of the war. If it wasn't over, the folks at home on the farms and in the villages and small towns whose sons had been called away and put in uniform would have led a political upheaval. That's how I saw it at the time.

Interestingly, when I talked to President Johnson about the pros and cons of calling up the reserves, he kept coming back to his son-in-law Patrick Nugent's experience during the Berlin crisis in 1961. Nugent's outfit was called up and he did nothing but sit around for six months.

"I got absolutely disgusted with it," Johnson said. "What the hell was he doing? He ought to have been back home working for a living."

The situation in Vietnam had many sides to it, but I think we could have pulled out—gracefully in my opinion—before Ngo Dinh Diem was overthrown and killed in November of 1963. Of course, withdrawing would have generated a lot of political heat among the right-wing Republicans because Kennedy's "We'll pay any price, bear any burden in the defense of liberty" speech was still ringing in the ears of America. Still, I think he could have justified withdrawal by saying we had sent fifteen thousand troops there, the political situation was a mess, the place was paralyzed, there was nobody we could work with to pull the country together, so we're getting out. But by sanctioning Diem's overthrow, we had assumed a moral obligation to stick with our commitment.

Long before I became COMUSMACV in June of 1964, I had made it a personal policy to keep my official problems and my family life separate. In other words, I didn't take my official problems into the bedroom. I don't recall ever talking to Kitsy about all the pins I was trying to juggle in Vietnam. And I didn't burden my kids with my problems, either. I think it would have been unfair to them.

I have a tough wife. Kitsy grew up in the army. Since marrying me in 1947, she has lived in thirty-six houses in seven states and three foreign countries. She has worked hundreds of hours as a nurse's aide in military hospitals, helping to care for wounded soldiers. She has written letters for them, made telephone calls home for them, scrubbed their backs, even helped sew up their wounds. While I was COMUSMACV, she sometimes flew on fixed-wing medevac flights between Vietnam and the Philippines, once going on to a hospital in Tokyo to give every Vietnam veteran there a red rose on Valentine's Day.

Kitsy and the kids lived with me in Saigon for about a year in a four-bedroom French villa on Tran Quy Cap Street, near the middle of the city. Unfortunately, the house was near a big pagoda that was the headquarters for a lot of radical Buddhists, some of whom practiced self-immolation on the streets of Saigon to protest the policies of the South Vietnamese government. Chanting mobs of these radicals occasionally surged by our house during their demonstrations, and that became a cause of some worry on my part for Kitsy's and the children's safety. Our only security was two

Vietnamese policemen, the so-called White Mice, who were stationed at a flimsy barrier at the entrance to the villa, and a couple of American MPs in the front room. I was afraid the radicals could get by the White Mice and break through the barrier, if they took a mind to do it, and rush en masse into my house.

I thought of one way to handle them. I told Kitsy that I wanted to get gas masks for her and the kids in case the Buddhists ever stormed the villa. She agreed and I had everybody fitted with one. Then I put a case of tear gas grenades under our bed. Everybody kept a gas mask by his or her bedside. If the radicals forced their way in, I intended to flood the house with tear gas. Fortunately, that last-ditch defense was never necessary, perhaps to the disappointment of the kids, who regarded this sort of thing as tremendously exciting. They were young and it was all a lark to them. In 1964 and part of 1965, Saigon was still safe enough for Kitsy to drive around the city alone in her car. But as the situation worsened, American dependents were finally ordered out of the country and she and the kids went to live in Hawaii. Later, they moved to the Philippines for the last two years of my service in Vietnam.

Now, what I'm going to tell you is a tremendous weakness on my part: I'm not much of a letter writer. Kitsy understands that. When she left Vietnam, she told me that my official duties had to come first. I kept in touch with her mostly by telephone. I mean, I lived with my job as COMUSMACV twenty-four hours a day, seven days a week. I would think about Kitsy and the kids at the end of the day, but I was usually too tired to write very much. When I could see my way clear, which wasn't very often, I flew over to Hawaii or the Philippines for a short visit.

My workday usually started at seven a.m. If I was lucky, I got to bed by eleven p.m. With Kitsy and the kids gone, I had three extra bedrooms in the villa, so I selected three of my key staff officers—one of them was the MACV surgeon—to live there with me. I found that I could keep abreast of their concerns, and save precious office time, by having breakfast and dinner with them. Office time was scarce because I had made a commitment to myself, rightly or wrongly, to spend four days a week in the field with the troops. I did this so I could talk to a cross-section of our officers and men and meet with their commanders firsthand. Of course, this policy left me with only three days a week in my office at MACV. It put a tremendous burden on my staff, but I was blessed with good people. I didn't have to attend to every little detail.

There was one detail, though, that I saw to every day. I signed the next-of-kin letters for soldiers who had lost their lives in Vietnam. I did that from day one as COMUSMACV and later when I was chief of staff. I didn't use one of those machines that reproduces a signature. I wanted every letter to bear my personal signature, and that's the way it was done.

On the days when I was in Saigon, I always had a chockablock schedule. There were always problems with the Vietnamese, decisions that had to be made on the conduct of the war, and endless gratuitous advice coming from Washington. I usually palmed a lot of the advice off on my staff, giving them a little guidance in a buck slip or a short telephone call on how to respond. A lot of this how-to-win-the-war advice came from Bob McNamara's "whiz kids" in the Pentagon. Since these people usually didn't know what they were talking about, I conveniently ignored many of their cables.

People sometimes ask me if I saw myself in a personal contest with General Giap while I was COMUSMACV. The answer is, not really. Giap had political as well as military authority. He could call the shots on the battlefield to a greater extent than I could because of political restraints that prevented me from sending troops into the DMZ, Laos, and Cambodia. Remember, there is also a big difference between the oriental and occidental ways of war. If Giap had been a general in the U.S. Army, the disregard he had for human life, the positions he put his troops into, would have cost him his command. But I guess the price he paid in lives didn't mean much to him. That complicated my situation in Vietnam because Giap didn't always act rationally. I had to assume, in fact, that he would not act rationally, as least as we Westerners define the word.

I have always tried to put myself in my adversary's position, to see myself through his eyes. I frequently did this with Giap. MACV had an analytical section that produced valuable studies on what the enemy could be expected to do, what actions he might reasonably take on the battlefield, in the context of scenarios that I gave them. These studies often paid off with good battlefield results.

President Johnson asked me in 1966, "If you were Giap, what would you do in Vietnam?" I told him I would attack across the DMZ, overrun Khe Sanh, go through the A Shau Valley and isolate the two northernmost provinces with a sweep through the Hai Van Pass to capture Hue, the old imperial capital. Quang Tri and Thua Thien provinces, the two northernmost provinces, were very exposed at the time. We had only two small airfields up there and no deepwater port. Now, I was trying to think the way Giap did, so before the Tet Offensive I reinforced the marines with three army divisions, built airfields and hardstands for helicopters, and developed port facilities. I was getting ready for an attack based on my analysis of what Giap could do, and so we were prepared for him when it came. Unfortunately, it's not obvious to the American people to this day that we stopped him in his tracks during Tet.

Now, we Americans made our share of mistakes in Southeast Asia, too. I have come to think that the biggest one we had to deal with in Vietnam points to Ambassador Averell Harriman. As our representative in Geneva in 1962, when we signed the accord on Laos, he made a tacit agreement with the Russians that if they didn't move into Vientiane, we wouldn't move into southern Laos. That agreement opened the way for Hanoi to build the Ho Chi Minh Trail, and it came to haunt us. With our Game Warden and Market Time operations, we stopped infiltration into South Vietnam by river and sea, but we were never able to shut down the Ho Chi Minh Trail because we couldn't go into eastern Laos to cut it.

People sometimes ask me if there has ever been a counterpart to the Vietnam War. Not to a great extent, but the Civil War comes close in some respects. The Civil War was not a static war, but one of movement; it was not a war one could follow very well on a map. Troops were tied down only to secure Richmond and Washington, along with a few other areas such as ports that were important for logistics.

In Vietnam, we held the major population and food-producing areas with static troops, mostly Vietnamese. We also defended the seaports and airports, but other than that, we couldn't afford to tie down troops. We didn't have enough of them to do that. We had to keep the troops mobile. One of the things about Vietnam that the American people have never understood was how we could win a battle and then leave the battlefield. They thought we were fighting for terrain; we weren't fighting for terrain, we were fighting to destroy the enemy's troops, fighting to hurt him enough to make him come to the conference table.

It was the same way in the Civil War. It was also a war of attrition and movement over distances similar to those in Vietnam. The Civil War had riverine warfare on the Mississippi, Tennessee, and Cumberland rivers; Vietnam had its own form of riverine war on the Mekong, Bassac, and Cua Viet rivers. The Civil War had wagons for transport; we had trucks. The Civil War had the horse for mobility; its counterpart in Vietnam was the helicopter. We would have gotten nowhere in Vietnam if it hadn't been for the helicopter. Remember, along the borders of Cambodia and Laos we had a wide-open flank more than seven hundred miles long, which we didn't have enough troops to defend. All we could do was lightly outpost the flank with Special Forces camps. Yet, when enemy units came across the border, we could use our helicopters to react with unprecedented mobility. If we'd had to move by ground, the enemy would have ambushed us constantly and we could have done little about it.

One of the biggest disappointments I suffered in Vietnam came from the media. I was quite disillusioned by their performance. We tried to get some visibility for the civic action and other nation-building work that was going on in the midst of the war, but that sort of thing wasn't sensational. It didn't attract readership because news, at least in the United States, tends to focus on the bizarre and the offbeat. In Vietnam, if there was nothing sensational going on, some reporters would make their own news. There was one incident in which a reporter pulled out a knife, gave it to a young American soldier, and suggested that he cut an ear off an enemy body. Some television reporters even talked soldiers into staging an event they could film and passed it off as live action.

Some of our media weren't sophisticated enough to realize they were being used by the North Vietnamese. LBJ said that when he lost the support of Walter Cronkite after the Tet Offensive, he lost mainstream America. By reporting Tet as a defeat rather than the victory it was, Cronkite was an unwitting participant in carrying out North Vietnam's very shrewd propaganda strategy. His ignorance of the war is still appalling. When CBS sent him to Hanoi to get some dirt on me during my libel suit against the network a few years ago, he quoted me as saying I could have defeated North Vietnam if I'd been given a few more troops after Tet. In the first place, I never said that. In the second place, how could I have defeated the enemy if I couldn't go after him in Cambodia, Laos, or North Vietnam?

There was no way we could win with the media, but I never really thought censorship in Vietnam was the answer to that problem. President Johnson told me a few months before he died that we should have imposed censorship. I didn't agree with him, but I didn't argue the point, either. In the first place, the Vietnamese government, as the sovereign power, would have had responsibility for censorship.

If we had opted for censorship, we probably would have worked with the Vietnamese as we did at the Port of Saigon. The port was a shambles when we got there, so we simply took it over and ran it under the guise of advisors. Under that scheme, every advisor had a Vietnamese counterpart; the advisor was training his counterpart to eventually take over his duties. We could have followed that model with censorship—and then watched it get undercut within a day or so. Here's how: assume you're a reporter. You've got a very sensational story, either written or on film. To get around censorship, you find someone, maybe an American, and book him on a commercial flight to Singapore, Manila, Taipei, or Tokyo. He takes your story to your news organization, and the rug gets pulled completely out from under us. I always thought of censorship in those terms; it just would not work.

However, we were not without some control over the media. If we gave reporters information on major troop movements, which we sometimes did, and one of them then broke the embargo on its release, we withdrew his accreditation to MACV. Embargoes were broken four times while I was in command. Losing his accreditation was a serious matter to a reporter: it meant he couldn't eat in our messes, he couldn't use our communications, he couldn't fly in our aircraft, he couldn't even use the PX. He was isolated and therefore ineffective.

When I came back to the states in 1968 and found so much misunderstanding about the war, I felt I should try to explain a little more about what we were trying to do in Vietnam. I did quite a bit of traveling as chief of staff, speaking mainly to such groups as the Association of the United States Army and other patriotic organizations. After my retirement in 1972, at a time when a lot of the troops were coming home, I felt so bad about the way they were being treated that I dedicated myself to talk to *any* group about Vietnam. I went to a number of radical campuses and received every discourtesy imaginable. Almost without exception, the anti-Vietnam group on campus was so well organized that it would pass out a leaflet to everybody going into the hall, accusing me of being a war criminal on eight to ten counts. When I began to speak, the radicals would try to drown me out.

I deliberately made myself a target for these people. I preferred to have them throw darts at me rather than at my troops, who were not psychologically equipped to handle that kind of abuse. I didn't let the curses and other hijinks get to me. I didn't sleep on them, I didn't let them haunt me. I mean, I think I was broad-minded enough to see that sort of thing for what it was, and I don't believe it affected me psychologically. I believed very strongly that I had an obligation to tell the story of what the troops did and come to their public defense, although I don't like to use that term because it implies they had done something wrong. I was not, however, going to stand aside and let them be called babykillers.

On the day Saigon fell in 1975, I felt sick about it—absolutely sick. We had done nothing to stop the North Vietnamese invasion. We had thrown away our trump cards and in effect washed our hands of Vietnam some three years earlier. The distress I felt was exacerbated by a phone call from the South Vietnamese ambassador in Washington, a man I had known and respected for some time. It was one of the most pathetic conversations I've ever had.

He said, "General, you spent so much time with us, you worked so hard trying to save us. I'm turning to you. What can you do? What can you do? We have no arms, no reinforcements."

I suffered with him as he spoke. "We've got about ten million dollars' worth of gold that we were able to get out. Do you think it will be possible for us to go into the international arms market and get arms that could help us?" All I could tell him was that it was too late to do anything. It was over.

I suppose I can say now, after all these years, that the whole Vietnam experience made me a stronger man, certainly in the psychological sense, than I would have been otherwise. I think it also made me more sophisticated in dealing with people and the institutions of our society. I've seen the American system at its best and at its worst. I had some temporary disillusionment about how well the system worked, but it hasn't lingered. The way I look back at it, that's the way the cards were stacked. I played them as they were dealt to me.

If we could project ourselves to the year 2050, the Vietnam War probably would look a lot different than it does now. History may well record that the so-called living-room war was one of the greatest international pacifiers that we have ever seen. It was very likely a crossroads in war. I don't think we will see this country send another expeditionary force overseas unless the American people are convinced their security is threatened.

I could be bitter about the way it all turned out, but I'm not. I've been around too long and I'm too philosophical to be bitter. I think we should just put Vietnam in the context of its time and go on. It doesn't do any good to brood about it.

Richard C. Ensminger

Blowing Rock, North Carolina

Marine forward observer,

1966–67, 1969

●

Richard and I first met at an informal gathering of Vietnam veterans in Boone, North Carolina. Afterward, we stood outside the Western Sizzlin' steakhouse in the hard blue glow of sodium-vapor lights for half an hour and talked in broad terms about the war. We agreed to meet at his home the next morning to continue our conversation.

Richard lives in a small two-level frame house on a paved road off U.S. 321, the busy four-lane highway that links Boone with Blowing Rock, a more genteel tourist haven eight miles to the south. The road to Richard's house took me through fields white with Queen Anne's lace as it wound up the saddle of a mountain. Look for the house with an American flag on the front, he had told me.

An amputee, Richard moved around at the veterans' meeting with the aid of an aluminum crutch. Now he greeted me in a wheelchair, where he spends most of his days. We gathered around a small table in the kitchen and talked for most of the morning.

"I grew up in a military family, traveling, never living more than a couple of years in one place," Richard said as he lit up the first of many cigarettes. "My stepfather worked in naval intelligence. I quit high school in 1963 after my dad went to Virginia Tech to teach military science. I moved from a big high school in Nashville—my dad taught at Vanderbilt—to a school of about nine hundred kids. To me, it was a hick high school, there was nothing to be involved in, and I was tired of moving, anyway. So I joined the marines."

A big man, easily six feet tall and two hundred pounds, Richard's emotions ran close to the surface as he recalled his tours of duty in Vietnam during 1966–67 and again in 1969 as an artillery forward observer. When he described the destruction by gunfire of a Vietnamese hamlet and its inhabitants, his voice broke and tears flowed down his face. I saw later how he deals with the pain of such memories. "Look at this," he said, pulling a large cardboard box from under a desk in a small room he has reserved for himself. The box was half full of brown plastic jars from the VA hospital pharmacy in Johnson City, Tennessee. I remarked that many of the labels bore the names of tranquilizing drugs. "Yes," he said, "it's the only way they know how to handle me."

I had been with the Second Marines at Camp Lejeune for almost two years when I got my orders to Vietnam in 1965. A lot of my friends were going over about the same time, and I can say now that we never really knew what a nasty situation Vietnam was. Most of us only knew war from movies and books and talking with higher-ranking sergeants and staff officers that had seen combat.

I went out to Camp Pendleton for three months of training before going on to Vietnam. I spent a lot of time in advanced combat courses and forward-observer training that taught me how to call for artillery fire and select the kind of fire I needed. I considered myself very good at calling in artillery before I ever got to Vietnam. I knew what I was doing. And, I had some idea of what it was like to be under fire. I'd been in Santo Domingo in 1965 during the Dominican Republic crisis and also down at Guantanamo Bay, where the Cubans liked to shoot at the guard towers.

I flew to Okinawa in February of 1966 and went from there on a naval transport ship to Danang, where I was assigned to the headquarters and service company of the 1/4th Marines as a forward observer for 81mm mortars. Just after I got there, I was attached to one of two rifle companies that made the second amphibious landing in Vietnam, near the China Beach area. While two other companies came in on helicopters, we ran out of our Mike boats into waist-deep water, and what did we see waiting for us on the beach but thirty little Vietnamese girls holding flowers. A bunch of dignitaries was with them, and I could see a big sign that said, "Welcome United States Marines." Combat photographers swarmed all over the place. We had only five rounds of ammunition for our M-14s, and we weren't even allowed to put them in our weapons. It was all a big show. From the beach, we walked eight or ten miles through the heat and muck to the other side of Danang. It would sprinkle for a little while and then get very hot, miserable conditions to do anything in, especially when nine men had to share a tent.

I guess I saw myself as another John Wayne for my first few weeks in Vietnam. I loaded myself down with extra grenades and ammo, but it didn't take me very long to learn that all that ammo was too heavy in the heat. On the other hand, it was an Article 15 offense to discard it in the field, so I finally worked myself down to one or two M-26 fragmentation grenades, eight to ten magazines for my M-14, and three or four canteens of water. Since I was a forward observer, I also carried a compass, a map case, a pair of binoculars, and at least one meal of C-rations. My helmet was decorated with bottles of Texas Pete hot sauce for the C-rats and bug juice to keep off the B-52 mosquitoes. We didn't wear underwear; it would rot off you because we were lucky to get a bath every two weeks.

My battalion ran a lot of short, sweeping combat operations along Highway 1 from Danang to Dong Ha. After a couple of months of that, I was sent out to a Fourth Marines firebase at Cam Lo, near the DMZ. The base had four tanks, four 105s, four 155s and two eight-inch howitzers, as well as two mortar units. Other than that, it was little more than red clay and heat. We lived in what we called lean-tos: two ponchos tied together. During the day we lived in what shade we could find or under the ponchos. They did double duty as body bags, too.

I worked on Operation Hastings as a forward observer, going out with units that had as many as forty men and as few as four or five. I called in harassing fire on Charlie. In Vietnam, a forward observer was supposed to have a radio operator with him, but most FOs carried their own radios. And we also preferred to carry our M-14s rather than M-16s because the M-14 was more reliable and accurate. I learned a lot of things in Vietnam that hadn't been taught to me in the states. For instance, I loaded my own rounds. I used wire cutters to snip off the tip of M-14 bullets. You'd be surprised what a cutoff M-14 bullet can do to somebody—it will tear him a new you-know-what. Of course, the M-14 was a big, long-range infantry rifle that wasn't designed for close combat in the bush. Some marines cut off the barrels of their rifles to compensate for that. Whatever weapon a marine had, though—and some had .357 Magnum pistols—he kept it cleaned and in good working order because his life depended on it.

I was always humping, always on the move. All of us worried a lot about ambushes. For that reason, we never had a set time for a patrol to go out. Sometimes we'd go in the middle of the day or late evening. If we set a schedule, Charlie got to know about it. He would know when we were out, where we were, and whether we followed the same trail twice. You learned this from guys who had been over there for a while. They knew how to stay alive.

When I first got to Cam Lo, the old-timers who had been in Vietnam for a year wouldn't have anything to do with me. They knew I knew my job, but their attitude troubled me at first. We new guys stayed together and little by little moved into the group. It was an initiation. I had to prove to them that I wouldn't get them killed. It was something that everybody went through. One marine warned me, "I'll tell you once: you mess up and you're on your own. Mess up twice and I'll kill you." He was a lance corporal, the same rank as me.

"Are you kidding?" I said.

"No, I'm not. I'll kill you in a moment's notice. You're not gonna get me killed." I figured the best way not to screw up was to stay in the back and watch everybody else. New guys in the back of a line couldn't trip bouncing betties or step on mines. But if a new guy took the point, people started getting very nervous.

Most marine grunts were good for only six to eight months of combat. It took from three to six months to learn the basics of staying in one piece. Then, for the last couple of months before a guy's DEROS, we just left him alone for the most part because he had the short-timer's attitude. This was when most of our courts-martial and office hours came up. Short-timers didn't want to go out in the field; they were afraid some guy would screw up their chances of going home. Second lieutenants sometimes did that. They were a dime a dozen in the marines. A second lieutenant who screwed up twice was a dead man, and not necessarily because of the enemy. He might get killed by his own men.

A lieutenant who came in and said, "Hey, I don't know what's going on" and looked to his sergeants to help him along usually did all right. But one who marched in and announced that he was going to run the show, that he was the boss out there in the bush—if he made it, he was damn lucky. His sergeant might turn around to him and say, "Nobody can hear you. Stand up and tell 'em." Charlie would pick off that lieutenant as soon as he did that. The sergeants, now they were the ones we paid attention to. Some of those guys were amazingly brave: they would walk rice paddy dikes under fire and never get a scratch.

I could usually have gunfire coming in on Charlie within a minute or a minute and a half of asking for it. If gunfire had to be cleared through the Danang Intelligence Center because of friendly troops in the area, it might take half an hour, which was entirely too long. Sometimes Danang would even deny gunfire because friendly troops were out there. Of course they were. *We* were the friendlies who needed fire on an enemy position. When the first round slammed in, Charlie would always look around in surprise.

If the round was close enough, he'd scramble around and try to scatter. If the second round was on target, I'd tell the gunners to fire for effect. Then I'd see bodies flying apart, vegetation being torn up, the earth just erupting, all hell in one moment. I've been on the receiving end of it, so I know what the enemy's feelings must have been.

If a forward observer gets spotted by the enemy, his life expectancy is about fifteen seconds. The same is true for snipers and scouts. I knew that before I went to Vietnam. As soon as Charlie saw you, he was going to try to kill you. I had a close call like that on Operation Prairie. I caught some Charlies in the open, but I didn't know they had small flanking units all around them. When they passed by a firebase, I called in 81mm mortars, maybe a hundred rounds pumped out from four tubes. We started taking automatic weapons fire from the side while I was on the radio, telling the mortar crews what was happening. Before it was all over, my radio operator and three or four other grunts got hit. It was a damned scary business.

I got wounded nine months into my first tour, in February of 1967, when a firebase basically got overrun during Operation Independence. It was a shrapnel wound. Charlie mortared the place on a cold, rainy night, dropping maybe forty or fifty rounds before he came at us—I believe he knew that firebase backwards and forwards. Before it was over, I burned out the barrel of an M-60, the 60mm mortars ran out of ammunition, all the LAWs were fired and not one radio worked. I was down to fifteen rounds for my .45 pistol when Charlie finally pulled back. If he'd hit us again, all of us would have been dead.

We fired a lot of 60mm illumination rounds and pop-up flares during the attack. Everybody carried two or three pop-up flares. To fire one, you pulled the cap off and put it on the rear end. Then you hit the cap and a little parachute flare shot about two hundred feet in the air. The flares let us see the enemy fairly well; I could tell that some of them were moving quickly, but others, for some reason, weren't. They were firing their weapons mostly from the hip. I'll tell you, I was scared to hell and back, but I think I fought to the best of my ability. There was always some fear in my mind that I was going to screw up, that I would let down one or two guys that I'd gotten close to. It was like walking a log across a river: one wrong step and you're going to fall in. The fear of screwing up was there all the time.

There were always some guys who looked for any excuse to avoid combat. One of them lives here in Watauga County. The way he tells it, he would put on his flak vest, his helmet, and his body pants—which I never saw anybody wear in Vietnam—and then he'd drop an M-26 grenade on the ground and walk fifteen feet away. That gave him enough shrapnel wounds in his legs to get medevaced out. This guy never really got hurt, but he picked up three Purple Hearts. He boasted to me one day that's how he got out of Vietnam. Frankly, I don't talk to the man. The only legitimate way to get out of combat in Vietnam was heat exhaustion, but we could sometimes con the company commander into letting us go to the rear to pick up some supplies. We never knew what might come out on the resupply chopper. I remember one grunt who talked his way into going back to make sure we got some hot food. A note came back with the chopper: "I couldn't get the hot food, but here's two fifths of liquor." We needed liquor in the bush like we needed a hole in the head.

I stayed in Vietnam ten days longer than I was supposed to on my first tour. I was in the bush in March of 1967, still seeing guys getting killed, when I figured I'd have to take some action of my own. I got on the radio to regimental headquarters. They said, "You're still in the field, huh?" A couple of days later, a chopper came out to get me. Well, as luck would have it, 122mm rockets started coming into Danang just as I was getting on the freedom bird to Okinawa. The plane had made it to the end of the runway when the captain announced that he couldn't take off because a rocket had blown off the tail section. Still another delay while we transferred to a new plane. On this one, I discovered that I had come out of the bush so fast I still had forty rounds of M-14 ammo in some of my gear.

I came back to El Toro Marine Air Station in California, where I took a shower, picked up my seabag and gladly took thirty days' leave, with fifteen days of grace travel to my next duty station. When I went to Vietnam, I weighed 235 pounds. I weighed 175 pounds when I came back, all solid muscle and red clay dirt. I rode a military bus down to San Diego to catch a flight to Miami, where I planned to unwind for a while. I had on my short-sleeve khakis, which were very wrinkled because they had been in my seabag for thirteen months, and my combat boots. I had slapped some black polish on them, but I really didn't care what anybody said. I was home.

As I got off the bus and started to walk up a ramp at the San Diego airport, a woman who looked to be about fifty years old jumped out of the crowd and pointed a .22 pistol at a marine twenty guys in front of me.

"You woman and child killer!" she screamed. She put six rounds in that marine at point-blank range.

When I heard her first shot, I hit the ground and rolled back under the bus. It was an automatic reaction—I had to find a place to hide. The marine who was shot had wounds in his stomach and side, but none of them was fatal. The woman was lucky to live through what happened to her, too. Some of the other marines threw her over a fence eight feet high. I understand the fall broke both her legs and several ribs. All of us who witnessed the shooting were held up a day because we had to give statements to the police and navy criminal investigators about what had happened. I simply wrote that I crawled under a bus.

I believe in God and country. When I went to Vietnam, I believed it was my duty to go over there and fight for my country. I came back as a corporal E-4 with a Purple Heart and a couple of unit citations. I knew I had done something worthwhile, but I wasn't prepared for the demonstrations against the war here, for the people who downgraded me for being in the military. As I saw it, there were three groups of people in the United States: the older people who didn't care about the war, the kids who didn't understand it, and those who were totally against Vietnam, against everything we were doing over there. The situation eventually got so bad that we were told to stay away from the civilian population as much as possible to hold down friction.

I went on to Miami Beach to spend thirty days with a couple of sergeants, but I cut it short after only six days. I was twenty years old, but I was supposed to be twenty-one to walk into a bar. I was old enough to fight for my country, but I couldn't get a beer. That wasn't all. If I walked up to a girl and asked her to dance, she'd take one look at me, like I was something with a bad smell, and wouldn't have anything to do with me. I had been back from Vietnam for only a week and already I was feeling like an outsider. And I was getting angry. I let my weight shoot up to two hundred pounds, I wore all my campaign ribbons, and I let people know I was one mean mother. I remember walking in one bar in Miami and some people said they wanted me out of there. I told a dude who shoved me that if he did it one more time, I'd gladly take on him and everybody else in the place. Another veteran was in there, a fellow who had lost an arm in Korea.

"I'll be more than happy to back you up," he said. The place settled down fast.

I went on to my next duty station at Quantico Marine Base in Virginia for training in crowd and riot control. In the fall of 1967, a big antiwar demonstration was being planned at the Pentagon, and a bunch of us at Quantico were trucked up there for security. I was one of several marines put on top of the building. I had a pump shotgun, body armor, and a helmet. Our shells had rubber bullets in them, but somebody high up must have thought it would be a bad idea to issue ammo to men who had served in Vietnam. Maybe they were afraid we would get mad enough to shoot somebody.

I had to work one more big demonstration, this one in front of the Capitol. This time, about fifty marines were called up from Quantico. We were issued full riot gear: helmets with plastic face shields, body armor, gas masks, and shotguns with five rounds of rubber ammo. Some marines in the line behind me had tear gas guns for backup protection. The people in front of me called me a babykiller, they called my mother every name in the book, and they did the same for my sister. I didn't like crowd control duty and had asked to get out of it. I tried to make it clear to my sergeant that someday a protester would come up to me and say the wrong thing and I'd shoot the bastard.

"You can't do much harm with a rubber bullet," he said. Well, I stood in that line and took the verbal abuse, but when a man spit in my face, I showed him what a marine with a shotgun could do. I got an Article 15 for my trouble and a transfer to other duty.

I volunteered to go back to Vietnam after a little more than a year in the states. I didn't feel comfortable going outside a military base. Somehow, I felt I wasn't wanted in American society. And I was getting tired of the petty, spit-shined mentality of the stateside marines. In Vietnam, I could do what I was trained for. Maybe I was also getting a bit paranoid—officers and authority were making me nervous. When I got back to Danang in April of 1969, the base had grown tremendously. It was now a big city of metal buildings. Naturally, a few things hadn't changed. I still had to go through Dogpatch, two miles of whorehouses outside the base, to get to a staging area where I got orders for the 3/5th Marines.

As I see it now, I think I wanted another tour in Vietnam to help keep marines from getting killed. It had become more important to me to keep Americans alive than to kill NVA. I was a sergeant by this time, and I figured I would be sent out to a rifle company as a forward observer, which was a good way to accomplish what I wanted to do. But Vietnam had changed and the marines had, too. We had draftees now. On my first tour, we were all volunteers. Now there was a drug problem that I hadn't seen before. Marijuana grew in every creek bed in Vietnam. Grunts were getting stoned on it, on hash and other drugs—you name it, and you could buy it. I could see this was a different war from the first time around, and I made up my mind not to trust the men screwed up on drugs. I would do my duty, but I intended to come out alive.

When I flew out to my company near An Hoa, south of Danang, I jumped off the chopper in the middle of a firefight. In a way, my arrival was a sort of metaphor for my second tour. Lima company never stayed in one place; it was always on the move. No rest, no sleep. After only two weeks in the bush, I was numb, worn out. All I wanted was a hot meal and twenty-four hours of sleep. I saw a lot more killing and mutilation during my second tour. For one thing, I was closer to it. During my first tour, I spent some time with the Combined Action Platoon program on hamlet security, but now the war seemed like one endless search-and-destroy mission. Since I was one of the few forward observers in my battalion, I spent almost all my time in the bush. I would go back to the rear with a company, then turn right around and go back out with another one.

I was so tired I started to act by instinct alone. I was lucky to get four hours of sleep a night. I know now that I was doing a lot of stupid things: I'd see two VC running out there and call in a fire mission, instead of letting my snipers and scouts handle them. I'd just blow the hell out of an area. I was even calling in false reports. I was out for blood. The one mistake in my life that I'm sorry for, that I still have nightmares over, came one day I was with Lima company. We took some small-arms fire from a village. Right away, I called for mixed air and ground bursts of artillery fire that flattened the place in less than five minutes. . . . It was a godlike display of power. After it was all over, I walked through a burning, smoky ruin of straw and bamboo huts. I could see parts of human and animal bodies scattered all around, and I noticed that the air was saturated with a sharp smell of gunpowder and urine. At this time, every marine unit in my battalion was supposed to meet a quota in VC and NVA—it was a meat quota. A lot of civilians who got killed were called VC. In fact, the village that I shot up became a VC village: four hundred confirmed kills, women and children. Lima company met its meat quota for two months with that one village alone.

I justified what I had done by thinking about marines that I had seen get shot and lay wounded, unable to move to safety, while the VC kept shooting at them. Sometimes the VC would shoot at a grunt even after he was dead. Seeing such things had a hardening effect on all of us. I think a lot of marines felt we were still fighting for a reason in 1969, but we weren't sure what the reason was anymore. The war had become a sort of perpetual-motion killing machine. We killed them and they killed us, and nothing seemed to change.

In June of 1969, I was in the bush with Kilo company, which had a new lieutenant who didn't like artillery. I could see why—he wanted to prove himself by getting marines killed in senseless infantry assaults. He wanted to punch his ticket and win medals for fast promotion. The fact that he didn't like artillery meant nothing to me. If I wanted artillery, I called for it. Now, this lieutenant had been brought in to replace an officer wounded in a minor ambush. He wanted glory, but he was green and scared, and that led to a snap decision to put me in charge of an infantry platoon made up of two other platoons that had lost half their men. Well, I had forgotten my fire-team tactics a long time ago and I tried to tell him that. We stood ankle-deep in rice paddy water eleven clicks from An Hoa while he warned me I would be court-martialed if I refused to take over the platoon. He also ordered me to sign off the artillery radio net and get on the battalion net.

"That's strictly against orders," I said. Again, he said he was the commanding officer, he had authority to make decisions, and I was headed for a court-martial if I disobeyed him. I had questioned orders before but never disobeyed them. So, I took over the platoon of fifty-four marines and led them toward a hamlet a short distance away.

There was enough bamboo in the area to limit our line of sight to about a hundred meters. The NVA were waiting for us in a classic L-shaped ambush along a creek bed outside the hamlet. They let the point squad walk into the hamlet before opening up on the rest of us. I believe we were hit by an entire company of NVA supported by a weapons platoon because those people laid down some fire on us. I was one of the first men to get hit, in the back of my left leg, and I'm sure it was my radio operator who did it. I felt a sharp, burning pain in my leg and swung around and saw the RTO frozen to his rifle, which was still firing. His head was gone. A round had taken it off and blood was spurting up from his neck like a water fountain. He must have had his M-14 on automatic and his trigger finger touched it off when he was hit. It put seven bullets in my leg. To this day, I don't know who he was or where he was from.

I can remember somebody dragging me into a bomb crater or some other kind of hole. My leg felt like it was on fire. I reached for my backpack and got out a shot of morphine to get some relief from the pain. By that time in the war, almost everybody was carrying little tubes of morphine. I popped off the cap, squeezed a bit of the fluid out, and stuck the needle in my leg. I still had some idea of what was going on around me—all hell was breaking loose. About twenty feet away, a gook in a spider trap was popping up now and then to spray the area with his AK-47. I shot at him with my M-14. A lot of marines were getting hit. A corpsman jumped in the hole to give me another shot of morphine and fell back in when he tried to leave. His guts were blown out. I could hear men screaming for their mothers, for God, for death. Those who got up to help others got shot themselves.

The ambush probably lasted less than an hour, but it seemed like days. I heard choppers coming in and the next thing I knew, a marine was trying to help me. I was certain he was an NVA, so I pulled out my .45 pistol and tried to shoot him. I woke up in a hospital, thoroughly doped up on morphine, and somebody told me I was one of four survivors of the ambush. I still had my wounded leg, but my right arm was in traction. I was also in a body cast except for my right foot. I had dislocated my shoulder and still had four or five bullets inside of me, not to mention some four hundred tiny pieces of shrapnel.

Later, I was told that I was trying to operate the radio when I was in the hole. How it got there, I have no idea. Radio operators back at battalion headquarters heard me trying to call in artillery fire, but I wasn't giving the right coordinates. They couldn't talk to me because I never let go of the key on the microphone. According to what I was told, I was calling for variable time fuses, which would have thrown shrapnel down on me and everybody else. I figured three-fourths if not more of us were already dead and that I was going to die there, too. Why not take everybody out?

I was shipped out to a hospital in Japan for a while, and then on to Bethesda Naval Hospital. I kept my leg for twenty-two months. The doctors kept saying, "We'll save it. You're going to walk again." Then one day they walked in and said it had to come off four inches above the knee.

I prayed to the Lord that I wouldn't lose my leg, but for some reason I couldn't fight off the infections in my bones and blood. I was in a clean, isolated room at Bethesda with blood going into me, IVs and heart monitors hooked up to me, but the doctors didn't know why I wasn't healing. Anybody who came in to see me had to wear a bibbed gown and a face mask.

I was released from the marines after recovering from the loss of my leg. I was taking six shots of morphine a day until I left Bethesda, when they gave me a six-month prescription for 180 tablets of Demerol a month. The VA gave me Percodan, a sleep medication. I had so much painkiller I hardly knew what was going on. That was the start of a drug dependency that took years to get under control. I went to stay with my parents, who were living in Greensboro, North Carolina, at the time. They couldn't understand why I slept so much during the day. My father, in particular, was puzzled by my tendency to fly off the handle, why I couldn't stay in a room any length of time, why I was taking two or three showers a night to get the sweat off me.

A lot of my emotional and physical problems came out of my second tour in Vietnam. In my nightmares, I relive calling in artillery on the village and seeing my buddies get killed in the ambush. I know of one survivor who killed himself. If the others remember as much about it as I do, they would be better off dead, too. I've been in and out of hospitals maybe sixteen times with kidney, lung, liver, and prostate problems. I've developed diabetes, which means headaches, failing eyesight, and failing hearing. Something made me sterile in Vietnam and I believe it was Agent Orange. I sprayed Agent Orange around some of the firebases with a backpack pump like the ones used to fight forest fires. Choppers would come around and spray, too. A couple of days later, we would burn the dead vegetation to make a kill zone two or three hundred meters wide.

Sometimes, I think the VA has caused me more pain and aggravation than anything else. I go and sit in the VA hospital in Johnson City for hours on end just to hear somebody tell me all these problems are in my imagination. Maybe I shouldn't be surprised, because it took the VA twenty years to figure out I have 50 percent PTSD. There are days when I lock myself up in a room. Nancy understands that. She knows I need time to myself. She's gone through a lot of counseling herself at the Vet Center in Johnson City and she's learned that she's not the only woman trying to live with a Vietnam veteran. Twenty or thirty other wives around here are going through the same thing. With my stepchildren, it's been more difficult. I think my stepson Franklin understands me now more than he did, even though he lived away from home for three years because the courts said it was a bad idea for him to live under the same roof with me. I have a twenty-year-old stepdaughter who lives in Florida. She won't speak to me because she considers me too unpredictable.

I have been so depressed at times that I've thought of suicide. I'm a forty-two-year-old man living in the body of a sixty-year-old. I really believe my health is failing, that I am slowly dying. A couple of weeks ago, I was told that I have a bad blood flow from hardening of the arteries. No one in my family has ever had that. No one has had diabetes or a nervous condition.

I have very few friends. I don't make friends easily because I can't get close to people. I spent five months at the VA hospital in Augusta, Georgia, in 1985 for treatment of post-traumatic stress disorder, but I'm still described as somebody with "a nervous condition with bad personality disorders." Maybe so. I've had a lot of jobs and ended up getting fired from most of them. Probably the only people I can really relate to are the members of the Disabled American Veterans chapter in Boone.

You know, I believe the war started out as a just cause that ended up being a very political affair. A lot of people made a lot of money off it; some of them are still making money off it. In one way, I'm proud that I served. I'm a true marine who went and fought for my country and for a way of life and I'm proud of that. But I'm not proud of what I did over there. It sickens me now to see a child cry, a child hurt. I can't watch a war story or an operation on television without throwing my guts up and having nightmares that night.

Col. James M. Addison, Sr.

Lipan, Texas

Air force reconnaissance pilot,

1966–67

•

Jim Addison's modern, ranch-style house sits atop a small hillock just outside Lipan, a town of three hundred in the sagebrush country an hour's drive southwest of Fort Worth. Lipan is one of those rural Texas towns whose weatherbeaten, Depression-era storefronts seem to have been hardly touched by the succeeding decades that changed so much in American life. Except for a new post office and funeral home, the town has the ambience of one that time chose to leave behind as a splendidly preserved monument to another era.

It was here that Jim Addison grew up and went off to college at Texas A&M, and here that he returned in 1977 to raise cattle after twenty-three years as an air force jet jockey. Jim flew one hundred reconnaissance missions over North Vietnam during 1966–67 in support of Rolling Thunder, the controversial on-again, off-again bombing campaign whose targets were sometimes dictated by President Lyndon Johnson himself. Like many of his fellow pilots, Jim approached the Vietnam War as a consummate professional—he was there to do a job. As he saw it, the political side of the war was something for the civilians in Washington to stay up at night worrying about. Thus, as we neared the end of my visit, it didn't surprise me that Jim seemed reluctant to discuss his personal feelings about Vietnam.

A big man, easily more than six feet tall, with a smile as wide as the Texas plains, Jim told me that he realized as early as 1964 that he would someday go to Southeast Asia. And when he did, he wanted to be doing what he was trained for, flying high-performance reconnaissance jets instead of electronic-warfare planes. "I told my squadron commander at Biggs Air Force Base in El Paso what I had in mind," Jim said, "and he let me go to Tactical Air Command Headquarters at Langley Air Force Base in Virginia to plead my case. At the time, TAC was looking for seasoned reconnaissance pilots to fly the RF-4C Phantom, which was just coming into the inventory."

After a long series of discussions with personnel officers at TAC and the Air Defense Command, and finally with the help of some well-placed friends in the air force hierarchy, Jim moved to Shaw Air Force Base in Sumter, South Carolina, supposedly to go straight into the air force's second RF-4C squadron. "It didn't quite work out that way," he said. "I was stuck in wing headquarters for a year before I was able to get down into the squadron and even check out the RF-4C."

The Phantom was the first airplane I had flown that could exceed the speed of sound in level flight. I had flown F-86Ds which could break the sound barrier if you went to forty thousand feet and pointed the nose down, but then I had regressed to airplanes that couldn't even do that. The Phantom had tremendous power on takeoff and was good for low-level flying to evade radar. It was the kind of high-performance airplane that most of us who had flown RB-66s had never known before.

The Phantom was a pilot's airplane, very easy to control. It would do anything you asked it to do. Of course, like any other airplane, it had its share of little quirks, one of them due to the way the wing tips were shaped. When you tried to turn the Phantom at very high G-loads, it had a tendency to want to snap on you. It took us a little while to figure out how to use that unusual tendency to roll. But once we understood the airplane, got to know it, we didn't have many problems with it. In fact, we saw that we could use some of the Phantom's flight characteristics to outmaneuver other airplanes. These characteristics became very important for the RF-4C because it carried cameras, infrared sensors, and side-imaging radar instead of rockets and bombs.

I can't recall the exact date when the order came down for my outfit, the Ninth Tactical Reconnaissance Squadron, to move from Shaw Air Force Base to Thailand, but we took off as one unit in July of 1966. By that time, I had about 150 hours in the RF-4C. My squadron had about twenty-five Phantoms assigned to it, and we roared off to Southeast Asia with eighteen of them. From the time we started training in RF-4Cs, we knew we would be going en masse to bolster the air force's reconnaissance capability in Southeast Asia.

I had a little mechanical trouble along the way to Thailand. My aircraft developed a generator problem and I ended up setting it down at Sheppard Air Force Base at Wichita Falls, Texas. From there, I hitched a ride to Hawaii on a Military Airlift Command plane to pick up another RF-4C, one that a squadron mate had some trouble of his own with. When that plane got airworthy, I tagged along with some fighter jocks the rest of the way to Udorn Air Base in northeastern Thailand. It took me twenty days to get there from South Carolina.

Udorn was the northernmost air base that the air force had in Thailand. It was only twenty-five miles south of Vientiane, Laos, which made it convenient for a lot of undercover people going in and out of that country. The countryside around the base was rather flat and covered with small trees. Some people believed that Udorn had been built across a river, and when it rained, that certainly seemed to be true. All I know is that plenty of water came up on the base during rainstorms.

My squadron stayed in two single-story barracks made out of redwood. Most of us thought that was really something, at least until we learned that redwood is a common wood in Thailand. Each barracks had ten air-conditioned rooms with one large latrine. Three men were assigned to each room, which was furnished with two military-style bunks and a cot. The lack of a third bunk wasn't really a problem, because the barracks was just one continual movement of people. My squadron flew missions around the clock.

I flew my first mission on August 20, 1966. I had been in Udorn two or three days by then, just enough time to get through the local-area orientation, get briefed by Intelligence, pick up my maps, and learn the order of battle. My first mission was a day flight over Laos, primarily to give me and my backseat pilot some experience over a low-threat area. I made a couple of these practice . . . well, I prefer to call them orientation missions. And then I went right into the fray in North Vietnam with my backseater, Lt. John Osborne.

John was a graduate of the Air Force Academy. He and a number of his contemporaries had come into the squadron directly from pilot training and it was a bit of a disappointment to them, I think. They were pilots who were going to be backseaters. They were more than navigators and we never called them that; they were pilots whose primary responsibility was to operate the radar navigation system and sensors on the RF-4C. The squadron had a highly skilled navigator who gave these men good training in navigation, but learning the radars had to be done on the job.

Unlike the fighter version of the Phantom, the RF-4C had flight controls in the front and rear cockpits. Most pilots, and I was one of them, let their backseaters fly the airplane as much as possible to get experience. With the kind of threat we faced in Southeast Asia, there were many occasions when the backseater had to bring the aircraft home.

I can't remember flying a mission in Southeast Asia without John. That's how close our crews were. There were times when a pilot or a backseater might be sick and we had to fly with other guys, but it's almost . . . I'd describe it somewhat like a pitcher and catcher in a baseball game. We learned what to expect from each other. Sometimes one word meant everything, just one word between a crew about what needed to be done. John trusted his life to me as the pilot; I trusted my life to him as the navigator and radar operator.

When I learned that I was going to Southeast Asia, I went to the Sea Survival School at Langley and then to the Air Force Survival School at Stead Air Force Base at Reno, Nevada. After three weeks at Udorn, I went over to Clark Air Force Base in the Philippines for Jungle Survival School. I felt I was reasonably prepared for going down, if it came to that, but I doubt that any of us was really prepared for the treatment that American prisoners of war received from the North Vietnamese.

There's an old saying in the air force, "A reconnaissance pilot is unarmed, alone, and scared to death." The only armament on an RF-4C consisted of two .38-caliber revolvers that the crew carried. That's all we had to defend ourselves with if we went down. Otherwise, each crew member generally carried what he wanted to in the way of survival gear. There's only so much you can put on your body, though, and a lot of people wanted to carry bullets. I remember one guy who carried enough ammunition to fight the war by himself with his pistol. Others wanted all kinds of maps, an extra survival radio, or freeze-dried rations. All of us carried chits printed in various languages, saying the U.S. government guaranteed money and other assistance if a person helped a downed airman get back to safety.

We knew the air force would stop at nothing to rescue us if it could. We had Jolly Green Giants, the big CH-53 helicopters, stationed at Udorn. The guys who flew them lived a kind of royal life and they earned it, because they had made so many rescues that were above and beyond the call of duty. A1-E Skyraiders were there, too. They could stay up a long time and carried a lot of firepower. Their job was to hold off enemy ground troops long enough for a Jolly Green Giant to pick up downed airmen. We went as far into North Vietnam as we could, right up to a prohibited zone next to the Chinese border, and we never doubted those rescue crews would come up for us if we needed them.

My squadron flew what I call a continual rotation schedule. That meant I would fly days for a while and then nights, and then the early morning, gradually working my way around the clock. Very seldom did I fly more than one mission a day, so there were no problems with my body clock on that kind of schedule. I didn't fly every day, though. Some weeks I flew four days in a row and took a day off between the next round of missions.

If I were scheduled to fly at, say, 4:30 p.m., John and I would go to the squadron building about four hours before takeoff time for our briefing. The intelligence people gave us the mission for the day and identified the target to be photographed. They also showed us the known locations of gun and missile emplacements in the target area. At first, some of the other crew members and me would go to the squadron operations area six hours before takeoff, but that was because we'd never been in combat. In South Carolina, places marked "gun emplacement" on a map never shot at us; in North Vietnam they did.

Some of the RF-101 jocks at Udorn that we were replacing had been there for quite some time and really understood the combat situation. They knew the North Vietnamese tactics for SAM-2 missiles and 85mm and 20mm anti-aircraft guns. They really took us under their wings when we got there. Some of our guys were a little too proud to let a strictly day-fighter jock tell them what was going on, but the first time they got shot at, they went back and talked to the ones with the experience.

Preparing the RF-4C for a combat mission was no different from a routine training mission stateside. I made a preflight inspection of the aircraft to see if it had all the equipment it was supposed to be carrying for our mission. Just like any other photographer, I always worried that my cameras might not have film in them! I started the engines about fifteen minutes before takeoff. Then John and I made the usual taxi checks, got our clearance, and rolled down the runway. I always tried to take off within fifteen seconds of our scheduled departure. Departure times were especially important when we had to be over the target at a precise time before or after an airstrike. Because we were only thirty-five or forty minutes from Hanoi, and we weren't carrying a heavy load of ordnance, we didn't have to refuel on most of our missions. The RF-4C had two external wing tanks and a centerline tank that carried plenty of fuel for what we had to do.

I'd climb to twenty-five thousand feet on most missions and go through another check of equipment, including the electronic countermeasures gear and cameras, while cruising over Laos and part of North Vietnam. As I neared the target area, I dropped down to fly through mountain valleys to try to mask the airplane from radar. I say "try" because it wasn't always something that could be done. I never ceased to be amazed by the North Vietnamese, who seemed to know when an aircraft was coming even if there was no radar around anywhere. I don't know how they did it.

When airstrikes went into North Vietnam, there might be from four to thirty aircraft involved. When we reconnaissance types went in, it was usually with a single RF-4C that had to do up to three jobs. We might go up early in the morning just to check the weather around Hanoi—see how high or low the clouds were—so a decision could be made on fighter-bomber missions. Or, we might be on a prestrike mission to photograph a potential target for a strike the next day or maybe two weeks later. And then there was the traditional poststrike mission for damage assessment.

The weather missions got to be rather routine after a while. They usually weren't very interesting because we'd invariably go up around Hanoi to see if the fighter-bombers could get to their targets. We would get up there about sunrise. It didn't take the North Vietnamese very long to learn that an airplane was going to be there at 5:30 a.m. every day, so they started sending MiGs up. We were never attacked by them, but they tried to chase us around a few times. Our air surveillance people would come on the radio and say, "You've got a bogey" in certain quadrants, and we would wander off somewhere else to avoid the MiGs.

But the North Vietnamese got to where they'd send up more and more MiGs to chase the weather scouts. Our reconnaissance wing brass got together with the fighter jocks over at Danang Air Base and set up a decoy weather recon mission. When the MiGs came up that day in January 1967, expecting to find RF-4Cs, our fighters bagged seven of them. It was one of the great air victories of the Vietnam War. Needless to say, the weather planes weren't bothered any more by MiGs.

To get to the Hanoi target complex, we'd usually come in through the mountains northwest of the Red River Valley. One of these mountains was Thud Ridge, called that because so many F-105 fighter-bombers were shot down in that area. Thud Ridge was a long, massive structure that was easy to identify either visually or by radar, and so for us it became a major navigational fix on most recon missions to the Hanoi area. We stayed down behind the mountains as long as possible, and then zigzagged at about five hundred knots over the Red River Valley until we did a "reconnaissance pop-up." This was nothing more than a sudden climb to five or six thousand feet to fly over the target, do whatever we were supposed to do, and get back down low to avoid the missiles.

We had sensors on the RF-4C that told us when we had been picked up by North Vietnamese radar. John and I both had small oscilloscopes on warning panels with several different warning lights on them. When a search radar beam swept by us, we could figure out how far away the radar was by noting how long the strobe was in relation to the center of the oscilloscope. We almost always knew where the radar was, so we also knew when we were going to be picked up. As we got closer to the target area, close enough for missile lock-on radar to pick us up, the oscilloscope would check that, too. The oscilloscope had three rings etched on the screen. If the strobe only went to that first ring, the lock-on radar was what we called a "one ring" and it wasn't very dangerous. Two rings meant we were much closer to the missile site. A three-ringer meant we were almost on top of it.

A lock-on signal didn't necessarily mean the North Vietnamese were going to fire on us. If we were outside their SAM-2 missile envelope, they couldn't do anything but look. If we got inside the envelope and they fired a missile, our sensors would pick up its guidance radar and a light in the cockpit marked "Launch" would come on; John and I would also hear an audio signal in our headsets. In the daytime, we could see a big dust cloud on the ground when SAM-2s were fired. Most pilots called them flying telephone poles. They were white and you could see them coming. They really weren't very hard to evade—if you could see them.

Well, the North Vietnamese were just as smart as anybody else. They began to realize we had something that told us when their missiles were coming up. They started firing missiles simultaneously from the rear and the front, which complicated things for us. I never had more than one missile fired at me at any one time, but I knew pilots who were sure they had four or five coming at them. You could see one missile and evade it, but with the shotgun method you might turn right into the next one.

The North Vietnamese also used their missile threat to force us to low altitude. Once you got close to the ground, of course, the anti-aircraft guns could be very nasty. Most of them could be aimed by radar, but I rather doubt it was used very much because the gunners weren't very accurate. They just shot a lot of shells into the air.

I learned something about anti-aircraft gunfire on my first mission. John and I were coming out of the mountains and over the Red River Valley at night, heading toward Hanoi. I will swear that just east of the city every gun they had was firing. Now, they weren't shooting at us because we were ten or twelve miles away. They were just filling the sky with flak and hoping somebody would fly into it. And would you believe it: John and I drew the same target the next night. We went back up there and flak was all over the valley again. I have to assume we were the only ones up there in the middle of the night. The navy might have been there, but I know of no other air force planes in the area.

"There's no way we can fly a hundred missions with that kind of flak," I told John when we got back to Udorn.

Luckily, it wasn't all that way. But for our first two missions over North Vietnam, we were scared—and I do mean scared—by all that flak. But we came to realize that it wasn't all concentrated on our aircraft. As I said, the North Vietnamese just shot a lot of metal up in the air. If it wasn't close to us, or right in front of us, we didn't have to worry too much about it.

My aircraft was hit only once in a hundred missions, and I didn't even know it had happened. One day John and I were just lazing along through the mountains, getting ready to go out into the Red River Valley, when I looked out the cockpit to my left and saw a small anti-aircraft weapon shooting straight at us. There was nothing to do but press on. Of course, it was all over in ten seconds or so. When we got back to Udorn, there was one small hole in the tail. We were lucky on that one.

I preferred night missions. They took about two hours from takeoff to landing, the same as most day missions, but I just felt that we could get in there and out more easily at night. Plus, the radar-aimed anti-aircraft guns weren't that good. We'd usually go in at two thousand feet for photoflash shots, and even though that let everybody in North Vietnam know where we were, it was too low for the missiles to do anything. We never had to worry about MiGs at night, either. MiGs were strictly day fighters.

On most of our missions, the air force had a multi-engine aircraft code-named Red Crown orbiting over the Gulf of Tonkin. This aircraft had surveillance radar and monitored the airspace over the Red River Valley. When we flew over Hanoi, we usually came out over the port of Haiphong and then made a radio call to the American air controllers. "Red Crown," I'd say, "this is Pogo 32. Feet wet." That meant we were coming off land and over the Gulf of Tonkin. Red Crown rarely acknowledged us with anything more than "Roger." I had already made sure our Identification Friend or Foe code was properly set for our return to Udorn, because this leg of our flight usually took us over southern North Vietnam.

Reconnaissance pilots didn't like to call attention to themselves with their radios. When we left Udorn on day missions, we'd call the tower and say, "Going to tactical frequency." That allowed us to listen to the radio traffic on airstrikes and find out what the situation was. But we seldom said a word to anybody on a mission unless we had to.

We didn't feel invincible and we weren't. But we felt after a while that we were learning tactics that allowed us to be as safe as we could be when somebody down there on the ground was firing missiles and shooting flak at us. We depended on the element of surprise and the maneuverability of the RF-4C. I knew pilots who just didn't believe anybody could shoot them down, but I never felt that way. Most of us lived with the realization that, no matter how good your planning, no matter how good a pilot you might be, somebody shooting up in the air just might hit you.

We lost our first air crew in December of 1966, four months after getting to Udorn. Bob Gregory and Leroy Stutts had gone up on a night mission and just never checked back in. Well, after two or two and a half hours, we knew they weren't going to come back; the aircraft was out of fuel. My squadron was very close and we were very upset when they went down. Both were prisoners of war; Stutts made it, but Gregory never did. I'm not sure to this day if anybody knows what happened to Gregory.

One hundred missions took about six months to complete. All of us had trained together, all of us had gone over together—well, I was the exception—and we came back together. Of course, I was the last of my squadron to come home because I got to Udorn twenty days late and never caught up with the rest of the guys in missions.

I stayed in the air force until 1977, finishing my service as the deputy for operations for my old wing at Shaw Air Force Base. In between duty in Southeast Asia and retirement were assignments at the Army Command and General Staff School, CINCPAC Headquarters in Hawaii, and the Pentagon. One of my duties at the Pentagon was assigning missions for the SR-71 Blackbird, which does a lot of classified reconnaissance work. My job was to clear every classified mission over foreign territory all the way up to the secretary of defense. The irony of that is I never got to see the SR-71 in the flesh. I wish I could have flown that fantastic machine, which is still a better reconnaissance aircraft than anything anybody else has.

I didn't think much about the war while I was in Thailand, and I really haven't worried too much about it in the years since I was there. I have never considered it one of my duties to defend or berate the war. When discussions of the war came up after I got back, they usually were not among air crew members or people in combat, but from those who simply knew I was there. People would ask, "Well, what'd you think about it? Do you think what we were doing there was right?"

I can look back now and say there's no reason in this world for a nation as powerful as the United States to go to a country like Vietnam and come back and admit that it could not control the situation. As far as I'm concerned, when we left Southeast Asia in 1975 we admitted that we could not control the situation. We were just going to give up. For all those people, whether they were air force, army, navy, or marines, who lost their lives over there, that was a disgrace. We didn't have to do that.

Just look at Southeast Asia now. Basically it's what most people said it would be: Communist. A lot of my friends used to fly out of Saigon, now called Ho Chi Minh City. We went over there to keep that from happening. But I guess a lot of things were against us in Southeast Asia. We tried to fight a war that had more political than military objectives. Yet, I think that if we had wanted to stop the war, we could have done it. We demonstrated what we could do with the B-52s and the saturation bombing of North Vietnam in 1972. Maybe we should have done that in 1965 and said to Hanoi, "All right, just like in Korea, this part of Vietnam is yours and the rest is going to be a free democratic country."

In the end, we gave up all that we had been fighting for in Vietnam. I just can't imagine Cam Ranh Bay, that big deep-water port, being controlled and used by the Soviet Union. If we weren't going to win, why did we go into Vietnam in the first place?

Manuel T. Valdez

Fort Worth, Texas

Marine rifleman, 1966–67

•

Manuel Valdez is a justice of the peace in Fort Worth. During an average week, he hears about a hundred cases—civil suits, criminal misdemeanor hearings, default judgments, and other legal proceedings—in his Police Building courtroom on West Belknap Street in downtown Fort Worth. "My only pleasant duty," he told me, "is performing five to ten marriages a week. Never a dull moment, and I love it."

Manuel was a marine rifleman in Vietnam from August 1966 to September 1967, serving with 1/1st Marines, First Marine Division, in southern I Corps. Now in his early forties, he is a trim, conservatively dressed man, every button in place, very polite, and, in the opinion of the *Fort Worth Star-Telegram*, one of Tarrant County's rising political figures.

Manuel entered college at UT-Arlington in 1965—"I remember seeing Vietnam on television that year, but I didn't pay much attention to it"—with no clear idea of what he wanted to do. He had graduated in 1964 from a technical high school that had pointed him toward the printing trades. "None of my friends ever thought about going to college," he said. "All they wanted was a car and a little money to run around with. I was the only Hispanic in my group to take the SAT, and I didn't even know what the word meant."

After a year of college, Manuel's father, who worked for the General Services Administration, the federal government's vast housekeeping agency, took a job in Corpus Christi.

"My family didn't have enough money for me to stay in college, and that's when I started thinking seriously about joining the marines. I knew I didn't want to be drafted. I wanted to make my own decision."

There were a couple of reasons why I wanted to be a marine. For one, my dad had fought in the Philippines during World War II with the First Cavalry Division and was very proud of it. He talked a lot about the war when I was a kid, and I looked up to him because he had been a soldier. The other reason had to do with a cousin. We were very close. He was one of the first marines to go into Vietnam in 1965, a very gung-ho guy. He wrote me some letters about what was going on over there—his buddy getting killed, things like that. Whenever I visited his mother's house, I liked to look through his books on the Marine Corps. I was very impressed with the pride marines seemed to take in themselves.

When I joined the marines in 1966, after a year of college at UT-Arlington, I didn't especially want to go to Vietnam. From what I could see, Vietnam was a jungle-type war, a pretty nasty place to be, but other than that, I don't remember having a very clear picture of what the war was all about. I went through boot camp at the Marine Corps training center at San Diego. Looking back on it, I think I handled basic training better than some of the other fellows. I had grown up in a neighborhood in which people got cut up in fights. When I was six, a man standing next to me got shot. So for me, the violence of boot camp didn't come as such a shock. The marines will push you to your limits and then take you beyond anything you ever thought possible. But the shock of somebody hitting you in the face or in the stomach—some of the recruits had never been exposed to any of that.

The DIs liked to zero in on Hispanics. They threw around a lot of racial slurs like "wetback" or "beaner." If the DI was a redneck, he might really mean those things, but if his purpose was only to get you to get mad, he was trying to test you, to see how high your emotions could go before you started fighting back. The marines were always wanting to break us, so that when we were told to do something, we didn't ask silly questions like "Why?" It was a kind of brainwashing that geared our minds to discipline. I didn't let the racial slurs bother me very much. As I saw it, boot camp was a sort of game. I took it seriously, but I was not going to let the DIs conquer me, no matter how hard they hit me or what kind of names they called me.

I think I was a good marine in boot camp. I didn't mess up very much. I had taken some ROTC in high school and that helped in drill and handling my rifle. When the DIs discovered that I was a bit ahead of the game, they made me an acting squad leader, and in some cases, a platoon leader. However tenuous those positions were, they saved me from some of the usual boot camp harassment. Boot camp was a valuable experience in more ways than one because it was my first real exposure to blacks and Anglos, to different varieties of language. Truthfully, one of the first things the marines made me realize was that we were all a team, and for that reason, there was very little discrimination in my training company. If one man screwed up, the whole outfit had to pay for it. Everybody was tied to everybody else, regardless of race or color.

After boot camp, I went through four weeks of jungle training at Camp Pendleton. We learned how to fight in mock villages and swampy areas. Right after that, I got orders for WestPac. Nobody ever said we going to Vietnam. Frankly, I think the marines were afraid people would go AWOL or even desert if they were told they were going to Vietnam, so we were simply told we were going to WestPac. I asked one guy, "Well, what does that mean?" "That means you can go to Hawaii," he said. "It's in the western Pacific." What it meant for most marines was Okinawa. When you got there and the supply sergeants started issuing equipment for jungle combat, you knew you were going to Vietnam. And then it was too late.

In boot camp, I had gone through a lot of testing that indicated I would be good in communications. "You might think in terms of radio," one of the sergeants said, talking about advanced training after boot camp. I liked that idea. I'd been through a year of college. Why not use what I had learned? Near the end of boot camp, one of the DIs said to me, "Valdez, you're perfect material for the infantry." I said, "No, sir, I had my tests. They showed that I had some communication skills. I'd like to try it." In fact, I did get some training as a radio operator, but it meant nothing beyond being qualified to be an RTO for an artillery or mortar unit. When I went to Vietnam in August of 1966, I went to the bush as a grunt in the 1/1st Marines at Chu Lai.

My plane came into Danang late in the afternoon, almost at dusk. The heat and smell from the villages around the base, the diesel fuel, the gunpowder and everything else, was oppressive. The smell was one of the first things that everybody talked about—we certainly knew we were in a different country. I remember being scared, too. In basic training, I knew those bullets weren't real, but now I was very apprehensive about where I was going and what might happen to me.

I had one buddy that I went through the whole tour with, an Anglo guy named Radke. He was from Malone, Texas, and as country as they come. Maybe we got along so well because we were so different. We never called each other by our first names; it was always Valdez and Radke. Radke died in his sleep from a heart seizure about a month ago. Like me, he was forty-one years old. Radke was very much into Vietnam; he loved to read books and articles about the war. I was a pallbearer at his funeral. Afterward, his family showed me a lot of the photos he had taken over there and they brought back a lot of memories. I didn't take a lot of photos in Vietnam.

Lt. Col. Van Bell, my battalion commander—he was known in the marines as "Ding Dong Bell, give 'em hell"—gave a pep talk to the new guys. Bell was one tough marine, a legend in himself. He had four Purple Hearts from combat in World War II and Korea. He told us what to look out for in the bush and how important it was to take care of our M-14s and other weapons. He wanted to emphasize the importance of those warnings himself; he didn't trust the lieutenants and captains to do it. Bell would even walk point on patrols, something a battalion commander wasn't supposed to do. A pretty crazy guy, but he was the only one who told us what to expect in the bush. And our battalion got results because he was a fearless combat officer.

I saw my first combat within four days of joining the battalion. My platoon had stayed behind to guard the company headquarters while the rest of the company went on a patrol. About five miles out, the other platoons ran into trouble and we were ordered to come up and give them some help. They had cornered some VC in a mangrove swamp. When we got to the area, I saw a sergeant standing behind a communications jeep that had a big radio mounted on it. He was calling in an airstrike on the VC.

The jets roared in, shooting up and bombing the mangrove swamp. I watched the show a couple of hundred yards away with some of the other guys. As one of the jets made a low pass, a couple of bombs dropped off its wing racks and tumbled toward the ground. One of the bombs landed directly behind the sergeant who was handling the airstrike. He disappeared in a ball of fire and smoke. After the airstrike, my squad was ordered to find as much of the sergeant as we could. A marine unfolded a big, green plastic bag. "Whatever you find," he said, "bring it over here and put it in the bag."

We were literally picking up pieces of the sergeant. I wasn't really trying to find anything, but when I saw something bloody, I picked it up with a leaf and took it over to the bag. I just . . . didn't want to touch it with my fingers. After a few minutes, I said to myself, "That's enough. I don't want to find anything else." I started acting like I was looking while the rest of the guys went on picking up pieces of flesh and bone. The first combat I had seen in Vietnam resulted in one of our own men getting killed by one of our own jets. I think the reality of Vietnam hit me right there: this was the real thing, this was a war. And I could get killed, blown apart, by my own people.

I didn't sleep much that night. I thought about the death of the sergeant. It had all happened so fast. It was real, yet in a sense it had the shadings of a nightmare. I told myself, "You've got a full year here. Don't even think about it. If it happens, it happens. If it doesn't, it doesn't." I decided to let that fatalistic philosophy guide me. I would take each day as it came.

My company went on a few big operations, but they were rare. Even a battalion-sized operation was unusual. Most of our work involved squad-sized patrols and ambushes in a particular quadrant that had places with names like the Mudhole or the Sand Dune. Every little place in Vietnam seemed to have a name.

I moved up from grunt to forward observer after a couple of months in-country. We were in a swampy area between the mountains and the coast when we came under mortar and machine-gun fire. Everybody hit the ground. I waited for the FO I was working with as an RTO to give me instructions for calling in countermortar fire, but he didn't say anything. I yelled to him. Still no response. He had been killed by the machine-gun fire. It was ironic: we had taken cover in a graveyard to save our lives, and that's where he died. The platoon sergeant told me, "Okay, Valdez, for the rest of the patrol, you're going to be the forward observer." "Fine," I said. "Let's get on with it."

Being the FO wasn't a hard transition for me. All it amounted to was reading the map and calling the coordinates back on the radio. An FO and his radio operator did basically the same thing. The only difference between them lay in the FO's authority to call for fire missions. I spent a lot of time in bush after becoming an FO. It made a sort of privileged grunt with an added benefit: I didn't have to spend much time in the rear. I didn't like it back there. It was too stiff, too regulated.

I remember hearing very little explanation about where we were in Vietnam or why we were there. It was up to the colonels and other officers to decide why we were going to a particular place or village. Mostly we just heard rumors: "Yeah, that village we're going to is hot, man. You'd better be ready." We never really knew the strategy behind anything; we just went where we were told to go.

My battalion moved up to the DMZ near the end of my tour. The terrain was different up north, more hilly. It was a different kind of war, too. In the southern part of I Corps, we didn't have frequent shellings. Up north, it happened almost every night. Although the NVA had big guns on their side of the DMZ that could reach us, most of the shellings came from 60mm and 82mm mortars. They kept us from getting much rest. My attitude toward the war started to change during this time. I had seen eight or nine guys that I had gotten to know get killed. Here I was getting close to going home, and yet I had been moved to an area of very hot combat. Fear started to creep into my mind.

I thought, "I've gone all this time and now my chances of getting killed are better than they ever were." Sometimes we'd see the NVA up close on ambushes or when they were trying to climb the concertina wire during attacks on our perimeter. I can remember the distinct closeness of them under the light of the illumination rounds. But they were only human. They could be scared, too. On one operation in the bush, we flushed some NVA and they came running right by us. Of course, they would have killed us first if they'd have the chance, but here they were running all over the place, coming face-to-face with us.

We captured several Viet Cong on a big operation and kept them for two days. Most were in their late teens, although the oldest one may have been in his mid-twenties. Few of us trusted them enough to even talk to them, but we did make them carry some of our equipment and packs. A couple of them managed to get friendly with some of the men in my squad. Suddenly, an order came down: eliminate the prisoners. The memory of that order carries a lot of emotion for me, even today. I don't know who issued the order, where it came from, or anything. Maybe somebody made it up. All we heard down the line was, get rid of them.

The order came after an FO stepped on a mine in a village. I mean, it was a huge mine, probably antitank, and it simply disintegrated him. The blast killed his radio operator and badly wounded a lieutenant. Supposedly this was a friendly village, but because of this one incident, bad though it was, a sudden, emotional response resulted in the death of the prisoners. Jesus, I don't know how many were killed, because other squads had prisoners, too. But I can tell you this: I refused to have anything to do with it. The VC weren't herded into one spot like My Lai. Each squad shot its prisoners where it happened to be when the order came down. Some of the VC were tied up, but none of them was blindfolded. I watched as some of the guys in my squad made our prisoners run a short distance before opening fire. Bodies were scattered throughout the village. Women and children were spared, for the most part. We burned the place to the ground when we left.

Vietnam was a very brutal war that hardened a lot of people to the value of human life. I remember seeing marines throw grenades into holes where women and children were huddling. The guys would yell, "Fire in the hole! Fire in the hole!" just before the grenades exploded. Compared to that, shooting prisoners was nothing, but women and children. . . . I know I had become hardened, but not to the point where I felt nothing.

Some guys asked me to toss grenades at women and children one time, and I refused to do it. "All right," they said, "we'll do it." Psychologically, the war had affected them. It had to, just as it had affected the marine who was standing next to me one day when he shot some Vietnamese in their backs and heads, and then slit the throat of a pig.

A friend of mine, a guy younger than me whose name was Diamond, liked to go out in the middle of the night to kill. "I'll be right back," he would tell me. "If you want to go with me, I'll show you a few things." Always back by morning, he would say, "I saw a couple of them," meaning he had killed two Vietnamese. What Diamond was doing didn't surprise me or throw me off. I think it was a form of revenge for marines who were getting killed or maimed in some of the villages. A part of me, at least, accepted what he was doing as "that's war." I preferred to use my spare time to work with children in friendly villages. I took a liking to them because they were brown-faced; they reminded me of my brothers and sisters and cousins. I gladly shared my C-rations with them.

The closer I got to the end of my tour in September of 1967, the more I began to think I would never get out of Vietnam. The days seemed to have more than twenty-four hours. My senses were telling me that I had lived a whole lifetime there. I had even forgotten the faces of my parents and other family members. In their letters to me, my mother and father begged me to write to them, something I did so rarely that my sister became a ghostwriter for me. She wrote letters to my parents and sent them to me to sign; I was supposed to sign my name to these letters and send them back from Vietnam. The letters would say something very bland like, "I'm doing fine and I'm coming home soon." Mainly, I didn't write because I was afraid my parents might get hurt. I didn't want to write an optimistic letter and then have them get the news that something had happened to me. And I especially didn't want to tell them that we were killing people over there.

I left Vietnam in September of 1967, thirteen months to the day after I got there. The marines didn't mess around with DEROS dates. I remember an eruption of yelling on the plane after it lifted off from Danang. It was as if everybody aboard suddenly burst out of his shell—a tremendous feeling of liberation. I've never felt quite so high because from that point on, Vietnam was behind me. I had held my breath for thirteen months and now I could breathe again.

I was nineteen years old when I came home. My plane landed at Edwards Air Force Base, east of Los Angeles, so I decided to go into the city for a few days before flying home to Texas. I was wearing my Class A uniform when I got off the bus in downtown Los Angeles. As I walked through the bus station, an older woman in an overcoat pointed at me and called me a babykiller. What she was saying didn't bother me; it went in one ear and out the other. I wasn't exactly expecting a hero's welcome, and, in fact, just wanted to slip back to the states quietly. I hadn't even called my parents to tell them I was back. As I saw it, I had accomplished something of tremendous value: I had survived Vietnam. But when I got a hotel room, the first thing I did was to take my uniform off and put on civilian clothes.

Then I walked across the street to get a sandwich at a small diner. I sat down at a table with an older man, Jewish, I think, and we started talking. I told him I was a marine, but not that I had just come back from Vietnam. Actually, I didn't care what he or anybody else thought at that point. I was so confident of myself that I walked through much of the heart of Los Angeles, soaking up the sights and sounds of the city. I was so confident I'd go anywhere, just walk and walk and enjoy the streets.

After a couple of days, I called my parents and said, "I'm back in the states. I'll be home tomorrow." I didn't want them to know I was back until they could meet me at the airport. They were elated when I walked off the plane at Love Field in Dallas. It was a real high for all of us. As we got to know each other again, I noticed that they didn't ask many questions about the war. Whenever we talked about it, I was the one who did most of the talking, and I found that I really didn't want to talk about it very much.

Maybe I didn't want to destroy the pride I had in my accomplishment. I didn't get involved in weighing the good and bad of the war. Serving in Vietnam was an obligation for me. I never questioned it any more than I questioned joining the marines. I was proud that I had fought for my country.

I finished my time in the marines at Camp Pendleton. You can imagine my shock when I got to my new company, in which I was supposed to be a mail clerk, and learned that it was almost ready to ship out for Vietnam. I couldn't believe it—the marines were about to send me back; my name was on the list. Khe Sanh was taking a lot of heat at the time and the marines needed every warm body they could round up in the states. Right then and there I started to think about taking off. I'm not sure whether I would have done it or not, but I really was on the verge of saying, "There's no way I'm going back. Nobody's going to make me go back."

While I was in Vietnam, I had sent money home for a car. I picked it up while I was home on leave, and now things were moving so fast I was having to think about what to do with it in case I did go back. I told my gunnery sergeant, "I just got back from Vietnam. Why should I go back?" He practically ignored me. He was far more focused on getting the unit packed up for Vietnam. Maybe he helped me to stay behind, maybe he didn't; I'll never know. I simply stood around while almost everybody else climbed on trucks and moved out for shipment to Vietnam. Nobody said a word when I stayed behind. It was, to put it mildly, a bizarre episode.

I stayed in Los Angeles about a year after my discharge to work for a moving and storage company. I was just a helper, but the company paid good money and besides I liked Los Angeles. The city was vibrant and exciting. I began to see after a while, though, that I was spending money as fast as I made it. I decided to come back to Fort Worth and enter UT-Arlington on the GI Bill. I started out in engineering, but as I started to get involved in community work, I switched my major to criminal justice. One thing led to another. A couple of months after I established a youth center in the Southside community of Fort Worth, some of the social services agencies came to me and said, "We'll pay you for what you're doing." Creating youth centers was easy. All I had to do was ask for help.

I worked for the city for ten years setting up big, multipurpose centers with gymnasiums. I enjoyed the work and must have been pretty good at it, because I moved up the ranks in the Department of Human Resources. Until six years ago, I was more interested in my job than politics, but an election was coming up for justice of the peace, and some of my friends urged me to run. In my campaign, I let the people of Fort Worth know that I was a marine in Vietnam and proud of it. I never tried to hide that part of my record.

So far as I'm concerned, I think I've put Vietnam in its place. Yet, I believe I gained something from the experience: I learned how to survive. Nothing in this country could ever be as bad as Vietnam was; nothing here could ever bring me down the way Vietnam might have. Knowing that helps me make decisions now. People come to my courtroom every day with all kinds of problems. To them, it's the end of the world. But I can listen to them and not get emotionally upset or lose my composure. I can see their situation with some perspective and tell them about alternatives.

I think I grew up a lot in Vietnam. An experience like that can certainly accelerate your maturation, but unfortunately that can't be said of every-body who was there. A lot of veterans came back truly affected by the war. They've never recovered from it. Somehow, the shock of it stopped them in time, so that they live with the war even today. I don't mind talking about the war when people ask me about it. A lot of the kids I come in contact with are very interested in Vietnam. I tell them the war has its place in history, that it was not all negative. I think it's healthy to talk about the war. And, you know, I always try to help Vietnam veterans. Any time they have an organizational meeting in Fort Worth, or just want to get together for some purpose, I support them.

Allen C. LoBean

Persimmon Community

Rabun County, Georgia

Navy Swift boat gunner, 1966–68

●

Allen LoBean told me on the phone that he lives so far back in the North Georgia mountains I would never find him. "Let's meet at the Hardee's in Clayton," he suggested. He arrived a few minutes after I did, wearing faded jeans, a work shirt, and a black cap emblazoned with "Vietnam Veteran" in yellow. A well-groomed man of medium height, he walked with a certain nervous caution that I had noticed in several other veterans.

Allen was a machinegunner aboard navy Swift boats for eighteen months in 1966–68. These lightly armed aluminum vessels resembled the PT boats of World War II. Fifty feet long and manned by a crew of six, they were used for offshore interdiction and river patrols.

After a quick breakfast at Hardee's, I followed Allen's Ford pickup along an asphalt road that led east into the mountains, where he lives on seven acres in the Persimmon Community. The road, full of hairpin curves, gave way after ten miles or so to what seemed little more than a graveled path. After a few more miles, we splashed through a small ford, then started up a gradual incline that led to Allen's cabin. The trip from Clayton had taken almost half an hour. Allen was right: I never would have found him on my own.

A housepainter and carpenter, Allen built the cabin, a two-story place of contemporary design, himself. I had expected something more primitive, but the cabin was comfortably and tastefully furnished, complete with a video monitor and a VCR.

"Back in 1965," he said as we began to talk, "the navy had what it called the 120-day delay program. That meant you could sign up and have four months to do what you wanted to before you had to report for basic training. Well, I had finished high school in Fort Myers, Florida, when I signed up, and I vaguely remember hearing something about Vietnam around that time—a skirmish or whatever—but I never thought I would go there."

I asked to go to the naval training center at San Diego instead of the one at Great Lakes, Illinois, for basic training, and oddly enough, I got it. I wanted to stay warm during the winter. I had asked for advanced training in aviation maintenance when I signed up, but the navy decided I really wasn't qualified for that and gave me one of those "do you like this or do you like that" exams and it turned out I liked everything to do with ordnance. So I ended up at Great Lakes after all, where I froze my tail off from October of 1965 to March of 1966 at the Gunner's Mate School.

Back then, the navy had two gunner's mate ratings you could strike for. One was gunner's mate guns and the other was gunner's mate missiles. And, God, I wish I'd had the foresight to choose missiles. But I chose guns, which was supposed to qualify me to handle everything from small arms up to the 16-inch guns on a battleship.

Gunnery school lasted for sixteen weeks. We learned about rotating machinery, AC and DC current, the velocity of a shell coming out of a barrel, how many foot-pounds of energy it had when hitting a target, and so on. Well, the passing grade for the school was 62.5 and I earned 65.93. I just made it by the skin of my teeth. I didn't hear a lot about Vietnam there, but I was naive enough to think I wanted to go. No ifs, ands, or buts. I wanted to go. I turned twenty while I was in gunnery school and at that age death doesn't mean anything. You just don't think about it. That's something that happens to somebody else or to people who're older, but it doesn't happen to you.

I was in gunner's mate school when I first seen Swift boats. One old boy we called Papa because he was married and had just become a father was watching TV one day when he said, "Hey, look, there's Swift boats on television. I want to sign up for that outfit." I was sitting there listening to all the horror stories about ship duty and how once you got on one, you'd never get off. You'd be stuck on it for the rest of your time in the service. "God bless it," I said to Papa, "I'm going to be a gunner's mate. I'll sign up with you."

My first request was denied, but I rewrote it, saying I could best serve my country that way. Then they sent me to Coronado, California, for Swift boat training. Swift boats was like fulfilling a childhood fantasy. They was neat—JFK, PT-109, the whole nine yards of "ask not what your country can do for you, but what you can do for your country." I got about two months of training on them. It was long enough and more training than most guys seen before going to Vietnam.

I ended up as the forward gunner with two .50-caliber machine guns, just what I wanted. When I was a kid, I always had these wooden guns and we played machine guns. We'd crawl and shoot everything. A toy shop had a plastic machine gun sitting on a shelf—it was way out of my price range—but I always dreamed of shooting a machine gun.

After the training at Coronado, I went to the Philippines for a few days in September of 1966 with my crew. That's where Swift boats was outfitted and put in running order before being shipped to Vietnam. I flew from the Philippines to Saigon. I could see the countryside was green and lush, a little like the states in a way. After I got off the aircraft, I walked across the airstrip wondering if I shouldn't be running. Here I was in Vietnam and nobody was shooting at me.

I stayed three days at the Capital Hotel, which had barbed wire all around it, and that was the first time I was able to drink something. I was twenty years old and I decided to find my limit. You know, this is Vietnam, I'm going to find my limit. So some of us went to a bar at another hotel and I drank and drank, but I was keeping track of the number. I had eight Singapore slings and eight vodka Collins, but they wasn't doing anything to me. I tried a stinger and a dry martini. God, all those people I've seen on television drinking a dry martini—they ought to use it for hair oil instead of drinking it. When we got ready to go back to the Capital Hotel, I went all the way to the back of the bus. I had eaten a great big dinner with seafood and the back of the bus was where all the motion was. I got sicker than a dog and I can remember some of the guys hauling me up the stairs of the hotel, my feet dragging. Lieutenant McGuire, the boat officer, was gung-ho and he came along and just shook his head because here was his gunner's mate drunker than a skunk.

The guys threw me in the shower. I had almost killed myself with alcohol and I didn't realize it. You know, I couldn't drink lemonade for six months after that because it made me so sick. The navy liked to give us lemonade.

The whole crew flew up to Danang together. At first, we swapped boats with another crew. This was called a turnaround boat. It would go out on patrol and come back in and be fueled up for another crew. It took about a month and a half before we got our own boat, PCF-15. Somebody had the foresight to box the ammunition for the .50 calibers on our boat so that I had an extra one hundred rounds for each gun. That gave me a thousand rounds total. I weighed 115 pounds at the time and really had to hit that gun mount to swing it because it wasn't electrical. I was always the little guy that people picked on at the beach and here I was behind something that could just flat destroy anything—geez, the power behind those .50s. I got to love those things. I got to be what gunners call a natural. If I could see a target, I could hit it by the fourth round.

Most of our time was spent on Operation Market Time, patrolling offshore to check junks and other Vietnamese boats for contraband. But on April 9, 1967, we got into it on the Troung Giang River between Danang and Chu Lai.

There was a sort of sandbar that came out of the north side of the river. It was shallow water over there and a couple of poles were sticking out of it. Everybody was at general quarters, flak jackets and everything, all the guns uncovered. All I had to do was jack my .50s back one more time to fire them. We fed past the poles to go over to a Green Beret base called X-Ray Delta. It was about eleven in the morning and already hot. We pulled up to an old wooden dock and Lieutenant McGuire went inside the camp to an old tin shack. We were sitting there facing concertina wire and Claymores, just acting the fool and watching an airstrike across the river. The pilot was dropping napalm. You could see the canister coming off the airplane as he flew over and it just slowly tumbled end over end and hit the ground and went off like an A-bomb. About that time, Lieutenant McGuire came back and said we was going up the river.

I was excited because I was looking forward to something. Swift boat duty could be pretty boring. Lieutenant McGuire said the marines was coming up the river from the west, trying to herd VC towards the river, and our job was to destroy any boats, sampans, or VC that we seen. It was a free-fire zone. About two in the afternoon, we had gone up the river a couple of miles, maybe three, and we could see these marines in the river. Some of them was swimming. Foster and Meron, who was on the aft gun, thought the marines was VC, and they was terrified. I was on the forward guns and knew what was going on because I could hear the Prick-25 and watch Lieutenant McGuire.

There was a little clearing along the riverbank, a sort of beach, and I could see a lot of coconut trees—it was beautiful country, very green. All the brush had been cleared out under the coconut trees. The beach was maybe a hundred feet long and thirty feet wide and the white sand looked like sugar sand, the kind you see in Florida. All of a sudden, three men broke and ran out of their cover in the brush. They ran across the beach and Lieutenant McGuire picked up his field glasses and looked at them, studied them for a minute. I had the .50s trained on them. All I had to do was pull the trigger. Then the men started running toward the marines.

I laugh about what happened next because—well, at the time I thought it was funny.

Lieutenant McGuire said, "Fire a salvo." A salvo is one round in each gun. I thought to myself, "God, surely he doesn't mean that. I can't—I'm not that good, I can't fire a .50 that good."

I opened fire, but it was the training in Coronado that actually saved some marine's life because I didn't fire high—I was looking for a backstop. The sand kicked up behind the guys running away and they disappeared over a ridge. The Prick-25 came on and the marines was yelling and screaming. They couldn't figure out who was firing because they didn't know where we was. And then a little bit later another group of VC ran out on this open stretch of beach. They was dressed in black pajamas and had BARs, grenades, and everything. Lieutenant McGuire picked up his binoculars again and looked at them, about a hundred feet away. I had the .50s ready to fire.

He called out, "Fire!"

I can remember to this day opening fire. And I can remember that the first burst was about sixty rounds and the thought in my mind was, "Back off, off, back off. Cut it down to short bursts or you'll burn up the barrels." I played the .50s back and forth on this group, just swinging the guns back and forth. The .50s had an acid smell and the shell casings was ringing out as they hit the metal deck of the boat. I was making what the navy calls body shots, from the shoulder to the waist. Anything else was a waste of time and bullets.

The next thing I remember was ceasing fire. There was nobody on the beach but one guy with a big red spot on his back.

"LoBean's got our first KIA!" yelled Turnbull, the radioman. I guess that was the first time we'd actually killed anybody in Vietnam. I got a Viet Cong and Turnbull was excited about it. "Did you see how that one flipped in midair?" he said.

"Yes," I told him, but the truth is, I can't remember it. All I remember is seeing a guy with a big red spot on his back lying on the beach. Williams, the helmsman, told me later that a marine officer walked over to the VC and shot him in the head with a pistol. I must have been checking my guns or doing something else, because I didn't see that. The marines checked the beach area and found seven more bodies in the bushes where the .50s had kicked them. They found three wounded VC. So I had killed eight Viet Cong right there and wounded three more. As far as I was concerned, my life hadn't been threatened at all. I had my orders to fire, I know. I have a Navy Commendation Medal citation that said we was receiving machine-gun fire, but I don't remember that.

My boat did a little more work on the river that day. We shot up some fishing gear and a couple of bunkers down the river before going back to the Green Beret base. I stayed up until ten o'clock that night. I was tired, but I still had a lot of trouble getting to sleep.

We went up the river again the next morning with another boat carrying the commodore of our squadron. I don't know why we went back because the operation with the marines was over. All we got out of it was a nasty little firefight that sent the commodore's boat flying by us in retreat at twenty-five knots. Bullets was coming at us so thick the river looked like it was in the midst of a rainstorm. Because of our position, we had to provide covering fire for both boats, but I couldn't get my .50s to bear on the targets for one reason or another, so I killed a few coconuts on the way out.

We got back to Danang about nine o'clock the next morning and I sat down and picked up my art book and little drawing pen and scratched eight crosses on a piece of paper. In a way that I didn't understand, I had become part of the machinery on the boat when the VC was being killed. I had no feeling, no feeling whatsoever, about killing those people. Even to this day I have no feeling and that bothers me to a point. I've heard grunts talk about their first kill, "Oh, God, I had dry heaves, I just went over there and threw up." For me, it was as if I had shot a bunch of tin cans.

On the streets today, when many of the kids find out you're a Vietnam vet, they'll ask you if you killed anybody. Their next question is always, "How did it feel?" Well, I had no feeling. In fact, in my mind, I didn't kill anybody, but the citation says I did and everything points to it, because the aft gun never did open fire.

I'm trying to get my crew back together. The first thing I want to do if we have a reunion is to sit down and talk about it. I want to talk about it because I really remember so little of it. When I went down to the VA Hospital in Atlanta and told them what I've told you, the medical people put me down as 10 percent disabled by PTSD.

The counselor said, "Why do you want to remember?" I said, "It was my job. I should have known what happened to those guys." And I really should have . . . I really should have known where they went, how many I killed exactly. "Well," the counselor said, "you should be happy that none of your crew was injured. You did the right thing." Well, how come I can't remember it? It scares me. It means I could go right out on the street and pull the trigger on somebody and never feel it because I was trained so well, trained over and over to kill.

You know, for a long time after getting out of the navy in 1971, I used to think the American people hated us. If you walked up to somebody on the street, even five years after the war ended, and said, "I'm a Vietnam vet," they'd just turn around and walk off. They wouldn't even talk to you, like we had done something downright dirty for going, for being there. But I also believed they felt sort of guilty for sending us.

A lot of the guys on Swift boats didn't have anybody to write to, so I sent a letter to the Mail Bag section of the Fort Myers newspaper and at one time had twenty-three girls writing me. Then I got to writing to one named Julie and basically came out of the navy and married her. It lasted two and a half years. I spent the time virtually alone. My dad had a stroke and I was appointed the guardian of him and his estate in Fort Myers. He moved in with us, which was hard on a married couple. I started working seven days a week on his estate. I didn't really have to, but I found that I liked to be alone. I'd get to the point—I don't know how to explain it, but I just liked to be alone.

So, the marriage failed, but I have nothing against Julie at all. Basically, I think I'm still in love with her. She wasn't happy and started coming home from work at seven or eight o'clock. I was always there at four or five o'clock, just the reverse of what you read in all the books.

I got married again two years later. We stayed together for about six years on a farm over in North Carolina. She had kids and I adopted them, but I had a terrible time getting close to them. We tried to have kids of our own, but I had mumps as a kid and I'm sterile; I didn't know that, but apparently the navy did. If I'd known I was sterile, I'd probably never have gotten married because I really wanted kids the second time around.

Part of my PTSD has to do with the episode up the river, the eight guys that I can't picture. I fell fourteen feet off a ladder once and you might say it happened so fast that I couldn't keep track of what was going on. But on the way down I told myself to let go of the spray gun and the paint: turn it loose, don't get tangled in it. The next thought was, "God, I hope this don't hurt much." Well, I should have remembered exactly what went on up that river. I can't, but it's beginning to slowly come out. I'm beginning to see faces.

The other part of the PTSD is that I'm alone. I've been alone since Vietnam, maybe even before it. I don't trust anybody and I definitely don't trust my government. I don't date and I don't go out. I keep a shotgun downstairs. A .30-caliber pistol is upstairs, and so is a .270-caliber rifle. I probably have enough ammunition to last me a month.

About three years ago, I became so depressed I put the pistol to my head one night. I was having money problems and in the middle of my second divorce: God knows, everything under the sun seemed to be going wrong. I said there ain't nothing out there; there ain't nothing to look forward to, that I had sort of done it all. And finally—I couldn't pull the trigger. So I asked myself, "What is it you really want to do, that you'd really like to change?"

I thought about the POWs and MIAs and how I'd like to give them a chance with their lives. And that's basically what saved my life, getting involved in the POW-MIA issues. I can laugh about it, but my God . . . the gun cabinet upstairs is nailed shut now. I guess my views on the war started to change about that time. I've been reading about Agent Orange and the other crap that's coming out about Vietnam. You know, I'd like to think we did *something*. I always tried to believe we fought for freedom, but I've read different things and, God, I've decided it wasn't freedom. It was political. The whole thing was political.

The one thing that held me together all these years was believing that Vietnam wasn't a waste. They yanked that away from me, too. To find out it was a waste. It was really a waste. It made some people poor and it made some people rich. And it made a lot of people sad.

Moses L. Best, Sr.

Fayetteville, North Carolina

Army signal specialist, 1966–67, 1969–70

●

Standing in his neatly trimmed front yard, Moses Best pointed toward a house on Broadell Street, then another and still another. "I knew them," he said, referring to their owners. All were friends who died in Vietnam. Like Moses, they were black sergeants who had seen in the army a way out of the segregated small towns of the South in the 1950s. Moses himself grew up in rural Lenoir County, North Carolina, one of ten children of a farmer whose attempts to secure school buses for black children earned him a savage beating from the Ku Klux Klan. "I watched them break his cheek open," Moses said as we talked in the family room of his house.

A wiry, energetic man who owns a small liquor store in Fayetteville, Moses saw service in Vietnam as an army communications sergeant in 1966–67 and again in 1969–70. The memories of coming back to a country badly split by the war are still hard for him to cope with. "Let me put it this way," he said, his voice quivering with emotion, "the American people weren't ready for the Vietnam War. I don't know why they were against us."

Moses was a platoon sergeant in the Eighty-second Signal Battalion at Fort Bragg when he went to Vietnam in October 1966 to join the First Brigade of the 101st Airborne Division. The year before, he had been in the Dominican Republic as the NCO in charge of special communication circuits that linked President Lyndon Johnson with the headquarters of American troops there.

"Even before the trouble in the Dominican Republic broke out, we'd been training at Fort Pickett, Virginia, which has a lot of hills and valleys that look like Vietnam," Moses said. "By the time a lot of us got in-country, we had a pretty good idea of what the terrain and the vegetation were like. A lot of NCOs at Bragg, maybe a hundred or more, were handpicked for Vietnam duty at the same time I was."

When I walked off the plane at Tan Son Nhut Airport in Saigon, the weather was so hot and sticky I thought I was going to pass out. It made my skin burn. And that smell—it was like I had just walked into a room where something dead had been closed up for a long time.

A bus picked up me and some other NCOs and we went over to the replacement battalion at Camp Alpha to spend the night. Along the way, I saw some Americans pouring diesel fuel on the roads to hold down some of that red dust that seemed to be on everything. The camp itself was overcrowded, with too many tents and not enough hot water to take a shower. I could hardly find enough water to fill my canteen.

Everybody at Camp Alpha was either digging holes or filling up sandbags for protection against rocket and mortar attacks. I filled up sandbags. While we were there, we also got lectures on how important it was to take our malaria pills and salt tablets. The most interesting thing to me, though, was airplanes that looked like C-130s flying around and spraying something on the jungle about a quarter of a mile away. I couldn't figure out what they were doing.

I said to a guy sitting next to me, "Man, why are they flying so low like that?"

"They're getting ready to burn the jungle off," he said. Pretty soon, some flame-throwing tanks rolled up and set the whole jungle on fire. In a way, it was a very sad thing to see because monkeys were burning up all over the place. They cried like a bunch of babies.

I drew an assignment to the First Brigade of the 101st Airborne Division, up at Phan Rang on the coast of the South China Sea. At the time, the other two brigades of the division were still at Fort Campbell, Kentucky. I picked up my first set of jungle fatigues and boots at the base camp. I wanted some new T-shirts and undershorts too, but the supply sergeant said, "You won't wear no T-shirts and shorts here. It's too humid and they won't do you any good." At first, I thought the sergeant was just having some fun with me, but he knew what he was talking about. A T-shirt was just extra weight and the shorts stayed too wet.

The area around Phan Rang was very dry. To me, it looked a lot like Texas—bushes and hills. A lot of little green snakes that the troops called Charlie Two-Step were around there. I had an experience with one of them when we went to Phan Thiet for a while not long after I joined the brigade. We were staying in five-man tents and only had candles for light.

So here comes a Charlie Two-Step parading right into my tent, where some of us were sitting around with M-16s loaded with 30-round banana clips. One of my tentmates hit the snake with the butt of his M-16 and that caused the rifle to fire, right through the top of the tent. He killed the snake, but it was a close call for everybody else.

Phan Thiet was a spooky place. I saw more graves there than I had ever seen in my life. The French had lost a big battle at Phan Thiet years before, and their cemetery seemed to go on as far as I could see. It was at Phan Thiet, in fact, that I saw my first combat in Vietnam. The VC hit us right outside the town. They had laid mines in the road, but the first two or three of our vehicles got by before anything happened. Then a jeep with a .50-caliber machine gun mounted on it hit one of the mines and flipped over—I think the machine-gun mount was all that kept the driver from getting killed. We got into a firefight with some VC and killed at least one of them, but the rest got away because they could blend in with the population so easily.

I tried not to get very attached to people in the brigade because so many were at risk of being killed, but I still lost a close friend at Phan Rang. He was a white guy named Chitwood, and he was in charge of the communications center when I wasn't there. A lot of guys in Vietnam who wanted to get the CIB or even a Purple Heart knew the quickest way to do that was to go to a rifle company. Chitwood was one of those guys. He wanted a CIB so bad he got his MOS changed and went to a platoon as a squad leader.

"Man," I said, "do you know what you're doing?"

He didn't want to listen to me or anybody else. He lasted about four months in the infantry. I heard he got shot through the head four times. A real nice guy, Chitwood. I often think about him. He was probably the closest friend I ever had over there.

You could get killed in strange ways in Vietnam. One soldier in the brigade got killed by a VC with a crossbow. The arrow from that teak-wood crossbow could plow three inches into a tree—I had never seen anything like it. I was so fascinated by the power of that crossbow that I brought it back and shot an arrow into one of the trees in my backyard to show my wife that I wasn't making the story up.

The First Brigade was a very aggressive outfit that believed in carrying the fight to the enemy. We lost a lot of men in combat. For some reason I never understood, we didn't talk about the ones who got killed. We'd line up their boots for a memorial service, render a salute at the end of it, and go back to work. There was really nothing else we could do.

At the base camp in Phan Rang, I would sometimes see bodies stacked up . . . well, like the bunk beds in ships. They were zipped up in green body bags and stored in big refrigerated containers until they could be moved to a mortuary. Some of the men in the brigade used the body coolers for their own purposes. They would put the free beer we got on standdowns in the coolers. It was hard to get upset about it because there was no other place to keep the beer cold. I had tried using fire extinguishers to cool down beer cans, but the first time I peeped in one of the body coolers and saw beer in it, I started putting mine in there, too.

When I was with the 101st, it had a lot of black soldiers, or so it seemed to me. We had quite a few black officers, too, but I can't remember a single one in a command slot. The whole brigade staff was white, but everybody seemed to get along pretty well. I think we blacks were treated fairly. If there had been any serious incidents, I would have known about them because the information would have come through me at brigade headquarters.

I made one parachute jump in Vietnam. It was a training exercise in December of 1966, and I remember that our parachutes had to be flown in from Japan. We were loaded with all our regular battlefield gear—rifles, machine guns, ammunition, Claymore mines, the whole nine yards. We jumped from C-130s near Kontum City a little before sunrise. I was the jumpmaster in the third plane, and as I was getting my guys to the door, I heard somebody say, "We're getting fired on." I started pushing men out the door, looking all the time at a hill coming straight toward the airplane. I heard the pilot say, "Let me turn back." I was the jumpmaster and was supposed to go with my men, but I decided to wait this time for the pilot to make another pass over the drop zone.

For some reason, my parachute didn't open all the way, and to make the situation worse, my left knee hit a stake when I tumbled on landing. My whole left leg began to swell like a balloon a few minutes later. Lucky for me, there was no ground fire at the drop zone. But I wasn't sure where I had landed, and neither was a PFC a few feet from me.

"Sergeant," he said, "where is everybody?"

"Right here," I told him. "Put your machine gun over there. Get set up now." I told him I had been hurt. I was on the verge of screaming with pain, but I crawled as well as I could to his M-60 position and waited with him until the drop zone got organized and a medevac chopper could be called to take me out. The chopper took me to the Eighty-fifth Evacuation Hospital in Qui Nhon, where I stayed until the morning of January 6, 1967. I remember the date because the VC rocketed a town outside the city the night before. The hospital was full of wounded Americans by morning.

My wound was bad enough for me to go on to the big hospital at Clark Air Force Base in the Philippines. One of the first people I saw as I was wheeled into the hospital was Mrs. Westmoreland in a nurse's uniform and cap. She was a volunteer at the hospital. I noticed that she was looking at the 101st Airborne patch on my jacket.

"He'll stop right here," she told the orderlies. She put me to bed, and then the doctors and nurses started coming—bunches of them. "I'm going to bring you something," Mrs. Westmoreland said. And she did, the next day. She walked in with some of the best chocolate fudge brownies I've ever tasted.

From Clark, I went on to a hospital in Japan, where some Japanese doctors got me back in shape, at least enough to walk. They wanted to operate on me, but I wouldn't let them. So they drew a lot of fluid out of my knee with a needle and prescribed hydrotherapy, sometimes three times a day. After four months of treatment, I went back to the 101st, but my knee was never the same.

Even before I came back to the states in October of 1967, I sensed that the American people weren't behind us in Vietnam. The first thing I saw when I got off the airplane at the Seattle-Tacoma Airport was a sign, "Stay Out of Vietnam." I took off my uniform and put on my civilian clothes at the airport because I'd heard about so many soldiers being hassled there by antiwar protesters.

Coming back was . . . a very bad feeling. Nobody seemed to want to talk to me simply because I was a soldier. And yet, I really don't think I was looking for very much. I just wanted to be treated normally. I came on home to Fayetteville, to this house that I bought years ago, and I didn't go anywhere for a few days. I needed some time to get to know my family again, to think and to adjust to what was going on in the country. I remember spending a lot of hours working in my yard before I even went down to see my mother in Lenoir County.

I came back to the First Brigade of the Eighty-second Airborne. I was home only eight months before the army said it needed me to go back to Vietnam with the First Brigade. NCOs with my experience were in critically short supply over there in 1968, but I got that hassle straightened out. I went to the inspector general of the Eighty-second and said, "Uh-unh, it's not my time to go back." I bought about a year by getting transferred to the Second Brigade.

My number came up for good in July of 1969. I decided to go back with a good attitude, with an open mind, and give it all I had. I also decided to be more careful this time. I went to the Fifty-fourth Signal Battalion at

Nha Trang as the operations sergeant, but I had another office nearby at I Field Force Headquarters as part of a two-man team that kept the commanding general linked by radio with the units in the bush. The Fifth Special Forces headquarters was there, too, and we supported their long-range radio communication with units in Laos.

The second time around . . . I don't know what was wrong. Everything seemed so damned disorganized. That's just my perspective, of course, but I do know for sure about two big problems at Nha Trang. One was white power and the other was black power. The black guys were into all that handslapping business, something I had no use for at all. I think the Vietnamese girls in Nha Trang—a lot of them had French blood—were at the bottom of some of the racial problems there because they would hang with both the white guys and the blacks.

When the troop cutbacks started in 1969, big combat operations became fewer and fewer to hold down casualties. There wasn't a lot for the troops to do in Nha Trang, and that made the racial situation and other disciplinary problems even worse. Too many troops were being confined in one area during the standdowns. People herded together like that could get killed by Charlie, or they might kill themselves. We had a big rocket attack the day before Thanksgiving in 1969, for example. One of those big, slow rockets came in early in the morning and hit an air force fuel dump. On Thanksgiving Day itself, a guy in the map section put the barrel of an M-14 in his mouth and blew his head off—why, I never knew.

I wanted to get away from what was going on in Nha Trang. After seven months there, I asked for reassignment to the 173rd Airborne Brigade at LZ English in Binh Dinh province. That was Charlie country all the way, but it was a better place to finish my tour than a rear area like Nha Trang.

When I came home in 1970 for the second time, the mood of the country was so bad that I didn't say much about the war to anybody. Even Alberta and I don't talk much about it to this day. Maybe if Fayetteville or another city had sponsored a welcome-home parade for Vietnam veterans, it would have been better for us. A lot of vets just can't cope with the rejection they got when they came back. Damn, they just can't do it.

A lot of guys, good God—you'd be surprised how many have been divorced. I didn't let that happen to me. I refused to feel sorry for myself. I could find too much to do. I started work on a degree in economics at Fayetteville State University after I retired, and I earned it, too. I started my own business. Alberta and I also had five kids who had to be raised, and I'm proud to say that all five of them went on to college.

Ted A. Burton

Poor Valley Community

Hawkins County, Tennessee

Army medic, 1967–68

•

Ted Burton lives in Poor Valley, eight miles over Stone Mountain from Rogersville as the crow flies, sixteen by car on serpentine State Highway 66. Ted, his wife, Joyce, and their young son, Joshua, make their home on a thirty-three-acre farm in this isolated part of northeast Tennessee, where Burtons have tilled the land and raised their families for generations.

Ted was waiting for me on the porch of his modest wood and cinder-block house when I drove up. He moved haltingly with the aid of a cane to lessen chronic back pain, the result of an accident while pouring concrete several years ago at TVA's Phipps Bend nuclear power plant. Fortunately, another in a series of back operations later gave him some relief from his discomfort.

Ted is an ample, friendly Tennessee mountaineer with a cherubic face that takes ten years off his age. In 1967–68, he was a medic with the First Infantry Division as it fought to clear the rubber plantations and jungles of War Zone C north of Saigon, long an untouched preserve of the Viet Cong. Unlike most soldiers, who expected to spend only six months in the bush and then go to a safer job in the rear, Ted spent almost his whole tour with line units because he believed that was where he belonged. Twice during our conversation, Ted broke out in tears. I became concerned that my questions might be invading some private corner of his world, a place where he preferred to keep his feelings about the war to himself. "No," he said, "I want to talk about it."

The oldest of seven children, Ted dropped out of high school in the early 1960s to help his parents. Later he went to Kokomo, Indiana, to work in a steel mill. An uncle was already there and Ted went north, too, convinced "southerners can get a job when northerners can't because we know how to work."

But Ted got homesick and came back after a year to work in an auto body shop. He took home twenty-four dollars a week. By 1966, Vietnam was a real war and Ted was looking for a better job. "I knew I was about to be drafted," he told me as we settled down for an interview that would last more than three hours. "Everywhere I went to look for work—Morristown, Kingsport, Rogersville—people wanted to know what my draft rating was. Even though I was married, it was so high I couldn't get a job nowhere."

With his name up for the September draft call in Hawkins County, Ted told the draft board to move him up to August. He volunteered for the draft.

"I'd heard of Vietnam, sure. I knew several guys from Hawkins County who'd gone over there. While I was in basic training at Fort Campbell, Kentucky, I got to figuring I was going to Vietnam, too."

During basic they called us all in for an interview and asked what we wanted to do if we had a choice. We had three choices. I said medic, medic, medic, and I was lucky enough to get it. The other guys there, a lot of 'em put down truck driver and they got to drive a truck in Louisiana. I went straight down to Fort Sam Houston for training to be a medic.

You see, I was a Primitive Baptist minister for four or five years before I got drafted. I preached the Gospel in Tennessee, Kentucky, and Virginia. I held revivals and baptized sinners. Preaching had a lot to do with me wanting to be a medic. I figured I could help people more that way than shooting at somebody. I didn't want to kill people; I didn't think I could do it. I didn't believe in killing, but after I got in, got over to Vietnam and seen my best friends die, a lot of them in my arms—if I could have, I guess I would have killed all them VC.

I spent ten weeks at Fort Sam, learning how to take care of wounds, just in general how to take care of sick people. I enjoyed it. I liked Fort Sam—it was a right pretty place. A couple of the instructors had come back from Vietnam and they talked about sucking chest wounds and that sort of thing, but for the most part, I don't believe the other instructors had ever seen somebody get shot. I remember we saw a lot of movies and trained on each other with simulated wounds. Quite a few of the reserve boys at Fort Sam talked about Vietnam more than us other guys did. When they finished up, they went home.

I got a six-day leave to go back to Rogersville after I finished up at Fort Sam. I had my orders then for Vietnam. Four of us rented a car in San

Antonio and drove it all the way to Knoxville. A friend of mine from Rogersville picked me up there and took me to my folks' place. Daddy, he didn't know too much about war. But he had a brother killed in the Second World War, and he hated to see me go to Vietnam. Mama, she hated to see me go awful bad. She cried, they both cried. Mama had to stay home and tend to the other kids when I left to catch an airplane at Knoxville and fly out to San Francisco.

I remember being very tired on the flight to Vietnam. I kinda figured what was coming. Everybody was pretty quiet. Well, just before the plane landed, the pilot announced over the intercom system that they was under attack on the ground and we might have to turn back to the Philippines. I looked out the window and could see things exploding down there. He circled for, I guess, five minutes and then he announced that he was gonna land. But he said as soon as we did, we was to get off and away from the plane. I was looking to be one of six people to unload the plane, and we unloaded it as quick as possible on to a deuce-and-a-half. We went right to the reception station at Bien Hoa with all the duffel bags and stuff.

I was in the back of the truck when we went through a village. Pigs and hogs was going through the houses and the women and men had on them big-legged britches that looked like pajamas. About the first thing I seen was a woman walking along the side of the road there, and she just pulled up her britches leg and went to the bathroom. It was the stinkingest place I ever experienced. It was nasty. I didn't know what to think. I was never used to nothing like that, never knew nothing like that existed.

I stayed at the reception station for only a few hours before I went up to the Big Red One headquarters at Di An. I stayed there my first night in Vietnam and was lucky enough to have to pull guard duty at the Donut Dollies' hut. I didn't want to carry no weapon, but I had to, a M-16. I had to open the gate so the officers could drive their Jeeps in. The hut had concertina wire around it. The girls was having a party—a lot of laughing was going on.

The next morning, I got assigned to Charlie Company, 1/18th Infantry. The people in Charlie Company were mighty glad to see me because they were so short on medics. I met Dave Simpson, a boy from South Carolina, at the aid station there and we got to be good friends right away. We still see each other about once a year. Then I got sent on down to the weapons platoon, and that's where I got to know Roosevelt Gore. I went on my first patrol a couple of days later. From that day on, I always carried the New Testament in my rucksack. I couldn't carry it in my pocket because of all the sweat.

One of my friends that I'd just met, he got blowed up and I seen what it was all about. I believe he stepped on a booby trap in the jungle. It blowed him all to pieces. I was about twenty or thirty feet from him. I helped pick him up and put him in the body bag. Just pieces left of him. He was a white boy. I don't know where he was from, but I prayed for his family. We was almost in to the perimeter when it happened, and that kind of made me realize what we was up against. We couldn't see the enemy, but he could see us.

My company was out in the field most all the time. I spent 363 days in Vietnam and I don't think more than three of them was back at Di An. When we wasn't on big operations, we'd be running patrols during the day and setting up ambushes at night. I usually went on an ambush every third night. Most of the time Charlie would get us before we'd get him. He would set up a homemade Claymore and blow it on us before we ever knew he was around, even during a cease-fire. Of course, we didn't pay much attention to cease-fires, either. If we saw a VC, we shot him.

If one of my guys got hit real bad, I'd give him a shot of morphine to keep him from going into shock. If he was bleeding a lot, I'd stop the blood and get an IV started. I always taped extra plasma bags on the strap of my aid bag. I learned right away that it was a good idea to have more than one plasma bag. Usually, a guy who'd been hit would holler for a medic with his next breath and away we'd go. A good medic cared about his buddies and he got to them no matter what was happening. We had one or two medics who didn't like to get out of their foxholes, so we got rid of 'em.

I got very attached to the guys in my platoon. I think we was all closer than brothers. It was hard not to get attached because we all depended on one another. Grunts look up to a medic. They know when something happens, they can depend on "Doc." That's what everybody in the infantry calls a medic. It was a two-way street: I appreciated them, too.

We all got together to talk when we could. Sometimes we'd talk about what happened that day, about home, or maybe about a grunt who was getting short. We might give him a short-timer's stick. That was a stick about a foot and a half long that he could cut notches in, one for every day left in-country. If a 707 happened to fly over, everybody would just go wild. That was the freedom bird to home.

One day we went out to an area where some guys from the 1/16th had been overrun the night before and almost wiped out. My company was ordered to make a sweep and knock Charlie around some if we could find him. We walked through jungle most of the time. The trees was about thirty-five feet high and had a lot of vines hanging on them. Everything was quiet until all of a sudden, a VC sniper hiding under an old tree in the underbrush opened up with an AK-47.

I heared somebody holler, "Medic!" I was the senior medic so I took off to see what had happened. I had to keep my head down until I could reach my platoon sergeant—well, he was the platoon leader, too, because we didn't have nary an officer in the weapons platoon. His arm had got shot off right above his elbow. A machinegunner with him had lost his right arm the very same way. My medic, he got shot right through the jugular vein. I run over to him first because he was in the worst shape. I reached down and cradled his head in my arms while I checked his pulse. His heart beat one time and then he was gone. His name was Stallings—that's all I remember—and he was about twenty years old. He was the only conscientious objector in my outfit, but he was a damn good medic and a real man.

When I crawled over to the machinegunner and started to give him a shot of morphine, he said he didn't need it. He didn't need it—with his arm just laying there, dangling.

"You do, too," I said.

"Naw, I don't feel a thing." He took the helmet liner out of his steel pot. Between the liner and the helmet was a big plastic bag of marijuana. "Here," he whispered to me, "give this to my boys. I'm going where I won't need it." I later gave the pot to one of the guys in the platoon. According to the army, I was supposed to turn in pot smokers, but Vietnam was such a rough place that I never could do it.

The sniper was still shooting—those little green tracers was flying all over the place—so the company commander pulled back the infantry a couple of hundred feet, just left me and my medic and two wounded men by ourselves. The captain kept sending his radio operator up to tell me to pull back, too. Well, I was trying to put tourniquets on the wounded guys and give them a shot of morphine. My body was already peppered with shrapnel from grenades thrown over my head by some grunts, and I was getting kind of mad.

"Tell the captain what I'm a-fixing to tell you," I said to the RTO. "You tell him I'm in charge here and that I'll move my men whenever I think they're ready. Tell him not to call back up here nary another time. You tell him this is Doc Burton speaking." I made him stay with me and tell the captain what I had said. Finally, I got this Puerto Rican guy to come up there and stand beside us and he shot the sniper; that VC wasn't more than six feet away from me. The Puerto Rican put a whole magazine in that sniper, killed him, and took about three steps. He picked up the AK-47.

The platoon sergeant looked up at the Puerto Rican. "Did you get him?" "Yeah, I got him, Sarge." "Well," the sergeant said, "put another magazine in him for me," and he did. I almost begged them boys to come up and help me carry the wounded people and my medic out of the woods to a clearing. Three guys finally ran up to help. I carried the medic on my shoulder and grabbed the end of one of the stretchers with my free hand so we could get everybody to the medevac chopper at the same time and get 'em out of there.

When I went back to where the 1/16th was set up, a lieutenant colonel from Dallas, Texas, walked right by every captain. He come up to me with his hand stuck out. "Doc," he said, "I heared what you said on the radio. You was right."

It wasn't all shooting and killing over there. I went on some medcaps. I didn't mind it if we was on patrol, because we was all there. But not long before I left over there, they sent us out to a village near Di An, just me and the doctor and three more medics in a Jeep. Didn't send no infantry or nothing with us. As soon as we rolled into the place, Vietnamese came running from everywhere to show us their little scratches. Me, my buddy Simpson, and another medic, a guy from Kingsport, set up our table. Right near us, the doctor and another medic set up their table.

Well, this old Vietnamese woman with teeth black as coal—I think they all chewed them betel nuts over there—came up to my table. She was jabbing at her mouth and patting her jaw. I motioned for her to sit down in a folding chair we had brought with us. "Beaucoup dinky-dao." She pointed at her jaw. "Beaucoup dinky-dao." She had a toothache. I dipped a Q-tip in some toothache medicine and swabbed the bad tooth. Well, she got up out of that chair, rattling off that Vietnamese and acting like that was the best thing that had ever happened to her. The other Vietnamese down at the doctor's table saw what was going on, so they started walking over to my table.

One of 'em was a Vietnamese man who looked to be about forty years old. He plopped right down in the folding chair and pointed at his jaw, rattling off another round of "Beaucoup dinky-dao." When I started to put some medicine on his tooth, I seen it was loose. I told Simpson to go get my forceps. "Doc," he said, "you ain't going to do that, are you?" "You just watch." I got them forceps locked on that tooth and made the man hold his hand up in front of him. When I came out with the tooth and dropped it in his hand, he tried to get up. I got him by the head and pushed him back down. I reached in there and locked on another one. It wasn't loose. When I gave a jerk on it, my forceps slipped off. Oh, he raised plumb out of that chair going "Ah! Ah! Ah!" I pushed him back down there and locked on that tooth again. I drug it up and dropped it in his hand. He started to get up again and I tried to push him back down, but he took off. The last time I saw that fellow, he was running off and rattling that Vietnamese.

Soldiers usually came to us medics instead of the doctors for help with certain problems, mainly VD. For guys with the clap, I'd give most of them 4.5 cc of penicillin in a shot. If I needed drugs, I just went down to the aid station and got what I needed. I had a little trouble once with a lieutenant and a staff sergeant, though. I reckon they was trying to show their authority or something. I don't know why the subject came up, but these two fellows told me one night when we was all sitting around talking that I couldn't do anything without their permission.

"You got to give me permission before I can do anything?" I said. They said, "Yeah, that's right." "OK, I need some medicine. I need to go to the pickup point, so I'll just wait for you'uns to tell me what to do. When somebody gets shot, I'll wait for you'uns to tell me what to do, if that's the way it's set up."

I stayed in the field too long, seen too much. I'd been over there eleven months and two weeks when I had a nervous breakdown. We'd been out on patrol all that day, and it was just before dark as we was coming into Di An. We was walking single-file fifteen feet apart on a company-size patrol, just like the book says, when suddenly there was this big explosion. A guy got hit by a Claymore. It blowed both his legs off right above his boots and blowed his arm off right above his elbow. The other arm and the rest of his body was full of shrapnel. I run in front of our guys a-shooting to get over to him when I heared the Claymore go off. I was between our guys and Charlie. I got over there and this boy, who looked to be about twenty years old, was crying and screaming. We had got in a new medic that day and he was kinda shook up. I told him what do, get the plasma started, and then I gave the boy a shot of morphine. I put some tourniquets around his legs, but he was bleeding so bad, just laying there crying and hollering. We got him out on a medevac chopper, but he said he would gladly die for his country and his family and his friends.

When that poor boy got blown up, I took it hard. I never did drink when I was a preacher, but that night I was in such bad shape that I got a fifth of Old Crow and drunk it in about three drinks. I got back to my hootch. We didn't have no mattresses, just springs on the bed, so I used my aid bag and pistol for a pillow. One of my buddies, a radio operator we called Magoo, came over and got ahold of my shirt. He was about drunk, too.

"Hey, Doc, wake up!" He started shaking me. When he did, they said I lost sight of everything. They said I hit him with my fist and knocked him a-flat of his back, that I knocked him clear across the hootch. They said I reached and got my pistol and was coming down on him, but six of them grabbed me and strapped me between two stretchers. They got me down to the hospital, but I didn't know nothing.

The medic on duty there called one of the hospital doctors and he told him to give me a shot of something—I never knew what it was. He gave me a shot, but it didn't take effect. After a while, he called the doctor and talked some more and he gave me another shot. He said I was spitting in his face, calling him everything. He was a colored boy and I was saying some pretty rough things to him. They left me between the two stretchers. I came to about two o'clock the next day. I don't know how my mind was working; I'd know what was going on partly for just a few seconds, and then I wouldn't know anything.

Everything was coming at me all at once, just like I was going down a road a hundred miles an hour. That's the best way I know to explain it— my thoughts, everything, just rushing at me. Finally the doctor came around that evening and put me in a bed. He came back to talk to me the next morning. I was still in bad shape, but I knowed enough about what I wanted to do to partly fool him. He said he'd let me out of the hospital if I would go back to the aid station and stay around there.

"I'll do you another favor," he said. "I won't put anything about this in your records." I went straight to the mail station that evening. When the mail chopper went out, I was on it. I got back to my outfit with about a week left in Vietnam. Of course, the doctors out there turned me around and sent me back to Di An. God knows, I just hated to leave those guys in Charlie Company.

The colonel, he came up to me a day or two before I left Di An and saluted me. He shook hands with me and said, "Doc, we sure hate to see you go. You're the best medic the Big Red One's ever had. You're more highly decorated than any man in the battalion, and that includes me." The rest of the guys shook hands with me and told me to get on back to the asphalt jungle.

I got spit on after I got back to the States. It happened at Newark Airport. Another medic and me, a boy from down here in Knoxville, was wearing our khakis. We got a taxi from Fort Dix to the airport to catch a plane to Tennessee when a young hippie-looking thing, a college-age girl, seen us as we walked into the terminal. She looked at our uniforms and spit on my chest. Then she just shook her head and went on. Well, I'd heard about what was going on in the States from replacements who came to Charlie Company. They talked about what was going on. If I could have got by with it, I'd have done a few things. If I could get by with it, I'd still do some things. These draft-dodgers, Jane Fonda, line 'em up against a wall. I'd gladly oblige 'em. I had a lot better people than they are die over there, and I ain't forgot them. Way I feel, they're just walking on their graves, what they done.

After I got back, I went to Fort Meade, Maryland, to work at the Twenty-eighth General Hospital. About all most of the guys done was mow lawns, work down in the hospital, and drive ambulances. Somebody's body come back, they'd go on "grave duty" to the guy's hometown. I never had to do it. I just stayed at Fort Meade most of the time, but they did send me up to the big army hospital at Valley Forge for twenty-three days to work on the communicable disease ward. One day I heared somebody holler "Doc!" I got to thinking, all these boys called medics "Doc" and I didn't pay no attention. I heared him again, and then I seen a guy running up to me. It was the machinegunner who got his arm shot off in the ambush. Well, he came up to me shaking my hand; they'd made him a plastic arm and he wanted to show me how it worked. He even hugged my neck. He was tickled pink to see me.

I got out of the army in August of 1968 and came back to Hawkins County. On the last day of the year, me, my wife, and our daughter went up to live in Pekin, Illinois, where I had got a job with the Caterpillar Tractor Company in East Peoria. It was pretty good money, and we stayed up there a year and a half. We came back home in 1971. The cost of living was too high up there and I missed these Tennessee hills. I did construction work for a pretty good while, learned to be a carpenter, how to finish concrete, even how to be a substitute mail carrier. I finally went to work for myself as a carpenter. When interest rates went up so much, though, people slacked off on building and remodeling, so I went back to construction work.

My marriage had been going downhill for years, even before I went to Vietnam. It finally came apart in 1976. I don't like to think Vietnam had much to do with the breakup, but I guess I just wasn't able to put up with some things very well after I got back. I got married again in 1979, but it lasted only a few months. She was in college and had to go in the service when she graduated. After she was in for a while, she decided she didn't want to be married. That was fine with me. I met Joyce about that time and we got married in 1980.

Thank God, she knows what it means to be married to a Vietnam veteran. I still have nightmares. I woke up one night not long ago and had her by the throat. That particular time, I thought I seen a VC coming through the bedroom window; he was almost on top of me by the time I woke up. I still have trouble with my temper, too. I just ain't got the tolerance I used to have.

I ain't preached for two years. I still believe there's an Almighty, but I don't believe it's his will that people do some of the things they do, and that some things happen the way they do. But I believe in an Almighty God and the Bible.

I draw $942 a month from the VA for non-service-connected disability. I can't work. The doctor done told me I'll have more arthritis in my back. I got hurt up at Phipps Bend. We was a-working one Friday night, making a big concrete pour. The regular crane operator, he had quite a bit of seniority and didn't have to work overtime if he didn't want to. So a guy from New York, we called him Radar, was working. It was Friday night and he was a-wanting to get off. He was handling that crane, jerking me around—liked to have jerked me in two. He was just mad because he was working overtime. I paid for it.

I don't know exactly how to put it in words, but Vietnam took more from me. It just wore me out; it took a lot from me mentally. I go back to the war every day . . . every day I see those little green tracers flying around and those booby traps going off. The way the war ended, why that was just all those boys' lives down the drain. It would have been worth it if they had went on and let us fight, let us win. Back when Vietnam first started, a guy I know said we need wars to build up the economy. I believe that's the way a lot of politicians think. I believe that was a politicians' war. I know of a lot of people who had connections, who had money, who was the same age and grade level as I was, and they never did have to go.

I don't talk about the war very much at all. People sometimes ask me about it, but there ain't much use in talking to them. If they wasn't there, they can't understand it, can't comprehend it. But you know, I'm awfully proud of what I did in Vietnam. If I had it to do over, I'd go again.

Roosevelt Gore

Nichols, South Carolina

Army mortarman, 1967–68

•

Roosevelt Gore lives with his wife, Rita, and their son, Jonathan, in farming country five miles outside of Nichols, a small town on the sandy coastal plain near the North Carolina border. He grew up in nearby Mullins, one of ten children of a sharecropper who raised tobacco, cotton, and corn. When I talked to Roosevelt, he was a foreman at AVM, an auto-parts division of the Maremount Corporation in Mullins, and a part-time student at nearby Francis Marion College.

Roosevelt was a mortarman in Charlie Company, 1/18th Infantry, First Infantry Division, during 1967–68. He became friends with Ted Burton and David Simpson, a medic from Columbia, South Carolina, who now works as an energy specialist for the state government. In the years since Vietnam, these three men, two whites and a black, all from a rural southern upbringing, have kept up with each other—a rarity among Vietnam veterans.

A stocky, gregarious man, Roosevelt talked with me on a warm Saturday afternoon at his unassuming brick house, much to the puzzlement of four-year-old Jonathan. He couldn't understand why anyone would come so far to see his father.

Roosevelt's father was a lay Baptist minister as well as a sharecropper. He believed strongly in Martin Luther King, Jr., and the principle of social change through nonviolent means. Nonetheless, Roosevelt told me, his father never protested against blatant cheating by the white owner of the tenant farm. "I think everybody in the family knew about it," he said. "The white man could get away with cheating because he wouldn't let my father or any of his other tenant farmers keep records of their crop production. Even if they could have, I don't think it would have made any difference."

What happened to his father was only a small link in an oppressive chain of discrimination that made growing up black in the early 1960s very hard, Roosevelt said. Blacks could only go to certain places in Mullins. In movie theaters, they had to sit in a balcony or in restricted areas downstairs. The doctor's office had one door for whites, another one for blacks. And the water fountains were marked "White" and "Colored."

"I felt like an outcast and that led me to grow up with a lot of resentment against the system," Roosevelt said. "I was actually glad to get drafted in 1966. I wanted to get away from the environment I was living in."

I finished Palmetto High School, a segregated school, in June of 1966. In August, I got my draft notice two weeks after I went to work for a factory in Mullins that made household furniture. I don't know how many whites was being drafted in Marion County at the time, but I do know a lot of blacks was being called. My father was very proud that I was going into the army. He wanted me to make a career out of it. I knew something was going on in Vietnam, but I didn't pay much attention to it. Two of my Palmetto High classmates had joined the marines and got killed over there, but Vietnam was still a long way off. I was more worried about my mother, who was very sick with heart disease at the time.

I went down to Fort Jackson for basic training and will never forget my drill instructor, a white guy who must have weighed two hundred pounds. He didn't like blacks. He always picked on blacks, maybe because we was from the South and he considered us to be illiterate. He used to kick us and spit on us, call us "niggers" and say, "All you black son-of-a-bitches are going to Vietnam." He liked to order me to get down on all fours and pick up cigarette butts with my mouth. Sometimes I've said, if I could see that guy again . . . but that's all in the past now.

He was a staff sergeant, big and intimidating with that Smokey the Bear hat that the DIs wore. Everybody in my outfit hated this guy but nobody knew what to do about him. We was so afraid we hardly even mentioned his name. As new as I was to the army, I thought all the sergeants and officers was going to be like him. All through basic, I kept wishing I'd never been drafted. AIT at Fort Jackson was much better, though. It was more professional and I don't remember any racial harassment. I got my MOS as a mortarman there and I liked it. I got to be pretty good with the 81mm mortars. I could set one up, adjust for elevation and deflection, and drop a round on the target within a couple of minutes.

I heard a lot of talk about Vietnam in AIT. It was obvious we was being trained for combat there, even though not everybody would be going. Quite a few of the guys I knew in AIT had brothers in Vietnam, which meant they couldn't get orders until their brothers came home. They liked to talk about Vietnam, maybe because they knew they wasn't going. I got my orders at the end of AIT. I came home to Mullins for thirty days, but there wasn't much to do except pull up cotton stalks. My daddy was more excited about Vietnam than I was. He thought it would make a man out of me. I didn't exactly see it that way because 1966 was one of the toughest times in Vietnam, and I was honestly afraid to go.

My mother never said much about Vietnam, but she broke down in tears the day I had to get on an airplane at Florence and fly up to Chicago. From there, I went on to Oakland Army Base for a couple of days of processing before going on to Vietnam. I didn't talk to very many people on the flight over. In fact, I spent most of my time writing a letter to my girlfriend back in Mullins. I had never been anyplace, so I told her about the Chicago airport, San Francisco, Oakland, our stopover in Anchorage, Alaska, and the time-zone changes.

We landed at Tan Son Nhut airport in Saigon at night and walked out into air so hot and sticky it was hard to breathe. Gosh, it had an odor—swampy like. It reminded me of the low country in the summer. I remember being very tired and wanting to lay down. I wondered if we would have a place to sleep that night, but before that could happen, we had to sign some papers at the airport and then load our duffel bags on a bus. I have no idea where we went to that night, only that it was a reception station out in the boondocks.

I got orders for the First Infantry Division while I was in AIT, so I didn't stay at the reception station very long. I flew out to Di An on a Huey the next day—my first ride in a helicopter. In fact, I knew so little about choppers that I didn't even buckle my seat belt during the flight; I thought I was going to fall out of that Huey the whole time. I was sent down to the weapons platoon of Charlie Company, 1/18th Infantry. I hardly had time to meet anybody, but I remember some short-timers saying, "Welcome to Vietnam. You can have it." The platoon sergeant told me to saddle up for a patrol with about twenty other guys that very night. Naturally, I had absolutely no idea of where I was or what was going on. But I do know that I almost drowned that night when we walked through a pond.

I stepped in a hole and went down like a rock. The guys walking behind me pulled me up. One of them said, "You can't swim?" The truth is, I didn't know how to swim. I was more concerned at the time that Charlie might open up on us, but thank God nothing happened.

I started to meet some of the other guys in my outfit after a couple of days at Di An. I could tell that a lot of them was from the South, but for some reason they didn't want to admit it. Not a single one of them would admit it. They wanted people to think they was from the North, and I can't tell you why. I told everybody I was from South Carolina. I didn't see any reason to make a secret of it, and neither did Dave Simpson, a medic who was from South Carolina, too, or Ted Burton, another medic from Tennessee.

Charlie Company had more blacks and Hispanics than it did whites. Most of the guys got along with each other pretty well, but there was a few blacks who liked to pick on the whites, especially when we was in Di An. Just the least little thing a white guy might say would set one of these black guys off and he would want to fight. The white might say "nigger" and that would be enough to cause trouble. I was never like that, though, and sometimes I felt the other blacks in the company resented me because I made friends with whites.

I saw my first real combat a couple of months after getting to Charlie Company. We was on a patrol when a VC hiding behind a tree with an AK-47 pinned down the whole company. My platoon sergeant got shot through the arm, and a medic, a white guy from Columbia, was killed with a round through his neck. Ted Burton was trying to put a bandage on the sergeant when I lobbed a hand grenade at the VC and flushed him out from behind the tree. A machinegunner killed him with a hundred rounds from his M-60. That VC looked like hamburger meat when he got through with him.

I was always the point man, maybe because I was black, until we went out on one patrol and set up for the night. We got attacked and the E-4 that was in charge of the squad, a white guy, cracked up. I got everybody back, no casualties, wounded, or nothing, because I was a pretty good soldier by then. I got my sergeant's stripes the next morning.

The worst time I had in Vietnam came on the night of November 2, 1967. I didn't know if I was going to make it or not. All three companies of the 1/18th was on Operation Shenandoah II in the rubber plantations around Loc Ninh. The intelligence people said a regiment of NVA and VC was in the area, so my company set up a perimeter in a field away from the rubber trees. The birds was so noisy after dark that I was sure somebody was moving out there. I tried to sleep, but I couldn't. About two o'clock in the morning, the birds got real quiet and that's when Charlie cut loose on us. A couple of patrols was run back to the perimeter by VC with flamethrowers. Rockets, mortars, and .50-caliber machine-gun fire started to come from everywhere.

I was in charge of the mortar squad and it didn't take us very long to start throwing it back at Charlie. They was about fifty yards away, so close we used only one or two charges on the mortar rounds. We was dropping them almost on the perimeter. We pumped a lot of rounds out there. Matter of fact, we fired so many illumination rounds we ran out of them for a while. When the illumination rounds was up, I could see the VC. They was dressed in green shirts and pants and helmets, and they was coming at us in a human wave.

I was standing up in a sandbag mortar pit directing fire. Another sergeant, a section leader named White, was outside the pit for some reason when a 82mm mortar round exploded about three feet in front of him. I heard the round that got him come whistling in. It was a real shame because White was scheduled to go to Hawaii on R&R to meet his wife. When the mortar round hit, I saw a flash of white light and felt a tremendous explosion, so loud that I have a ringing in my ears to this day. I felt something hit me in the stomach and butt, something that didn't hurt so much as burn.

I hollered, "Medic!" Dave Simpson came running up to me. He picked out some slivers of shrapnel and put bandages on my wounds. "You've got your Purple Heart," he said.

I went right back to directing mortar fire—I guess I was a gung-ho soldier. The attack went on most of the night. Before it was over, we had to call in airstrikes on the perimeter to help keep Charlie back. The jets dropped bombs so close to us some of our own people got hurt.

We didn't lose many people that night, but I counted 142 Vietnamese on the perimeter after the sun came up. They was about my age or younger. Most of them was torn apart and dead, but a few was still alive, moaning and groaning. I noticed that quite a few of them was carrying marijuana. The wounded ones tried to talk to us, but I didn't know what they was saying and I didn't care. They would look us in the face and stick out their arms, reach out to us, but I'll tell you I had no sympathy for them. None whatsoever. I wouldn't let them grab me or touch me in any way.

Somebody brought in a backhoe and scooped out a deep trench. We threw the Charlies into it, dead and alive. The wounded ones wasn't going to live very long, anyway. I knew it was a violation of the Geneva Convention, but what we did that morning has never bothered me. I wasn't in command. It was kill or be killed in Vietnam, and this time we had done the killing.

I didn't hear much news from the states while I was in Vietnam. To tell you the truth, I wasn't very concerned with civil rights and everything else that was going on back home. I was more concerned about staying alive.

After six months, though, I did begin to wonder what we were doing in Vietnam. It seemed like the more Viet Cong we killed, the more we had coming at us. I don't know how the Vietnamese civilians in our area felt about us, but some of the things I saw probably speak for themselves. The biggest thing that bothers me has to do with some of our soldiers who would use their rifle butts to hit Vietnamese kids on the side of the head. The kids was begging the GIs for food, asking for a piece of C-ration candy or whatever, and the guys would just knock them out. I don't think anybody cared.

I told my folks about a lot of the things that was going on in my letters home, but it was a telegram that caused the most trouble. A day or two after the big attack in November, my mother got a telegram saying I'd been killed. She told me after I came back that the mailman got out of his car and walked up to the house with the telegram. He said he was sorry to have to deliver it. Of course, she knew right then what the telegram said. It was a big shock to her and she fell sick for a while, at least until the Red Cross could get the facts straight.

I finished my tour in February of 1968 and came back to Fort Hood, Texas, where I went into a ground-surveillance radar outfit for my last six months in the army. It was easy duty after Vietnam, but after a while I came to hate life in the states more than I had over there. There was a lot of reasons, I guess, but one of the biggest of them had to do with an incident at Fort Hood. A couple of white guys and me tried to go to a dance at the enlisted men's club one night. Well, some soldier had married a Vietnamese woman and brought her back here. She was taking up a cover charge at the door—I think it was a dollar—and when we walked up to her to pay our money to get in, she wouldn't take my dollar bill.

"Niggers can't come in here," she said, looking straight at me. Her remark almost tore me apart. I could hardly believe what that woman had said.

"I just spent a year over there trying to help you," I said, "and you're going to turn white on me?" I was angry, terribly angry. All three of us walked off. I didn't do a thing about it—but I should have.

When Martin Luther King, Jr., was killed in April, it seemed to me that the real war wasn't in Vietnam, it was in the United States. My company was ordered to Chicago. We loaded up two C-130s with men and jeeps and flew up for riot duty. Nobody wanted to go. I thought, "Why did I have to go to Vietnam and then come back here to fight our own people?" Our officers had live ammunition with them when we went out on the street, but it was never issued to us, even when the rioters threw rocks at us. If we had been ordered to fire on them, I really don't think I would have done it. That kind of decision was never made, thank God. For the most part, the whole exercise didn't amount to much more than spending a week in a warehouse in Chicago.

I got out of the army in August and went back to Mullins, back to the farm doing the same thing I had always done. I had no idea of what kind of work I wanted to do, but I was lucky enough to get on with AVM in September. I went to work in the electroplating shop at forty-three dollars a week take-home pay. I'll always remember that amount because it was three dollars a week less than I would have got on unemployment.

Not much had changed for blacks in Mullins during the two years I was gone, and so far as I could see, it didn't show much inclination to change. I felt I had paid my dues in Vietnam, though. I had been a leader over there. I had been a noncommissioned officer with responsibility for the lives of other men. I couldn't see why I should sit in the back row anymore.

About a year and a half after I came home, my supervisor at AVM, a white guy from New York named Doug Lewis, went with me and a black friend, Gilbert Woodberry, to a run-down little pool hall called the Mullins Grill. All we wanted to do was shoot some pool, but Bunny, the white guy who ran the place, blocked the door when we tried to get in.

"Niggers ain't allowed to come in here," he said.

"The hell they can't," Doug said. He pushed open the door and we all walked in. I went over to rack the balls on a pool table, but Bunny took them off and dropped them in the slot.

"I'm going to shoot pool," I said. I took the balls out of the slot and put them back on the table. This time, Bunny took all the balls except the cue balls off the tables. Why he left the cue balls I don't know. I was about to break out the windows with the cue balls when I heard a lot of sirens on Main Street. I looked out a window and saw the whole street blocked off by cars and policemen. After about twenty minutes in the poolroom, the three of us was hauled off to the police station. The chief tried to strike a deal with Doug Lewis. Gilbert and me was in another room, but we could overhear what was being said.

"Tell me you wasn't with those niggers," the chief said, "and you won't be charged with anything. I'll let you go."

"I'm not going to say anything," Lewis told him.

The chief said, "You're a damn fool, too. All you got to do is admit you wasn't with those niggers and I'll let you go. But we're going to lock those niggers up."

We was all charged with inciting a riot. Doug called the boss at AVM and he came down to the station and paid thirty-five dollars apiece in fines for us. The next day, Doug got fired. He was told that if it hadn't been for him, Gilbert and me wouldn't have gone to the Mullins Grill. It wasn't fair. Doug stood up for us and lost his job.

Two weeks later, I was in the VA hospital in Fayetteville, North Carolina. Some gauze that had been left in my butt wound had caused an infection and had to be removed. While I was stretched out on my hospital bed, taking it easy and watching the TV news, I saw all hell break loose in Mullins. A black girl named Valerie—she had more nerve than I did—had seized on the trouble at the grill to agitate for civil rights in Mullins. She started a small riot, and I honestly think a lot of black people in the town was glad to see it. Some railroad box cars was burned and some windows was broken in the grill. I wished I had busted those windows the first time. Of course, I didn't tell my father I was involved in the business at the grill. I was more afraid of him than the cops in Mullins.

Like a lot of other Vietnam vets, my first marriage didn't work out. My wife and I got divorced in 1975. She claimed the war was behind the breakup, but I'm not sure I believe that. Despite what she told the judge, I was never violent in our relationship. Rita and I got married in 1981. She was divorced from a Vietnam vet and sometimes says—I hope she's joking—that us vets are all alike. I don't know. I only know that I don't think much about Vietnam. In a way, it was a big dream, and a lot of times you forget about dreams.

If I remember much about Vietnam at all, it's about a black guy who had just come back after going home on emergency leave to Detroit. His father had died. I still walked point sometimes, but I had only eight days left in Vietnam and this guy offered to take my place on a patrol through a rubber plantation. He walked into a Claymore and just took the whole damn blast. I was the third man back and almost went blank when that happened, seeing this guy turned into ground meat on his first day back. The worst feeling I had in Vietnam was seeing that guy get killed.

Other than thinking about him, Vietnam's not a big part of my life. And I can say that honestly, because today is the most I've talked about it in twenty years.

Brenda Sue Casto

Somerville, Alabama

Army nurse, 1967–68

•

Brenda Casto grew up in an Alabama coal miner's family, the third of eleven children. Her uncompromising father ("people trembled when that lion roared") insisted that his daughters take up either teaching or nursing in the belief they would always be able to support themselves. Brenda chose nursing, the occupation that would take her in 1967 to the army's Eighth Field Hospital in Nha Trang.

Since she and her husband Paul would be visiting her mother in Cordova, Alabama, on the morning of the day we were to meet, Brenda and I agreed to get together that afternoon in Birmingham. We talked for almost five hours at my motel off I-65.

Brenda is a pleasant blonde woman with deep hazel eyes that belie serious health problems. Three heart attacks since 1984 have left her with half her normal heart capacity. Whenever her breath grew short during our conversation, she would politely ask to stop for a moment while she applied a slow-release nitroglycerin patch to her skin.

She talked freely about the human side of the war, but I could see that it was not always easy for her. At times, her eyes grew misty and she turned to cast long, thoughtful glances out the motel window while framing answers to my questions.

"I joined the Army Nurse Corps in February of 1967 because I wanted to go to Vietnam," Brenda told me. "I had graduated the year before from St. Vincent's School of Nursing in Birmingham and was working as the evening and night supervisor at a small hospital in Hartselle, Alabama. It was a good hospital and I got a lot of experience there, including supervisory work, because I was the only registered nurse in the hospital at night.

"I liked what I was doing, but I was also young and single, with no ties, and American men were being shot and killed in a foreign country and I honestly felt American women should be there to take care of them. I guess it came from being raised with a very strong sense of family and duty. I looked at my younger brothers and thought, 'My God, if they go to Vietnam and get shot, who would take care of them? If I don't go, would it be right for some other nurse to go in my place to take care of them?' It sounds very dramatic now, but over the years I've tried to figure out why I went, and that's basically it."

I was one of only three people in my class of 240 nurses at Fort Sam Houston who knew how to administer IVs. I had taken a class in nuclear disaster medicine at St. Vincent's, so I knew how to give them when we all gathered in a big room to learn how to puncture each other's veins. It was pretty traumatic for a lot of the girls, who simply had no idea they would have to make far more important decisions—life or death decisions—in Vietnam. I carefully chose one who knew how to give an IV so that my arm wouldn't get mutilated.

I didn't hear a lot of talk about Vietnam at Fort Sam. Most of the doctors and some of the nurses figured they would be going at some point. In fact, word got around very quickly that the fastest way to get to Vietnam was to go to one of the hospital schools—surgery, for example—and flunk out. That punched your ticket for sure.

When it came time to get orders, I found out that I was going to Fort Hood, not Vietnam. I went to the chief instructor and said, "Why am I going to Fort Hood? I'm supposed to go straight to Vietnam."

"Oh, Brenda, those are just interim orders for six months," she told me. "We don't send anybody straight from basic to Vietnam."

"Yeah, you do," I said. Let me tell you, I was mad. We talked about my orders for a little while. I explained to her that my agreement with the army called for me to go from basic to Vietnam. I said that if I didn't get my orders, I was going back to Alabama because I considered my contract with the army cancelled.

I got my orders.

I went home in April for three weeks of leave before going over. It was a good leave, even though Mother was upset and frightened about my assignment to Vietnam. Naturally, my younger brothers and sisters thought it was all a big adventure—their sister was going to war. They didn't even know where Vietnam was. My dad had never gone off to

World War II; he was exempt because of the coal mines. None of Mother's brothers went to war, either, but here was one of her daughters about to go. It was pretty rough on her. Much later, I learned that she saw some television pictures of a hospital being overrun during Tet and suffered some kind of spasm. After that, she would turn off the television set anytime the war was mentioned.

I left for Vietnam at Travis Air Force Base, wearing my summer uniform, a skirt and short-sleeve blouse with the little green cap. I was the only woman on the airplane. The mood among the troops was light-hearted, almost exuberant, but I suspect it was bravado more than any-thing else. A couple of times the sergeants had to get up and remind them that a lady was aboard. The guys were getting carried away with stories about their last night in the states. The cabin got quiet, deathly quiet, as we made our approach to Cam Rahn Bay. You could have heard cotton wool fall on the floor. It was as if somebody had said, "No more noise, you can't laugh anymore, you can't stay on the plane. This is it."

Bless their hearts, all the guys wanted to carry my bag as we got off the plane. I remember saying "sir" to one of them. "Ma'am," one of the sergeants said, "any woman who says 'sir' to a private doesn't have to carry her own bag." Being from the South, I had been taught to say yes sir, no sir, yes ma'am and no ma'am. It seemed like the polite thing to say to the private, even if I did have those little butterbars of a second lieutenant on my uniform.

I'd been on an air-conditioned plane for eighteen hours when I walked off into that ungodly Vietnamese heat at eight o'clock in the morning. I was tired, of course, and maybe that had something to do with picking up a bit of heat exhaustion. I decided to spend a few days at the reception station at Cam Ranh Bay, which struck me as just one big, scorching pile of sand with countless long, wooden buildings, before flying south to Saigon.

The hootches at the reception station had chicken wire for windows. They were hot day and night. The one I was assigned to temporarily had a latrine in the back of it, and I'm sure that single outhouse worked overtime to make its contributions to the choking smells that were all over that base. The first thing I wanted to do after getting to my hootch was to stand under a shower and get cleaned up.

"Wait until tomorrow, we'll have one built for you by then," a GI told me. I remarked that a shower was already there. "Don't use it," he said. "That one's for the B-girls." At first, I didn't know what kind of girls he was talking about, but I learned he was talking about showgirls. I don't want to give them a bad name, but the truth is that a lot of these girls got too close to the GIs. Maybe that's why the guys wanted to build a private shower for me.

The next day, just as they promised, I had a fifty-five-gallon drum with a Seven-Up can for a shower head. I thought it was the most marvelous thing in the world, and so did the B-girls—theirs only had a pipe.

I had been at Cam Ranh a couple of days when I got invited to a beach party complete with steak and corn on the cob. We even had beach umbrellas. The sky at Cam Ranh was incredibly blue, and the water was so clear you could see a hundred feet down. A bunch of guys were running around the beach, carrying on and playing volleyball. F-4s were taking off and landing at the airfield, and here I was, in the middle of a war zone, wearing a pair of cutoffs that I'd borrowed from somebody. I felt I was in a time warp.

I liked the people at Cam Ranh. I guess having a woman at the reception station gave the fellows a touch of home. They didn't want me to leave, but I finally had to put my foot down and say, "Get me out of here or I'll hitch a ride out." I flew down to Saigon on a C-130. The sergeant in charge of the transit billet there turned out to be from Decatur, Alabama, and he didn't want me to leave, either. He just wanted to hear the sound of a southern voice. I could have been there a month and nobody would have known I was in the country.

When I finally got to see the chief nurse, she was very nice and listened patiently as I explained everything that had happened. Then she asked what I wanted to do in Vietnam. I told her I wanted a job with responsibility because I knew how to handle pressure. She mentioned an opening at the Eighth Field Hospital in Nha Trang.

"They've had a lot of casualties up there," she said, almost as a warning. When I got to Nha Trang, I was welcomed with open arms—thank God, another body! Doctors and nurses at the Eighth Field were working around the clock, seven days a week, week after week. One of the male nurses, a major, gave me a tour of the hospital and told me I would be working in tropical diseases: malaria, bubonic plague, yellow fever, and black water fever, among others. A few days later I watched a kid die of yellow fever. He was a good-looking guy, blond, blue eyes, real Joe College. Twelve hours after he came in as sick as a dog, he was dead. He literally vomited and evacuated his bowels for twelve hours and there was nothing we could do except put IV fluids in him and keep him clean, knowing the whole time what the outcome would be. I had never dreamed of seeing a young man die like that.

The bubonic plague patients were hard on everybody. They came in with huge boils under their arms and on their groins. If the boils weren't punctured quickly enough, they would explode and shoot excrement all over the place—on me, the patient, everything. I had to take a plague shot every time I had a plague patient because the shots were good for only one exposure. I dreaded those shots because they made me very sick, but when I thought about the alternative, they didn't seem so bad after all.

A lot of people think combat produced most of the bad wounds in Vietnam, and it did. But one day I had a sergeant come in with a severe case of jungle rot. The skin had fallen off the bottom of his feet; I could literally see the ligaments and bones. He didn't want to leave his men in the field, so he didn't report his jungle rot until it reached a critical stage. Tropical medicine was very difficult to practice in Vietnam. I had to deal with dehydration and diseases I'd never heard of in the States. I found it extremely depressing to watch somebody vomit himself to death; I couldn't believe such things were happening in this modern world of penicillin and astringents. But in Vietnam every little scratch got infected and every little bug that came along embedded itself in your body. I didn't enjoy any special protection just because I was a nurse. Amebic dysentery stayed with me for six years after Vietnam.

I was anxious to get out of tropical medicine. I had come to the Eighth Field with ambitions to work on the surgical ward. I finally got my chance when one of the hospital administrators called on the phone and said my records indicated mass casualty training.

"Yes," I said, "that's right."

"Good," he replied. "Look out the back window." I turned around and saw an empty hootch. He said that was where I was going to set up a mass casualty unit. There was nothing in the hootch but some cots, a table, a chair, and a dirty floor. A medical corps sergeant named Blount was assigned to help me. To put the unit together, we had to make do with what we could find. We tacked up chicken wire from one end of that hootch to the other so we could hang IV bottles. I got some clothespins from one of the girls who didn't need them so we could pin the bottles to the wire.

Blount was a big man about thirty years old. He was from somewhere in the South. He was also an alcoholic. He couldn't function without a drink, but give him his booze and the man could do cutdowns, put in tubes—he did beautiful work. When he sobered up, he couldn't walk straight. I didn't drink, so I gave him my liquor allowance. In a situation like Vietnam, you did whatever you had to in order to get the job done, and getting the job done meant keeping Blount functional, which is to say drunk.

We hadn't had the mass cal unit set up more than twenty-four hours when we got word that eighty casualties were coming in from the French bordello down on the beach. I suppose a few of the guys had stopped off to see those French-Vietnamese girls who worked at the bordello, but most of them were in the restaurant and the bar when Charlie hit the place with satchel charges.

Eighty wounded and bleeding people are a lot to take care of. Not ten nurses in this country see that many wounds in a month. I'm talking about traumatic wounds: legs hanging by a thread of skin, faces blown away, eyeballs lying out on a cheek, penises and scrotums blown away. I'm talking about putting somebody over to the side because he was bleeding to death from an artery wound and nothing could be done for him. I remember saying to myself, "He's dead and he doesn't even know it." It was screaming, bloody damn murder.

I made the decisions on triage. The more massive the wound, the less care a man got. It was as simple as that. They got IVs, their wounds were cleaned and dressings were slapped on them. Then they were taken outside on the sand to wait in 118-degree temperatures. Yes, it sounds inhuman, but that was the way it had to be done. If you're going to die, it's a waste of time to do much for you. Soldiers who can be sent back to fight are the ones who get cared for first. I was so busy during triage that I tried to shut my feelings away, but I did remember one of the points we discussed in detail in the disaster nursing class: if your mother were brought in with massive wounds, how would you deal with her?

After so much blood and pain, there had to be some levity, some lightness. I found it in a soldier who had picked up a wound in an embarrassing spot. "When your son asks how you got your Purple Heart," I asked him, "are you going to tell him you got wounded in the butt in a bordello?"

"Hell, no, Lieutenant," he said. "What am I going to do?"

"Well, just say you were bending over to pull a buddy out of a foxhole," I suggested.

The Eighth Field was the first permanent American hospital in Vietnam. To me, it always had the sickly sweet smell of burned flesh and Lysol. It sprawled through nine or ten wood and stucco buildings and had only twenty-five nurses for 348 beds. Two or three of the nurses were men—and they were very good, experienced nurses. They were impressive role models for young nurses just coming into the hospital. Even the medics at the Eighth Field knew a lot about procedures: one of them taught me how to put in IVs with eighteen-inch tubes. By the time I left Vietnam, I could do twenty of those a day.

Surgical ward work was very hard and tiring. It wasn't unusual to work twenty hours at a time. I did a lot of irrigation of catheters and milking of chest tubes. Everybody on my unit had a catheter, but I can say with a lot of pride that we didn't have a single major infection the whole time I was there. We could usually save our patients unless they had severe head wounds. Most men with those wounds died in surgery. If they did live, by the time they got to me they were going to be vegetables for the rest of their lives. Very few of the head wound cases that I saw ever became functional again. Most of these wounds came from bullets or shrapnel, and some of the worst occurred among the helicopter pilots. It wasn't unusual to see a helicopter pilot with the back of his head blown off because the bullet had gone through the faceplate of his helmet and curved around inside to strike the back of his head.

I think the hardest part of caring for these men was knowing that although their bodies still functioned, their minds were gone. I held their hands and tried to talk to them, tried to give them a sense of presence. Sometimes I sat on the concrete floor of the ward and rocked them. You see, it wasn't me who was holding them; it was their mother or their wife or their sister. I tried to literally rock away their pain. Often that was all I could do.

Looking back, one of the most traumatic events for me in Vietnam was the first time I found myself standing over such a soldier with a litany going through my mind: "Die, die, just go ahead and die." All the way through nursing school, I'd been taught that nursing was a duty to mankind, a way to make positive changes in people's lives. Once I got home I could cry, but I couldn't do it in front of a patient. Maybe it would have been better if I had.

What I saw at the Eighth Field began to take its toll on me after only a month there. I found myself becoming more introspective. I'd go back to the nurses' villa after work and just read or stare at the walls. I realized after a while that I was staying away from people. I wasn't socializing or talking very much. I knew vaguely that the girl in the next room was Puerto Rican, but I didn't have the energy or the interest in finding out how she got into the Army Nurse Corps. All of us got fairly close to our roommates, but never close enough that we'd talk shop after duty, about how we'd lost a patient that day. These nurses had lost patients, too, but nothing could be changed by talking about it. So we just closed off that part of our emotional lives.

The beach was two blocks from the hospital, but I only went there three times with some of the other nurses, a couple of doctors, and two of my medics. We talked about home and the *mamasans* on the beach selling little bananas—small talk, very superficial. We talked about what life would be like after the army. I asked Dr. Morellis, a major in his forties who was about to make lieutenant colonel, what kind of medicine he wanted to go into after the war.

"Well, Brenda," he said, "I'm a surgeon. I think I'll always be a surgeon, but I'm not sure I'll ever use a knife again." At the time, I thought that was such an odd thing to say.

None of us at the Eighth Field had a lot of time to socialize, but when we did, we made the most of it. The first social event I went to was a dance in a big open hootch. Everybody was there to party down. Did you ever try dancing for four straight hours in combat boots? For the nurses, of course, it was like being the belle of the ball. Nobody used vulgar language or tried to touch us. I suppose I came across as the girl next door you could get sassy with.

A guy might say, "Brenda, you've got the cutest buns in town," and I'd shoot right back, "You wanna pat 'em?" It was back-and-forth talk, nothing serious or suggestive.

A few months after I got to the Eighth Field, I met a Special Forces lieutenant, a good-looking guy who thought he was the cat's meow. He came strutting onto the surgical ward one day, undoubtedly convinced that I'd let him do anything he wanted to. He announced that he had come to see his sergeant. We had a little to-do about who was in charge, and I told him he would have to come back to see the sergeant. What he really wanted was a date with me. He thought he was going to overwhelm this southern girl with his Ranger and Special Forces patches.

"You cute little ol' thing," he said, "I'd like to rassle you all over the beach." I told him to back off, that I didn't have time for tomcats.

Bless his heart, I finally had to tell him that I wasn't interested in dating him. He came back to see his sergeant and we got to be good friends. I could see that he was a nice guy once you got through all the bluster, so I told him that he might enjoy meeting my roommate. She was about five foot two, wore her hair in a pixie cut and had a very bubbly personality on the wards. At the villa, though, she tended to keep to herself.

I was delighted to see an instant bond between the two of them. Young love is a wonderful thing to be close to. . . . People are so caring for each other. Over the next few weeks, their romance grew into a marvelous contrast between the reality of the war and the idealism of their dreams. My roommate extended her tour to stay in Vietnam with him, but the army required people who extended to take a thirty-day leave home. The last thing she said to me before flying out was, "Don't let anything happen to him."

Two weeks later, the lieutenant came over to the ward and told me he was going on a long-range patrol. He gave me a couple of letters to mail to my roommate.

"Take care of her when she gets back, Brenda," he said as he turned to walk away. The next night, one of my medics woke me up. In a kind of reflex reaction, I told him to go away and let me sleep, but he wouldn't. He said a wounded Special Forces sergeant in the hospital was refusing treatment until he could talk to me.

"He's just saying your name over and over," the medic said. By that time, I had been in Vietnam long enough to get into fatigues and combat boots in under three minutes. When I got to the hospital, I realized the sergeant was one of the men from the lieutenant's patrol. He was the only survivor of an ambush. He said he was afraid that he would die under anesthesia and wanted to tell me that the lieutenant was dead and where he had been killed. He couldn't tell anyone else, he said, because the lieutenant was in love with my roommate.

I got treatment for the sergeant and then called my roommate at her mother's home in Buffalo, New York, to tell her what had happened. Her brother answered the phone. I told him who I was and asked if my roommate could come to the phone.

"Where are you calling from?" he asked.

"Vietnam," I said.

"Oh, my God," he whispered.

I said, "Get a chair and stay with her, because I have something really bad to tell her."

The lieutenant's death was very hard for both of us. . . . It's hard even after all these years to talk about it because it was one of the first things that came out when I started having nightmares and depressions after the war. I guess I never knew what the word cannon fodder meant until I went to Vietnam.

Yet, we all had our little triumphs at the Eighth Field. One I'll never forget was a young soldier who had lost a leg. His other leg was dying, and he was badly traumatized and depressed. He wouldn't eat or drink. All of us had tried to reach this kid, but nothing seemed to work. One day I just went over to him and held his nose while I poked a water bottle down his throat. I gave him 400cc and put the bottle on the table next to his bed.

"When you decide to drink the rest, let me know," I said. He started ranting and raving. He threw a tray off the bed. I immediately picked up a pair of bandage scissors—big steel scissors—and rapped him on the arm.

"Damn you," I screamed, "I've got something to say and you're going to listen to me!"

I called all of the medics over and told them to stand at the foot of the bed. Dr. Morellis walked in to see what was going on. I ignored him. I said to the kid, "We've all worked our butts off to help you. We've spent twenty hours a day on you. You've lost one leg. The other leg looks like Swiss cheese, it stinks, it's rotting away. Only one person can do anything for you. You've got to eat what it takes for your body to heal itself. You can die on the plane, you can die at home, but by damn, you will not die on me."

Then I told him he would be fed nothing unless he asked for it. I also told everybody on the unit, "This is a direct order. You will not offer this man anything. If he wants anything for pain, if he even wants a bedpan, he must ask for it in a polite tone of voice." Dr. Morellis started to speak and I said, "Don't say a word." God bless his heart, he backed me up all the way.

About three o'clock in the morning, somebody woke me up and said the kid was hungry. I went to the ward and asked him what he wanted to eat. He looked up at me and said softly, "Ham and eggs with a biscuit and some chocolate cake."

I started crying. I looked around and even the head cook, who was standing a few feet away, was crying, too.

When Tet broke out at the end of January, the Eighth Field worked for seventy-two straight hours without a break. We emptied and filled the hospital several times. We were so busy with casualties for a while that the cook stood behind us and held a sandwich so we could take a bite out of it. The neurosurgeon got blisters on the palms of his hands from nonstop surgery—his hands were actually bleeding. To stay awake, we took any kind of stimulant we could get, from coffee to Ridilin to Darvon Compound 65 mixed with Coca-Cola. I gave dexedrine to my medics to keep them going. When I finally got to sleep, I curled up under my old gray army desk while Charlie pounded Nha Trang with mortars.

The town was almost overrun during Tet, and in fact the civilian hospital was. At one point, we were told that VC were on our hospital compound. I had twenty-four patients, every one of them hooked to an IV bottle and in critical condition, to look after. They were wrapped in mattresses on the floor. All I had to defend them with was an M-16, and I intended to use it if I had to.

People were supposed to call out and identify themselves when they got to the ward door. I saw the door start to open.

"Who is it?" I yelled. Nobody answered.

I said, "Look, damn it, you'd better answer. I've got a gun." I had the rifle leveled and ready to fire when I realized it was the hospital commander who was opening the door. I came very close to killing him.

I wasn't afraid during Tet. I didn't have time to be afraid. But if I'd had time, I would have been terrified, especially when the VC started dropping mortar rounds near the napalm depot, which was across the road at the airfield. If that napalm had gone up, it would have blown all of us away.

For a while, I had to care for a VC prisoner and I didn't like it. I told the chief nurse that I hadn't come to Vietnam to take care of VC. The man, who was in his early twenties, had a massive chest wound, but I wasn't really concerned about him as a patient; I was concerned that I was having to take care of a man who may have mutilated the bodies of American soldiers. I had seen a body with its chest chopped open. The heart had been ripped out and stuffed into the anal area.

I decided to use the VC to teach a new medic, a conscientious objector, how to give shots. "Don't worry," I said. "This guy can't feel anything. He's still recovering from surgery." The medic gave the prisoner a shot and promptly passed out. I mean, he fell right on the floor. Of course, the needle was sticking out of the VC's leg, so I revived the medic, made him take the needle out, and watched as he put it back on the syringe. The VC got shots until the medic stopped fainting. And that's how I worked through my anger.

I thought I held up in Vietnam pretty well. I guess most of us nurses thought we did, even though we weren't emotionally equipped to handle the constant waves of pain and despair. None of us really wanted to leave. Maybe a part of us wanted to go, but another part was saying, "If you do, somebody is going to die. If you don't take care of him, who will?" It was hard to leave those healthy, ordinary kids who were being denied a chance to live, who were being blown apart for people that could not have cared less about what was happening to them. I doubt to this day that more than 10 percent of the Vietnamese ever wanted us there.

My roommate and I had the same DEROS in May of 1968. We continued working up to the magic day when a jeep came by to pick us up, along with our trunks and duffel bags. We flew up to Cam Rahn for a couple of days before going on to Seattle. Both of us went down to Fort Lewis, where my roommate processed out of the army. Just after we got there, the big guns opened fire on the artillery range. My roommate and I both dove for the floor of the building we were in. I rolled under a desk, and I guess that should have told me something.

Despite all the emotional baggage I was carrying from the war, I had decided to stay in the army. While my roommate went back to civilian life, I went to Fort Rucker, Alabama, where the army's helicopter pilots took their advanced training, as the night supervisor at the post hospital. The casualties that came out of helicopter accidents at Rucker were a constant reminder of Vietnam, but the post was also fairly close to home. I felt the tradeoff was worth it.

Two years later, I was in Aschaffenburg, West Germany, as the chief nurse at an army dispensary that served fifteen thousand troops and their families. A lot of the field medics there knew I had been in Vietnam, and they would come by my office and ask me what it was like to be over there. Before long, I found myself trying to talk them into applying for nursing school as a way to delay an assignment to Vietnam.

My dispensary, which was part of the Ninety-seventh General Hospital, won the European-wide mass casualty exercise. I was very proud of that. But not long afterward, something happened that made me aware of Vietnam-related stress for the first time. We were alerted one night that a helicopter had crashed and burned with fifteen men aboard. Their bodies were brought to the basement of the dispensary. I was the only nurse and the ranking officer on the scene, so I had to take them out of the body bags and tag them for identification . . . fifteen young, burned bodies. Suddenly, it was Vietnam all over again.

I decided that I had to get out of the army. I had managed to hide the fact that I wasn't well from others, but when I looked in the mirror, I could see that I'd pushed everything into the can and put the top on. Already I was having nightmares, and now I began to experience flashbacks when I smelled blood and death. I tried to work around the nightmares and flashbacks, but then to have fifteen bodies—that shook me into doing something. I left the army in 1973 after five years and ten months.

I married Paul, who I had met in Germany, after we came back to the states. He's from Ohio, and that's where we went to start our civilian lives. I decided to go into psychiatric nursing there because it offered interesting work and good pay. But I was having a lot of trouble sleeping, and what sleep I managed to get was filled with nightmares in which I saw eyes staring at me from formless faces and sometimes hands reaching out to me, trying to touch me. I started to throw up with every little hospital smell.

I know now that I was trying to do too much. I was working full-time and driving 160 miles round-trip several days a week to Columbus, where I had started working on my bachelor's degree at Capitol University. I did that for eighteen months. Finally, I quit my job, a good position with a lot of seniority, to reduce my level of stress so that I could finish the work on my degree. There were times when I would drive over to the university and be unable to remember that I had made the trip, or I would forget to bring papers to my teachers.

Not long before I quit work, I was talking to one of the psychiatrists. I walked over to the window and looked out. "What's wrong with me?" I asked him. "Why do I have bubbles in my throat? I get very angry and I must throw up seven or eight times a day. I have patients that I can't deal with. What's happening to me?"

We talked for an hour. He put me in touch with some people who were working with PTSD. I'd never heard of the term. It took three years of therapy before I could even bring myself to apply for disability under PTSD. Maybe it's middle-class southern pride, but nobody in my family had ever drawn disability, unemployment, workmen's compensation, or food stamps.

Paul and I had hoped for some peace and quiet when we moved to the cabin outside Somerville in the late 1970s, but the nightmares and flash-backs came back because of the heat and army choppers that fly around there. Still, I went to work for a year at an alcohol and drug treatment unit, a very positive type of nursing that helped patients realize they weren't the worst people in the world. I think I needed that realization, too, when PTSD finally forced me to give up nursing in 1983.

To be honest with you, I haven't liked myself very much since Vietnam. I've felt very empty. I think anybody who went to the war left behind an enormous part of his youth and vitality. You see, we Vietnam veterans burn out quicker. There isn't enough energy left in us to last a lifetime. I'm sure Paul feels cheated because I held myself together all those years and reinforced my sense of self-worth by being the same supernurse I was in Vietnam—the one who could take on everybody's problems. That way, I didn't have to deal with what was left of Brenda.

I've suffered three heart attacks since September of 1984. The first one was a massive coronary that destroyed 50 percent of my heart muscle. There was no warning whatsoever of the first attack. My family doesn't have a history of cardiovascular disease, and the doctors said they didn't have any other firm answer. Personally, I think the heart disease came from PTSD and Agent Orange. The air force was spraying Agent Orange in the Nha Trang area when I was there. Some of my patients came in saturated with it. They didn't take showers every day, as the air force claims. If you even drank the water, you got exposed to it. Since Vietnam, I've had seven miscarriages and a hysterectomy because of cancer, as well as aching joints and discolorations on my body. Aging? I've had these problems for twenty years.

Vietnam was such a waste for our country. In some ways, the people who stayed home were victims of the war as much as the veterans were. So many people come up to me now and say, "I protested the war, I'm so ashamed." I tell them not to be ashamed. I gave a talk at one of the local schools and a kid said he was ashamed of an uncle who ran away to Canada. I told him to be glad his uncle exercised his right as an American citizen. Once I didn't agree with that. But maybe people like his uncle exercised their rights more than I did.

Every Vietnam nurse that I know has grown old before her time. As for me, I know that I am going to die, and I can only say I won't be sorry when death takes me away. I come from a very close family. I was honest with every one of them when I said I look forward to death. These twenty years since Vietnam have been no more than a façade. I'm very, very tired, and I don't want to go on with it any longer.

Rev. J. Houston Matthews

West Columbia, South Carolina

Marine rifleman, 1967–68

●

As I walked up to the door of the parish house at All Saints' Episcopal Church at nine o'clock on a crisp fall morning, the door handle began to turn before I could touch it. The door suddenly swung open to reveal a smiling, black-haired man wearing loafers, khaki slacks, and a clerical collar. "Houston Matthews," he said, extending his right hand to me. "Glad to meet you."

We walked down a short hallway decorated with children's drawings to his utilitarian office, there to spend most of the morning hours talking about his war. In March 1968, Houston had lost a leg and an eye after being wounded in a rocket attack on an outpost of the big marine combat base at Khe Sanh. "I don't hold any bitterness about it," he remarked near the end of our interview, and I had no doubt that he meant what he said.

For Houston Matthews, Vietnam was the fiery crucible that forged a marine rifleman into a priest. Now, twenty-two years and half a world away from the dusty killing fields of Khe Sanh, he ministers to a flock of four hundred parishioners drawn from the middle-class neighborhoods of West Columbia. He and his wife Sharon Rose are the parents of two girls and a boy.

"I was intrigued by what I thought was the glamour of war, John Wayne and all that sort of thing, when Vietnam was coming along in the mid-sixties," Houston told me. "I had spent a year in a military high school in Chattanooga and knew something about discipline and teamwork. I rather liked that kind of life. Just before graduating from high school in Gastonia, I told my father that I thought going into the military might be the best thing for me. I felt I was too unsettled to go right into college."

Following what he called a "spirited discussion" with his father, Houston ended up at Wingate College, a small Baptist school near Monroe, North Carolina.

"I spent the summer and fall semesters of 1966 there and was a dean's list student, but I just didn't feel I belonged in college. I was too free-spirited. I still thought some time in the military would help me get my bearings."

Like a lot of other southern families, mine has a military tradition that goes back to the Civil War. My father fought in the Battle of the Bulge with General Patton's Third Army and was very proud of that, but he didn't want me to join one of the services, especially the marines, with Vietnam heating up. He had suffered a nervous breakdown after the war and spent eighteen months in a hospital during his recovery. After I went down to the Marine Corps recruiting office in Charlotte and signed up, he got very upset and told me that war was serious business. He was certain that I would go to Vietnam and get killed or injured. As a man of some influence in our community, he tried to pull some strings to keep me from going into the marines. My mother was more realistic about my decision.

"He's of age now," she told my father, "and he signed the papers. As much as I don't want him to go do this, we've got to let him follow his path."

I wanted to be in the marines because I believed they prepared their people for combat better than the army did. At least, that's what some of the people I talked to said. They had been through marine boot camp and extensive infantry training afterward. I liked the idea of being a grunt and even thought of going into special reconnaissance units; I was just intrigued by the excitement of that sort of thing.

I had just turned twenty when I got to boot camp at Parris Island. I was a year or two older than most of the other guys, and maybe that's why I didn't have much trouble with boot camp except for some of the psychological games the DIs liked to play. I never felt anybody was badgering me, though, nor did I ever see a DI hit anybody.

I got my orders to Vietnam while I was at Oceanside, California, for three weeks of advanced infantry training. I guess 85 percent of the guys in my company got orders for Vietnam as either machine gunners or riflemen. My parents were in a state of shock when I told them I was going, even though they knew the handwriting was on the wall. I went home to Gastonia for my thirty-day leave and soon began to feel something was being left unsaid among us. We all went down to Fort Lauderdale for a week, but even in that relaxed atmosphere, my father and mother couldn't bring themselves to tell me how afraid they were that something might happen to me in Vietnam.

I landed at Danang in what must have been hundred-degree heat. When the tailgate of the C-130 that had brought us over from Okinawa dropped down, I couldn't believe the heat, the smell, and the dirt of Vietnam. Most of the marines I got thrown in with at Danang were dirty and grungy; they were half-shaven and hadn't had a shower in at least a week. I stayed at Danang for two weeks in a staging area before I got to my unit, Alpha Company, 1/9th Marines. I remember getting on a H-34 chopper with six or seven other guys and flying from Danang up to Dong Ha, which was almost on the DMZ. I kept all my unit locations written in an old Bible that I took with me to Vietnam.

The guys at Alpha Company kidded me a lot about being a greenhorn. Fortunately, a young buck sergeant from Puerto Rico took me aside and told me about the things to watch out for. Apparently, he had lived most of his life in Puerto Rico before moving to New York City with his family. He knew about tropical places and how to get around in them. This guy was almost like an Indian—he had a sixth sense in the field. He could look at a bush and tell if somebody had passed that way.

I also went through a two-week training program at Dong Ha in which I and the other new guys learned how to maintain our health in Vietnam, which meant taking malaria pills and purifying water with Halazone tablets as much as anything else. But we also learned about ambushes and using our M-16s on "rock and roll," which meant automatic fire. My marine unit apparently was one of the first to get M-16s and we soon found that it was much harder to hit a target on automatic fire than on semi-automatic.

I started going out on small patrols of five or six guys after I finished this course. A buck sergeant or a corporal was usually in charge when we went a couple of miles or so out in the hills, which resembled the Appalachians to a great extent. The company-size patrols that sometimes went out might go seven or eight miles.

The first time I went on a patrol, we were going through some woods when all of a sudden small-arms fire opened up on us. I heard a scream and looked around to see that a young guy about my age had been hit in the back. He was bleeding from three or four wounds; Charlie had really nailed him good with an AK-47 or a light machine gun. We all started shouting "Corpsman! Corpsman!" I ran back to the wounded grunt, but the corpsman beat me to him. He flipped the kid over and tried to put a big bandage on him, but there was nothing he could really do. The kid died within a few minutes of being hit.

While all this was going on, everybody was flat on the ground, firing wildly into the woods. We never saw the people who killed one of us. What we couldn't see, we couldn't hit.

The kid's death was a real shock to me. The only other dead person I had seen was at the site of an auto accident, when I was a child. It really brought the seriousness of Vietnam together for me. I think my whole process of living out each day began then and there.

My outfit stayed at Dong Ha for three weeks and then moved on to the combat base at Con Thien. We took a lot of incoming rocket and mortar fire at Dong Ha, but Con Thien was much worse. I had been at Con Thien only three days when a 122mm rocket sailed over and hit a command bunker under construction. The rocket went right down the tube, instantly killing a lieutenant and a radioman, because the sandbag roof hadn't yet been put on the bunker. I vividly remember a captain, a guy from New York, being carried half alive out of all that smoking wreckage. He only lived a couple of days.

Con Thien was the first place I saw airbursts. The guys were always talking about them. One day I saw a puff of black smoke suddenly appear in the air. Somebody yelled at me, "That's an airburst! Get down, get underneath something!" As I scrambled to find some shelter, a shower of hot metal hit me from the explosion. I was lucky that time. Marines were constantly getting killed by incoming fire at Con Thien.

They could get killed in a lot of other ways, too. We tried to run a patrol one time from Con Thien and came up against some North Vietnamese who were dressed as marines. They drew us into an ambush before we realized what was going on.

We had gone into a cleared area about five hundred meters down the hill from the combat base. Ahead of us was a tree line. A squad got to the tree line and starting drawing terrific small-arms fire. Guys started to drop like flies.

The lieutenant saw men dressed in our combat gear. "Don't shoot," he screamed. "They're marines!"

Only when he looked through his field glasses did he realize they were NVA. The "marines" in the tree line were wearing black sneakers. We fell back and called in artillery and airstrikes, including napalm, but by that time we had lost five or six men. After the area was blitzed, we went back in there and found a massive bunker complex practically on the doorstep of Con Thien. Some of the bunkers even had piles of hot coals in them. The NVA had been heating tea when we stumbled on them.

I went to Khe Sanh in January of 1968 and it was like Con Thien all over again, only worse. One day we took seventeen hundred rounds of incoming fire; nobody could move without risking death. My battalion had a perimeter outside Khe Sanh proper, maybe a mile and a half from the base. We formed a kind of human tripwire, sent out there to help keep the NVA away from Khe Sanh. While I was there, another outpost on a little knoll a mile farther out was overrun by four hundred NVA. They charged a sixty-man platoon of marines and killed most of them in hand-to-hand combat. I had to go out there after it was all over to help secure the outpost and pick up the bodies.

By this time, I had seen a lot of people get killed in Vietnam. Every day to me became another day to survive, another day closer to going home.

I went to Vietnam as a spiritual person. I had grown up in the Presbyterian Church and flirted with Catholicism during high school, much to my parents' distress. Back in those days, Catholics in the South were regarded about the same way as Martians. My father and the local Catholic priest in Gastonia were old golfing buddies, but my father had little use for the church itself—a typical southern response to such a situation.

I felt a calling to the ministry, but there were certain things about papal authority that I couldn't buy into, so the priest steered me toward the Episcopal Church. It was there that I had a spiritual experience during communion. I believe I felt the presence of God at the altar rail. It was not an intellectual feeling, but something more physical, a feeling of warmth and security. In my mind, it was much like the times my grandmother would hold me close to her and assure me everything would be all right after I had been hurt.

And so, I looked at the things that were happening in Vietnam and I began to question the whole idea of war and why God could let these things happen. I didn't feel that God was doing something terrible to us, but rather that we were doing something terrible to each other.

Let me give you an example. I saw the face of the first person I killed in Vietnam. We were in a village outside Cam Lo that had been infiltrated by VC and started to draw some fire from the rear of a building about forty yards away. I had an M-79 grenade launcher at the time and quickly dropped a couple of rounds in the area where the fire was coming from. When we went to check things out, a dead woman was back there. Beside her was some kind of bolt-action rifle I had never seen before, maybe a sniper rifle.

The woman was about twenty years old. She was wearing typical VC clothing, a conical straw hat, black pajamas, and sandals. I was responsible for the death of this woman, and even though I was well aware that she had been trying to kill us, what I had just done bothered me immensely. I tried to rationalize my way out of it: I didn't really want to fight anybody, but this is war, I had to defend myself. Still, I felt a burning sense of guilt about the woman's death.

I tried to talk to some of the other guys about it, but most of them were at the point where killing just didn't really make a damn to them. They had been close to buddies who got killed, and their hearts had become hardened. I know it was difficult for a lot of the guys to avoid hating the Vietnamese, but thank God there were a few exceptions. One of them was a navy corpsman with a real sensitivity to people; he would help everybody. But his kind of compassion seemed rare.

I got wounded on March 28, 1968, while I was on the perimeter outside Khe Sanh. My company commander had warned all of us to stay in bunkers because the NVA had a habit of sending in rockets and artillery around noontime, but this was a bright, clear day, a good day to be outside. I had just come off a patrol and was standing around talking to some new guys when somebody asked me to distribute little cans of Dole pineapple juice around the area. I scooped up a bunch of cans in my shirt and started across the red dirt road to a bunker. Suddenly—*bam!*—I was thrown flat on the ground. I felt like a football player who makes it to the end zone and gets tackled by somebody who isn't supposed to be there.

I heard a couple of rockets go overhead and then the voice of Henry Radcliffe, my company commander. He was kneeling beside me.

"What are you doing?" he yelled. "What are you doing? I told you not to get out of that bunker!"

I think a 122mm rocket got me. The explosion didn't blow off my leg; it just filled the front of me with shrapnel, including my right eye. I started praying almost automatically when I felt the blast, and the same warm presence that I had known two years earlier at the altar rail in Gastonia flowed through my body. I asked God to pull me through whatever had happened to me. I knew, spiritually, that he was present with me and that he would not abandon me.

People kept pushing me down every time I tried to get up because a corpsman was putting a tourniquet on my left thigh. He popped me with morphine and put a patch over my bleeding eye. All the while, rockets were whistling over us, maybe twenty or thirty in all, on their way to Khe Sanh. The one that got me probably was a short round.

The marines who were helping the corpsman put me on a mule, a little flatbed utility cart used at a lot of firebases in Vietnam. The corpsman jumped on it and rode with me down to the underground surgical hospital at Khe Sanh. The people there put IVs in me and checked the extent of my wounds. I was moving in and out of consciousness because of the morphine, but I do remember that a medevac chopper came in later with several more wounded marines. The NVA fired mortars at the chopper when I was rushed out to it on a stretcher for a flight to the USS *Repose*, a big white hospital ship on station off Danang. On the ship, I saw a long line of stretchers, Americans from all over Vietnam. I was just another body waiting for help.

When I finally got to the operating room, I was taken through doors that had blood all over them. The OR was a massive room inside the ship. On the operating tables were guys moaning in pain, and seeing and hearing them shook me badly.

My surgeon was a lieutenant commander from Atlanta. I asked him, "Are you going to amputate my leg?"

"Not unless I have to, son. Not unless I have to."

Then I asked him, "Am I going to die?"

No, he said, I wasn't going to die. I think I needed more comfort than that. I yelled to no one in particular, "Do you have a chaplain?"

Somebody said a Catholic priest was in the operating room. When he got over to me, I said: "Start praying, Father."

The next thing I knew, I was out. I woke up five days later with a feeling of sheer terror: both my eyes had patches on them. Everything was dark.

"Oh, my God," I thought, "am I blind?"

I was truly frightened. Then I ran my left hand down my leg, but there was no left leg to feel. All I could do was scream in horror at what I was learning about myself. The surgeon heard me scream and came over to my bed.

"What's worrying you?" he said in a reassuring voice.

I told him I could see nothing and that I was afraid I was blind. He said a piece of shrapnel in my left eye had caused a traumatic cataract to form. A bandage had been put over it for protection.

"Your left eye is fine," he said. "And with surgery, your right eye should be corrected."

Unfortunately, that didn't happen and I lost the right eye.

A lot of people who got badly wounded in Vietnam were sent to hospitals in Japan, but I went straight to the United States after five days on the *Repose* and a couple of nights at the army hospital in Danang. The layover in Danang was very uncomfortable for me. In the bed next to me was a South Vietnamese soldier who had been hit by a flame thrower. He was burned over much of his body and screamed all night long in pain.

The nurses gave him sedatives and put wet sheets over him, but there seemed to be little else they could do.

I went from Danang to Philadelphia Naval Hospital, where I stayed until November of 1968. The first time my parents came up to see me, they just went to pieces. It was tough on them and on me. But after that first time, they started to adjust to what had happened. They stayed a week in Philadelphia on their first visit and came to see me every day. After that, they came up once a month until I started going home on short leaves.

A lot of thoughts about my future were going through my head. I was twenty-one years old; I had lost a leg and an eye. Would a woman ever be attracted to me? Would I be able to get a job or finish college?

I was badly depressed for a month after getting to Philadelphia. The hospital had counselors who would come by and talk to patients if they wanted such help. The counselors didn't force themselves on anybody, though I sometimes wish they had. A lot of guys there didn't take advantage of the counselors, therapists, or ministers who were available to help them. The local Episcopal priest had a ministry in the hospital and he came to see me once a week. With his help, I started to work through my feelings and gain strength to overcome what had happened to me.

I was really back in battle. I think I won it when the spiritual side of me allowed the emotional and physiological sides of me to be healed. I believe all of us are three-dimensional beings: mind, body, and spirit. If one of those dimensions is not in union with the others, we are out of balance. The spiritual dimension unlocked the door that allowed me to accept my disability and overcome it. That did not mean I had dealt with Vietnam in its totality or everything else that had happened. But by the time I left the hospital, I was happy with myself.

I went back to Gastonia and lived with my family for six months, doing very little. I was weak and had to get used to the prosthesis. I did nothing more strenuous than visiting friends at Wake Forest, Chapel Hill, Duke, and the University of Georgia. Although some of my friends were from families that didn't support the war, most of them didn't seem to hold the fact that I had fought in Vietnam against me. A couple of my friends at Chapel Hill and Wake Forest who were involved in protesting the war were very critical of the soldiers in Vietnam, however, and their attitude upset me enough to get into a fight with one of them.

I felt such comments attacked me personally. For about a year after I came back I gave talks to high school kids and civic groups about the war— you know, the hero comes back. It seemed to me that most people in their thirties and forties supported the war, but the young people were all mixed up about it.

By late 1969, though, I had come to believe the war was a futile effort. I thought we really needed to get out of Vietnam, and I backed off from giving talks. I had begun to hope that the country would have enough sense to get the war over with.

Several events came together about a year after I returned to Gastonia. My father died in a car accident and I got married to a girl who was four years younger than me. The marriage lasted all of four months. I had intended to start college at Chapel Hill, but after my father's death I felt I should stay close to home so that I could help my mother. Since Belmont Abbey College was only a few miles north of Gastonia, I enrolled there and earned my degree in psychology in 1974.

I was thinking seriously about entering the ministry during this time of transition. I went to see the Episcopal bishop of western North Carolina in the fall of 1972 and talked to him about my interest in the ministry. As a result, I met with the Commission on the Ministry several times and received enough encouragement to enter the General Theological Seminary in New York. I was married to my second wife when I began three years of study for the ministry there in the fall of 1974.

After my ordination, I served Episcopal parishes in Louisiana for nine years. I was in Lafayette for three years and in Opelousas for six as the rector of a small parish before coming to West Columbia.

Yes, I think about Vietnam. I can see it now as a time and a place, one that in the end was a good experience for me. Coming from an upper middle-class white background, it brought me together with people I might not have otherwise met—people who lived different lives, who had different religions and beliefs. It let me experience life in a way that showed me people are more important than money, power, or status.

It may seem paradoxical to say this, but Vietnam put my life back together. I think I was moving in a very destructive direction when I was in high school. I was a party boy and a hellraiser. Vietnam made me realize that the world contains a lot of suffering as well as joy.

I'll never be able to rationalize why we were in Vietnam or why we did the things we did. But I can truly say it was an experience that enabled me to be who I am today. I thank God for that and I'm glad I went.

George D. Riels

Sunrise Community

Forrest County, Mississippi

Marine rifleman, 1967–68

●

Visiting with Danny Riels in his comfortable ranch-style house east of
Petal in the Sunrise Community brought back a lot of memories for me.
Sunrise was a part of my childhood world in the early 1950s, when my
maternal grandparents worked a one-mule farm a few miles away in the
Macedonia community. For a while in the middle part of the decade, I
attended the same high school in Petal that Danny graduated from in
1966.

Danny went to Vietnam in late 1967. That was the "year of the big
battles," so called because of the many search-and-destroy operations
mounted against main-force Viet Cong and North Vietnamese units. For
Danny, however, Vietnam consisted of one small battle in Quang Tri
province, a battle with no name that left the former Petal High wingback
partially paralyzed and destined to lose his left leg.

A quiet, courteous man who sports a full, dark beard, Danny spends his
waking hours in a wheelchair. He was very tired on the day I saw him, and
understandably so, for he was recovering from one of his occasional
kidney infections. A catheter slowly drained urine into a plastic bag on the
floor next to his wheelchair as we talked.

"In high school I had been mainly interested in football," Danny told
me. "I played wingback and we won our conference championship my
senior year. I weighed about 130 pounds, real small, but I was fast. I
worked at a drugstore and pumped gas at Webb's Texaco on Central
Avenue for about a year after graduation. I was just a mechanic with no
real interest in cars, but I'd worked at the gas station while I was in school
and just stayed on after getting out."

Unsure of what he wanted to do, Danny went to Jones County Junior

College but dropped out after a few weeks and went back to work at the service station. In 1967 he and two of his buddies from Petal enlisted in the marines. "We felt it was the patriotic thing to do. We had two weeks at home before we had to go to Parris Island for boot camp. It was an exciting time for us. We stayed pretty busy during those two weeks—mainly by hanging around and drinking beer."

Before Danny left for boot camp, a high-school friend who had joined the marines a couple of years earlier tried to talk Danny out of his commitment. "I think he really made an honest effort to talk me out of it. He said the Marine Corps was a tough outfit to be in, but I had done joined and there was nothing to do but go ahead with it."

At first, we didn't know what we had gotten ourselves into at Parris Island, but we hung in there and it really wasn't that bad. The drill instructors yelled at us a lot, but I never saw one hit anybody. I had a bit of an advantage anyway because I was still in pretty good shape from my football days, so I didn't have any problems with the obstacle course and things like that. Some of the other recruits did. The DIs liked to scare us now and then with talk about Vietnam—you know, if you didn't do this or that just the way they said, you'd get killed. I think that was just to help us along with the training more than anything else.

I got separated from my buddies during training. One had got hurt during football season in high school and had a bad knee. He really shouldn't have been there to begin with. He went over a wall on the obstacle course and hurt his knee again, and got sent home. The other boy got into supply or something after boot camp and I never did see him anymore.

After boot camp, I went up to Camp Lejeune, North Carolina, for advanced infantry training. I was just another rifleman, a grunt who carried an M-14. When I left Camp Lejeune, I had my orders for Vietnam and thirty days of leave at home before I had to report to Camp Pendleton for another month of advanced training. We spent a lot of time out in the field in California, just physical training, mostly. We had some rifle training, but not on the M-16. We watched demonstrations of the flame thrower and that was about it. Really, that was about the extent of it. I noticed that nobody talked very much about Vietnam while I was at Pendleton. Maybe not talking about the war was a way to hold down worrying about it.

I went from Pendleton to Okinawa and from there to Vietnam in

December of 1966 in a big cargo plane, just stuffed in there like a sack of flour. When I got off at Danang, it was hot and muggy and a lot of planes and helicopters was coming in and going out. Somewhere in the distance, I heard gunfire. It was exciting to be in Vietnam, but it was scary, too, because again I didn't really know what I had gotten into.

I was assigned to the Third Marine Division somewhere in Quang Tri province, but I can't remember which specific battalion or company. I do know that I stayed in a holding company in the rear for the two weeks before Christmas, standing guard duty, cleaning rifles every day, and training a little bit. The guard duty took me out on the perimeter, but the most interesting part involved keeping an eye on some Vietnamese prisoners of war. They didn't look very tough or bad to me. There were only three of them, and every one looked like a kid. They didn't give me or anybody else any problems.

I went out to my rifle company in a truck. I had a M-16 by that time and liked it. It was lightweight, and easy to clean and take care of. Of course, if you got sand in it, it wouldn't fire sometimes. There was still some kinks in it at that point. The M-14 was a lot heavier, but you never had a problem with it.

The guys in the rifle company treated me pretty bad for the first week or so. They were the old-timers, the survivors. They liked to scare me every now and then, and they'd give me and the other new guys all the dirty details like cleaning latrines and pulling guard duty.

I think the guys who'd been there a while wanted to test the new guys coming in. They was probably right in what they did, because I don't think my training prepared me very well for Vietnam. If I had done what they had told me to do in the States, I would have been killed in a second over there. You had to be a little bit smarter and use more common sense. You couldn't go by the book.

We was in an area with a lot of rice paddies. The land was flat, most of it, and the weather was real hot and muggy. At night, though, it'd get to where it was pretty cool, which was good for us because most of our operations was after dark. We'd stay out all night on ambushes. When the sun came up, we humped back to the base, cleaned our weapons, and tried to get some sleep.

Just before dark, my squad almost always walked to an old bombed-out church a mile from our base camp. From there we'd go to where we were supposed to be. Sometimes, though, we'd just stay at the church. We done that several times, just stayed there and slept. It would get cold enough in that church that we'd have to cover up with our ponchos.

My squad leader was a corporal, not much older than me, but he had been there for a while. There was two blacks in my platoon and I got to be friends with one of them. We got over there at the same time and spent a lot of time on guard duty together. The platoon sergeant was a Yankee. You could tell he was a Yankee, so us southerners sort of stuck together, but it wasn't really a North-South thing.

We walked through villages now and then, but didn't see any young men. We'd see a lot of older men and women, and a few younger women, and kids all over the place. We sort of figured the young men was in the army or with the VC. Most of the people in the villages were very nice to us, in my opinion. Some of them would come over to our perimeter to sell us Pepsis and things. Some of them done our laundry and cut our hair. We never had any problem with them.

I didn't see any casualties until the day I got wounded. That's the only time we really got into firing. I wasn't over there but five weeks, and two and a half of them was in the rear.

One morning we got a report that some VC was in the area and we was supposed to go check them out. Normally, we didn't go out in the day-time, but we got the whole platoon together and everybody went out on patrol. The VC was supposed to be in a wooded area that we was going to surround. Some of us went on the front side and some of us around the back side. The VC was going to be flushed toward us, in the front. And they ambushed us before we even got a chance to get in position.

We was in rice paddies with water a little more than ankle deep. It was like walking through weeds. We was on line about three feet apart. The only thing that I can remember is somebody hollering "VC!" when we got about twenty-five yards from the tree line.

As soon as I heard "VC!" I hit the ground, down in the water, and that's where I got wounded. They told me later that somebody was in a spider trap over to the left. I got hit just a few seconds after I hit the ground. I heard some firing and remember getting hit, but I wasn't hurt, just numb. I was paralyzed from the time I got hit. I knew that because the only thing I could move was my hands. My rifle was in the water, but my face was out of it and I threw my helmet over my face and held my head down as far as I could. Not in the water, just enough to keep my head covered.

I yelled, "Corpsman, I'm wounded! Corpsman, I'm wounded!" as loud as I could. I was scared to death. The first thing I did was pray. I wasn't no saint, but I was a Christian and was saved when I went over there and I read the Bible almost every night. I just turned it over to God.

"Lord," I said, "it's in your hands."

The corpsman rushed over to me with a shot of morphine and I was pretty much out of it after that. A couple of the guys carried me about 150 yards on a stretcher to a place where a medevac chopper could land. I wasn't in no pain because I couldn't feel anything.

The helicopter flew me to the aid station at Danang, where I stayed for eight days. Because I was torn up so bad inside, I couldn't have anything to eat, no water, no anything, for eight days. They didn't do any surgery on me other than emergency surgery. I was living on antibiotics and was doped up most of the time, but I was conscious of what was going on around me. I remember being more interested in the other men laying there. A lot of them was in worse shape than I was, with tubes coming out from all parts of their bodies.

I got my Purple Heart at Danang, and that made me one proud marine. I was happy about something else, too. I knew I was going home.

I went to Japan to an army hospital and stayed there about two weeks before going on to Clark Air Force Base in the Philippines. I stayed at Clark for more than a month and that's where I had my surgery done. The bullet had hit in the side of my hip. It went all the way across my stomach and struck the tip of my spine. That's what paralyzed me. In fact, the doctors who took out the bullet gave it to me. I still have it, a round from an AK-47.

I believe the doctors at Clark did all they could to save my leg during that time, but they eventually had to take it off because of gangrene. I had some artery damage; the blood would go down, but it wouldn't come back up, so gangrene had set in. They took off the leg above the knee.

Of course, I didn't like it. The doctors kept me pretty well out of it with Demerol because I was feeling pain by that time, but I knew what was going on enough to call home and talk to my folks. My brother-in-law, who was a captain in the army, was in Vietnam the same time I was, and he came over to visit me at Clark. That helped quite a bit because we was good friends, very close. He stayed with me there several days.

The medical people at Clark was very good, very nice and understanding. They was just tremendous as far as I was concerned. The Red Cross ladies came around and some professional football players did, too. Lance Alworth was one of them. The Red Cross ladies would write letters for me and bring around Cokes and sometimes a beer.

People ask me if I was depressed at the time. The only thing I was depressed about was wanting to get home, because it seemed like it was going to take forever to get out of Clark. But I couldn't move because they had just taken my leg off and I had to have whirlpool baths twice a day.

The pain—I mean, can you imagine having your nerves exposed like that, getting in water and having to pack your wound twice a day? It was very painful.

When I finally left Clark for home in April of 1968, I made a stopover in Japan and my wounds got infected. How, I don't know. But they did and I had to stay in Japan for almost another month at the army hospital. Finally, when all that got cleared up, I got on a plane and came back to the States. I was flown from San Francisco to a VA hospital in New Jersey, and from there I went to the Philadelphia Naval Hospital. I got there in May. As soon as I got settled in, the family came up to see me. I stayed at the hospital for a month and took physical therapy.

I had no feeling from the chest down. My arms, neck, and head were fine. To start with, I couldn't move my legs or stump, but the physical therapists worked with me and I got to where I could move my leg, but I couldn't walk. They fitted me with a prosthesis and I tried walking on that for a while, but I never could get it to work.

So, I came on home. I flew down to New Orleans about the middle of June. Coming home was real nice. The people of Petal gave me a big ol' welcome home party as soon as I got here. Some of the merchants and the people that I had gone to school with put the party together at the Petal High gym. After that, we went over to my mother's house for coffee. We just had a real good time.

You either deal with the sort of thing that happened to me or you don't. I had made up my mind at Clark that I was going to deal with it, that it was just a part of life. And I did. I still more or less do the things that I used to except run and walk and go up steps. I work and drive my own car. I don't have to have hand equipment and that sort of thing. For the most part, I've worked ever since I got back from Vietnam. I was an office manager for an insurance company for twelve years. After I left there, I ran a little grocery store for a year and a half and then was an apartment manager for two years.

I got married a year after I came home, to a girl I had gone to school with. We gradually grew apart, though, and the marriage failed after seven years. We left the best of friends and still are today. Diane and I went to high school together, too, and we've been married for almost nine years now. We've operated a little grocery store, the Beverly Hills Food Mart, for the last two years. When I'm not able to go to work, she goes in my place. I enjoy the work because it's easy and something I can do.

Unlike a lot of other vets, I've never been down on the VA. I went up to the hospital at Memphis for a month of therapy after I got back home and later took some therapy at the hospital in Jackson, and I had the best of care. Recently, they've tightened up on a few things, though. I can't get a prescription from a doctor down here filled up there. You know, I've been doing it for twenty years, but now all of a sudden I've got to go to Jackson to get a prescription from a doctor there before the hospital will fill it. I'd just as soon pay for it than drive up there and get it. I guess that's the way they do things, but I don't understand that part of it. A prescription is a prescription.

It's something of an issue for me because I have these kidney infections now and then. I've also suffered from some abcesses that sent me to the hospital for treatment. On the whole, though, I'm doing all right. The antibiotics will clear up the infection I have now in a couple of days.

I suppose war is inevitable, but I don't like it. I find it hard to believe that anybody could. Still, if another one broke out, and if I was able to go, I would do it. I think it's our duty to do that. I would never dodge a war because I disagreed with it, and that's why I think the ones who deserted to Canada should have been left there.

I don't know that much about Jane Fonda, but I can understand her reasoning behind what she did. I really don't think she did that much. She went to North Vietnam, I do know that. But I think she was more or less trying to find an end to the war. She don't bother me. If that's what she believed in, fine. Now to desert when you're called on, that's a different story. It's certainly not fair to the ones who lost their lives for the deserters to just be able to come back to the States and start *their* lives over again.

My stepkids Stephanie and Jason ask me about the war once in a while, about the bullet and the Purple Heart and where I was. It don't bother me to talk about it. But looking back on the war, I've come to think it was for nothing. At the time we got into Vietnam, I think it was for a good cause. But the way they ended it, just giving up and pulling out . . . it didn't accomplish anything so far as I can see. I don't like that part of it because it was political. It ended up being a political war, and the only people who got anything out of it was the politicians. To be honest with you, it just wasn't worth it.

William U. Tant

Memphis, Tennessee

Marine rifleman, 1967–69

●

When I first saw Bill Tant, he was wearing what I took to be a policeman's uniform: white shirt, gold badge, blue trousers. In fact, he was a private security guard for a sorority house at the University of Alabama. A few months after I talked to him, he went to work as a crewman aboard the M/V *Charles F. Detmar,* based in Memphis.

Bill was among the first marines to fight their way into Hue, the ancient imperial capital of Vietnam, at the outbreak of the Tet Offensive. The battle to wrest control of the city from the North Vietnamese Army lasted twenty-six brutal days. In April 1975 he returned to Vietnam briefly to help evacuate the last Americans from Saigon.

Bill and I talked on the day he had come to the VA hospital in Tuscaloosa to be fitted for new dentures. Although he took obvious delight in telling stories of himself as we began to talk, he grew introspective about the war as we neared the end of our conversation. "It's been twenty years since Hue," he said, "but I think about it all the time."

A muscular man a little under six feet tall, Bill, with his lanky frame and ruddy complexion, is almost a stereotype of the southern "good ol' boy." He grew up on a farm outside Cottondale, Alabama, but disagreements with his father led him to live with an uncle in Webster Groves, Missouri, during his last year in high school.

"When I was a kid in 1967," he told me, "I wasn't as blessed as some of the other kids my age, the ones I called 'political scientists' because they was so much smarter than me about the whole situation in Vietnam. I had no idea what a war was like. I didn't have a very firm idea of what I wanted to do after high school, either, so I signed up for the marines. After all, I was eighteen years old and thought I knew everything.

"But I seen one thing about that time that sticks in my mind today. I saw a news clip on TV, I think it was the battle of Con Thien, and they showed a marine. He was sitting by a tank and the news people was talking and showing parts of the hill where the battle was going on. The newsman said 'Oh, my God!' and the camera switched back to the tank. It had taken a RPG right in the back and the guy that had been sitting there was gone."

I went to Parris Island for eight weeks of boot camp. Physically, I don't think the marines was tougher than any other boot camp. But mentally, I don't believe you can compare anything to it; I haven't run into anything since that could mess with your mind like Marine Corps boot camp. It was a propaganda program, and when I came out I was convinced that I could beat anybody in the world. I didn't have enough sense to be afraid of anything. I didn't question why or how to do something, I just did it.

The drill instructors would hit us in the stomach or punch us in the kidneys, but I saw one get so mad at a recruit that he broke his dress sword across the guy's head. He knocked the guy out. Then he marched the whole platoon off and left the guy laying there. Evidently the recruit was a total screwup. This was in the fifth or sixth week of training, and he should have knowed his left from his right by then.

The only time I got in trouble was a time when we was taking what we called a navy shower. The DI turned the showers on and the whole platoon stripped and just walked under the shower to rinse the sweat off. That was a navy shower. Well, I had to pee. I snuck off to the head and thought I could get back in line before the last guy walked by. While I was in the head the DI walked up and propped his hand on the door. I saw the last guy go by.

"Sir, excuse me, sir," I said when I tried to get in line. The DI went berserk. He yelled and screamed about catching a marine whistling in the shower one time and sending him to the big navy brig at Portsmouth, New Hampshire, for a year. Now, I believed anything the Marine Corps told me. And I thought, "My God, if he could do that for a guy whistling in the shower, I'll get four or five years for peeing when I'm not supposed to."

Everybody had to take a battery of tests at Parris Island. The highest score I got was on radio and communications. I said to myself, "Well, I don't have to worry about being a grunt. I'm going to be working on radios." On the day before I was supposed to leave for advanced training at Camp Geiger, North Carolina, I got my grunt MOS. I knew then I was going to Vietnam.

I went home to Cottondale for ten days of leave in November of 1967 before going out to Camp Pendleton, California, to a staging battalion. On the day I had to leave, my mother went with me to the Birmingham airport. She started crying as I walked toward the airplane. "Don't be squalling," I said. "I'm going to be home for Christmas. They've done told me that." I reported to a gunnery sergeant at Pendleton and there was this blackboard behind him with "Debarkation date: 22 December" written on it.

I said, "Gunny, what's that?" He told me that was the day I was going to fly overseas. "Well," I said, "I'm in the wrong building, 'cause I've already been told I'm going home for Christmas." He just kind of laughed and looked at my orders. "No, Tant," he said, "you're in the right building."

I landed in Danang on Christmas Day. It was hot, it stunk. I guess it was the water buffalo crapping in that dirty rice paddy water. The place just had a different smell to it. I didn't really cry when I got off the airplane, but tears—you know, I got kind of teary-eyed. And I thought, this is for real and I realized I didn't really want to be there. I wanted to be home in Alabama, pulling corn for my daddy.

All of us had to line up in a big building that looked like a hay barn. A sergeant was sitting at a desk at the front of the line and he was handing out orders. He had a little rubber stamp and he'd say, "First Marine Division, Third Marine Division, or FLC," which meant Fleet Logistics Command. Those guys didn't go out in the bush.

People consider me a redneck sometimes, but I'm not totally stupid, you know. I started counting and figured I was going to get the First Marine Division, so I got in front of another marine to try to get one of them FLCs. I got up to the desk and the guy handing out orders said, "You're going to the First Marine Division." I never saw the man look up, but somehow he knew I had jumped the line.

I thought, "Oh, Lord." I knew right then and there that 1968 wasn't going to be one of my best years.

I went out to Golf Company, 2/5th Marines at An Hoa. The guys more or less ignored me. The only man who shook hands with me was my squad leader, Corporal Lucas. I was just in awe of those guys. I mean, some of them were no older than me, but they were just—they just had a different way about them, a different look.

I fired my first M-16 at An Hoa. I went through boot camp with an M-14 and used an M-1 carbine in advanced training. In Vietnam, everybody talked about the M-16. "You've got to keep it clean," they'd say. "*Keep it clean!*" Well, you could have wrapped an M-16 in an airtight garbage bag and it wouldn't have done no good. The M-16 jammed itself. It produced so much carbon it could jam with a twenty-round clip; it didn't have to have any dust or dirt in it.

I didn't see much combat for the first month, nothing but a few snipers. There were a lot of booby traps around An Hoa, though. An Hoa was supposed to be one of the most booby-trapped areas in Vietnam. Every time a patrol went out, somebody got hit by a booby trap. Most of them were just hand grenades designed to create casualties and tie up four guys to take care of one. It's a hard thing to say, but if a guy's dead, you don't have to worry about him.

My fire team leader was Jack Fields, and he's the first man I can vividly remember getting hit. He had tripped a booby trap or somehow been hit in the butt before I got to Vietnam. He tripped a booby trap after dark and got hit again in almost the same place. Jack was from Massachusetts. I don't know if you've talked to many people from Massachusetts, but he had a real high voice—a Boston accent. And he was laying there and cussing about where he was hit, and I couldn't help but laugh. I guarantee you he made more racket hollering than the hand grenade did when it went off.

About a week before Tet started—and this was no brilliant move on the part of the American military, contrary to what they might say now—my outfit moved from An Hoa to Phu Bai, south of Hue. They had no intelligence telling them what was going to happen in Hue. I believe one of the reasons we moved was because of Khe Sanh, which was getting a lot of pressure. And then Tet busted open and we never got there.

I was on a hill northwest of Phu Bai with Kenneth Buchanan, an Arkansas boy, and some other guys on the night before Tet started. We had an M-60 with us. It was just mountains and jungle as far as you could see. About eight o'clock, a marine recon team two hills over from us got hit by the NVA and airstrikes and artillery came in all night long. The recon guys was talking on the radio to a relay station, telling Phu Bai what was happening, and they said they were up against fifty NVA. The marines said they was going over one of the hills, and on the other side they ran into more NVA. Before it was over, the recon guys estimated there were three hundred NVA in the area. I believe they had hit NVA that was going into Hue. They was only five or six miles from the city. We never got hit.

The next morning, we flew back to Phu Bai and the platoon sergeant came up and told us to get our gear ready. We was going to Hue City to stand lines around the MACV compound. We loaded on the trucks and I asked Corporal Lucas—it still took guts to ask him anything, I had so much respect for him—"Are we going to see some gooks?" He was too busy to say anything. We was about three miles from Hue on Highway 1 when we started hearing machine-gun fire. Just before we went across a canal outside the city, we saw an ARVN tank that must have been hit by a RPG. The driver was hanging half out of the tank. It looked like the NVA had caught him with a flame thrower as he tried to get out.

Corporal Lucas looked at me and said, "Yeah, I think we're going to see some gooks."

There was a mile or two of rice paddies ahead of us before we got to Hue. Some big French houses was on both sides of the highway, which was really just a dike with a paved road on top of it. We started taking fire and somebody yelled for us to get off the trucks. I had been through all that training on how to disembark when a convoy gets ambushed—don't stop, keep moving if you can—and all that training just went out the window. I ran straight out of the back of the truck. Of course, nobody had dropped the tailgate and I didn't bother to pick my feet up. I hit that tailgate and went off head first onto the asphalt. It was a right good drop and it's a wonder I didn't get killed right there. I had already seen a lowboy flatbed truck that had body bags all over it, ARVN and army and guys from Alpha company 1/1 Marines, which had gone in before us, and I was scared.

We was taking small arms fire, RPGs and 57mm recoilless rifle rounds from the houses. The NVA had sandbagged them things up, fortified them, and we ran right into an ambush. We started moving down the road and there wasn't any cover except the trucks and some trees. We finally got up to a Shell filling station on a traffic circle, and that station provided two of the three maps of Hue City that my battalion had. Right before we got there, I saw an ARVN APC off in a rice paddy. I saw what I thought was bodies, but when I looked again, they was moving. It was ARVNS pointing and yelling, "Beaucoup VC! Beaucoup VC!"

I thought, "Jesus Christ, don't we know they're there? And what are these guys doing out here hiding in the mud?" That was what they was doing, hiding in the mud.

Our trucks got through the ambush, but we didn't get back on them. I guess Captain Meadows, my company commander, had enough sense to know that if we got back on the trucks, the NVA was going to hit us again. And so did a black staff sergeant named Levi Jones. I probably have more respect for that man today than any man I've ever met in my life, which is ironic, me being from Alabama and supposed to be prejudiced. But this guy had charisma. I mean, there was just something about him. I puppy-dogged him. Wherever he went, I went.

We got up to another crossroads and there was a guy on a truck, firing a .50-caliber machine gun. He was working over everything because the NVA was everywhere. He got hit in the upper left shoulder and it knocked him off the truck. When he got hit, I remembered something I had learned in advanced training. They had told us, if you get in a building, don't silhouette yourself. In other words, don't get in front of a window that's got a window behind it. I looked up and saw this gook that was about five feet back from a window—he had gotten in between two windows.

I told Staff Sergeant Jones, "Staff, he's up there. He's in that building." Jones told me to get on the machine gun and "When you see him, open up." I had never fired a .50-caliber, but the guy that was hit was laying there. "What do I do?" I asked him.

He said, "Just grab a handle and take both thumbs and press the button." I got up there on the gun and waited until I saw the NVA move and I opened up and didn't quit shooting until the ammo box was empty. Some of the guys went into the building and came back and I had hit the NVA one time, took half his face off. I must have shot two hundred rounds and I hit the guy one time.

A lot of the marines who were at Hue will disagree with me on this, but I don't believe the NVA was making a 100-percent effort to stop us at this point. I think they wanted to inflict casualties and let us get in because they was sure they could wipe us out. We kept pushing and taking casualties, but they was what I guess the military would term "acceptable." In fact, we wasn't getting chopped up that bad. We was causing more casualties than we was taking.

We was still on foot, but now we had a couple of M-48 tanks with us. Both of them had been hit two or three times by RPGs. The RPG was not nearly as devastating as a lot of people think. I mean, it will kill you, but I saw a lot of tanks take seven or eight or even nine hits a day and still keep going. We was heading down the street to the MACV compound, which was one block south of the Perfume River and the only place we had a chance to hold out. It was either get there or get our butts kicked back out. I would say we had been under fire for almost three miles from the time the NVA first hit us. Now, there were periods of time when there wasn't any firing and we would move for a while, but the next thing, we'd hit a bunch of them. We got to MACV about noon or one o'clock, but then we got orders from Phu Bai, from some guy back there who had no idea of the situation, to go across the Perfume River bridge with what was left of us. And that wasn't very much.

At the time, I thought Phu Bai wanted us to go across the bridge and secure it, which made sense. But years later I found they wanted us to link up with an ARVN general in the Citadel. Now, he had way more people than we did, and they wanted us to link up with him! We lost just about all of the second platoon getting across the bridge. When I was in Washington a couple of years ago, I looked at a map of Hue and that bridge was, I think, a click and a half long. You hear a lot about the German bridge at Remagen in World War II, but this bridge was a lot longer. It was a typical old steel-structure bridge. The NVA had snipers on top of it and sappers under it throwing satchel charges at us. And there was a machine gun on the far end. Corporal Tulley, a Louisiana boy in the second platoon, got a Silver Star for knocking out the machine gun. I don't know how he ever got to it, but when he did, we got on across.

In less than four hours, we had over fifty casualties. In less than four hours! A truck came along behind us to pick up the wounded and dead. We took a left after getting across the bridge and I remember seeing a big movie theater. I swear it was showing *Gone With the Wind*. Somebody on top of the theater or another building close to it fired a RPG into the truck, and that caused even more casualties.

Corporal Lucas went up a little alley next to the movie theater and he got shot, just a nick in the arm, a flesh wound. He came running back down grinning from ear to ear. He had ten days left in Vietnam and he was telling everybody that he'd got a Purple Heart. This guy had been through three of the worst operations up to that time in Vietnam and never got a Purple Heart.

We went about a block up the street and there was another street coming in from the right. My squad was working the left side of the street and another squad was on the right side. I was walking point along a wall that was about ten feet tall, old and French-looking. I saw some buildings and an archway up ahead, but I didn't know at the time that it was the entrance to the Imperial Palace of the Citadel; it turned out to be one of the most fortified positions the NVA had.

I was walking point because it was my turn. Corporal Lucas told me—I don't think he even knew my name—"Point man, speed up. Catch up with the guy on the other side of the street." I started to run and just as I did, the NVA opened up with a machine gun and missed me and the guy behind me. They hit everybody else in the squad except Doc Kirkham, the corpsman. Another machine gun opened up on the squad on the other side of the street and it hit a guy seven times in the chest and stomach. Believe it or not, he lived and was back in Vietnam six months later.

I was up against the wall and that gun missed me when it started firing at my squad, but it nailed Corporal Lucas. Bullets started coming back up the street toward me. I could see the rounds coming and I had no place to go, but it was like when you shoot automatic bursts and let your fingers rest—well, the bullets stopped on one side of me and started again on the other side. He missed me. I didn't get a scratch.

I ran over to a tree and could see the door to a building, about fifteen feet up the street. I ran up there to go in the building and the damn door was boarded shut. The NVA had nailed the windows and doors shut so we couldn't get off the street. There was nothing to do but run back and get behind the tree and I looked at Lucas and I knew he was dead. I . . . just knew. You don't have to take somebody's pulse; you can tell when a guy's dead and I knew he was dead.

Doc Kirkham had done pulled a couple of guys off the street and was starting back up to Lucas. He was crawling and I tried to tell him there wasn't no need, that he couldn't do no good for Lucas. But just as he got to Lucas, the NVA shot Doc right in the jugular vein, just clipped it. One of the books on the Battle of Hue mentions Doc Kirkham and says he got shot dead instantly. Well, he didn't. I wasn't ten feet away from him and he looked at me and shook his head.

"I'm dead," he said. He knew he was going to bleed to death and there wasn't nothing I could do. I could not get to the man. I guess it took thirty seconds or a minute and he was dead.

I looked back around the tree and saw an NVA flag on a parapet of the Citadel. The guys back down the street couldn't see the flag because of the leaves on the tree. They didn't know where the machine gun was, but I did: I could see it. I was trying to holler and tell some of the guys across the street where it was. Buchanan was over there with an M-79. Well, the guys thought I was trying to tell them I was hit. I knew the NVA was behind a damned parapet. I turned around and started shooting and that's when my M-16 jammed. I shot about fifteen rounds and then there was nothing I could do. I cleaned my weapon every chance I got and *nobody* will ever convince me my weapon was dirty. For the next two hours, I used my cleaning rod to punch out shells every time I fired the rifle. It had turned into a single-shot and before that day was over, I threw it in the Perfume River.

Staff Sergeant Jones got hit in the stomach and Buchanan got it right through the hand. I took his M-79, his rounds, and a .45 pistol. About a day later, I picked up a Thompson submachine gun that was laying in the street with four or five clips. I carried it until I broke it down one day to clean it and wound up throwing it in the Perfume River, too, because nobody knew how to put it back together. I had springs and screws laying everywhere.

I kept the M-79 the rest of my time in Hue. I loved it. All I had was high-explosive rounds and maybe a few white-phosphorous. I didn't have any buckshot rounds at Hue, but the nice thing about the M-79 was that I could miss somebody by ten feet and still kill him. I wasn't a very good shot on the rifle range at boot camp, but with the M-79, I made up for it.

When Lucas got killed, my fire team leader took over the squad—all four of us—and we pulled back across the Perfume River to the MACV compound on the first day. My company couldn't make it to the Citadel. In the marines, you don't retreat, you pull a retrograde movement. That's what it amounted to. We had a little bit of fire going back, but nothing like we had coming in. All the tires on the casualty truck were flat from bullet holes and it rolled across the bridge on rims.

When we straggled into the MACV compound, I saw a guy being carried on a stretcher. He had been ambushed on a convoy and his foot was dangling from a piece of skin. They didn't even take him to a hospital or infirmary. A doctor walked over with a pair of scissors and just snipped off the guy's foot. A piece of skin was all that was holding it on.

We spent the night at MACV and I had a bed, the first one since I'd gotten to Vietnam. Another marine and me had a room with a refrigerator and cold beer. The room belonged to a couple of army officers, a colonel and a major. They came in there and we started to get up. "No, you go ahead and sleep," one of them said. "We're going to stand lines." Colonels and majors at MACV stood lines that night with marine grunts.

The Battle of Hue was basically house-to-house, room-to-room. We spent days clearing LeLoi Street, the main street that ran parallel with the Perfume River. It seemed like some days we couldn't—hell, we couldn't go a block, or maybe even a hundred feet.

When a guy got shot, we always tried to get his body. We wasn't going to leave a body laying nowhere. A guy I knew got shot and four or five other guys got shot trying to get him back. Eventually, they did. He was all shot to pieces in the arms and legs. I think he had seventy-four bullet holes in him. But the NVA kept shooting the body up; it was like a game to them, something to draw us out. Well, they did that. I saw guys beg somebody to come out and get them and then I saw guys say, "I'm all right, don't do it." Some of them was doing it because they didn't want us to get hit and some was doing it because they was afraid if we did come there and move them, they was going to get hit again. Different people reacted in different ways.

I don't know what the casualty rate for the corpsmen was in Hue, but I assume it was very high. In my opinion, you'll never find a more gutty bunch of people than navy corpsmen. When people got hit, they called "Corpsman!" but it was almost a useless statement because he was already on the way. I never saw a corpsman that hid behind anything and waited for an opportunity to get to a marine. That's why we lost so many of them.

By the fifth or sixth day in Hue, we started getting mad. We got to the point of still being afraid of dying, but more or less just said the hell with it. We got smarter and learned how to fight in a city. We learned how to work with each other, how to use the tanks. When I saw a window or a door or a tree, I shot at it. The best weapon we had in Hue was the flame-thrower tanks. Instead of taking a house room by room, the tanks would just hose the place down and we'd go on about our business.

I got hit in Hue. Me and another guy was in a room that had steel bars on the windows. He was standing above me shooting and I was laying down when my neck burnt real bad. I thought some of his shell cases had come down my neck. Come to find out, it was pieces from a round that had hit one of those steel bars. If it hadn't hit the bar, it would have hit the other guy dead center in the chest. I didn't even get a Purple Heart and it's never bothered me until the last few years. I got a knot there because calcium has built up around it, but it's no big deal. I was lucky because only three guys in my platoon went through the whole battle without getting killed or badly hurt.

After Hue, I was on several operations around Phu Bai and Danang. My company stayed pretty busy. In late June or early July, we went up on top of a mountain and was searching a cave. We found a NVA hospital. Somebody came running out and one the guys shot him from ten feet away with a .45 pistol, right through the belly. Come to find it wasn't a guy, it was a woman, and she walked down off that mountain.

Then and there, I said to myself, "If the women are this tough, how in the hell are we going to beat the men?" The North Vietnamese reminded me a lot of what I think the old southern troops was like. They was fighting for a cause that they believed in and they just wasn't going to give up. We was going to have to kill every one of them to win. The only good feeling I got from killing one was knowing, well, that's one guy that can't kill me. But I also knew I had killed somebody's son, somebody's daddy, and that didn't make me feel good.

I came back to the states in February of 1969. I never had anybody spit on me, but I heard some people say some pretty hard things about killing innocent people and stuff like that. If anybody had spit on me, I'd have gone berserk and probably would be in jail today. Most of the time back then, we didn't wear our uniforms in airports in California. We had just got out of one bad situation and by wearing the uniform we was going to be in another one. We was tired of fighting. Even in Tuscaloosa, people I have known all my life didn't feel comfortable around me in my uniform.

I got out of the marines in 1970 and joined again in 1972. I couldn't find a decent job and I think being a Vietnam veteran had a lot to do with it. In fact, I think I'm being punished to this day because I served in Vietnam. The good jobs was all taken when I got back.

If it hadn't been for the evacuation of Saigon in April of 1975, I probably would have stayed in the marines. But while we was flying from the aircraft carrier *Hancock* to Saigon to help provide security for Americans leaving Vietnam, a young trooper asked me a question. "Tant," he said, "why did we let something like this happen?" *Why* is not a word in the Marine Corps. You know, it's just not in the vocabulary. I started trying to find a reason. Why *did* this happen? Why did all those guys die for nothing? We was going back to pull out, it was over. I simply couldn't find a reason to justify training seventeen- and eighteen-year-old kids to go die for no damn reason.

I got out of the marines again in 1976. I hated being a garrison marine. I resented a staff sergeant with a fire-watch ribbon telling me what to do. I had paid my dues; I knew what being a grunt was all about. I had to travel a lot to find work after I got out. I put in time as a roofer in Houston and as a crewman on a shrimp boat in Florida. I even worked construction for a while with Jack Fields, the guy who was my fireteam leader. Then I got married in 1979, when I was in Houston. I was thirty and she was nineteen.

The first time I asked her to get married, I was as drunk as a road lizard. I called her the next morning after I had sobered up and said, "Look, I don't really want to do this." About a month later, I got drunk again and asked her to marry me. I figured I loved the girl, so why not?

First thing she wanted me to do after we got married was to quit drinking. She wanted to change me and I wasn't going to change. I've always had nightmares about Nam, and really, I think that's the reason I drank so much. You get drunk and you don't dream, at least I don't. She didn't understand Vietnam and that was one of our problems. I tried to talk to her about the war, but I just couldn't communicate with her. I just talked about the war with guys who was there. Finally, my wife and me couldn't seem to talk about anything, so we got divorced about six months after our boy was born.

If you ask me, Vietnam will never be understood except by the people who was there. And even at that, you could ask twenty different people about Vietnam and hear about twenty different wars. An army grunt down in the Mekong Delta didn't see the same war a marine on the DMZ saw. Vietnam was not one war. It was a bunch of nasty little wars.

Col. Benjamin H. Purcell

Clarkesville, Georgia

Prisoner of war, 1968–73

●

"Come out to the house for lunch," Ben Purcell said on the phone. "We'll have a sandwich and talk during the afternoon." A retired army colonel, Ben lives in the country a few miles east of Clarkesville. His brick two-story home, built atop a knoll, offers a clear view of the north Georgia mountains, distant green waves that shimmer on the horizon in the heat of midsummer. Ben spent sixty-two months as a prisoner of war, most of them in solitary confinement in North Vietnam. After we talked, I knew why he built his house on a hill.

Ben Purcell was a hero in a war never destined to be heroic. He waged an intellectual struggle against his North Vietnamese captors, never giving in to their ceaseless demands, never giving up on his determination to outwit them. In retaliation, he was not allowed to write his wife, Anne, or receive letters from her. Incredibly, he escaped from his captors not once, but twice—and was plotting his third escape when the war ended.

A native of nearby Baldwin, Georgia, Ben is a brown-haired man of medium build and military posture. Forthright but courteous, he possesses a tremendous reservoir of inner strength that rests on an abiding faith in God and country. It was this unshakable faith that the North Vietnamese came up against time and again in their attempts to break his will, only to reap a disappointing harvest of frustration.

"I was a professor of military science at Kemper Military School in Boonville, Missouri, when I received my orders to Vietnam in 1967," Ben told me. "When I arrived in-country, my orders to report to the First Cavalry Division at An Khe were changed and I was assigned to the Danang Sub-Area Command as its deputy commanding officer."

Ben's command was a housekeeping unit that supported all army units in I Corps, as well as marines in the northern part of the country who were using army equipment, such as the big cannons firing across the DMZ. His job required frequent helicopter flights 110 miles north and south of Danang. Like most other Americans in Vietnam, Ben hitched a ride on a chopper when he needed to go somewhere.

"I had been in Vietnam for five months when I was captured," he said. "The day before it happened in February of 1968, just after Tet, my boss had gone to the DMZ, where the 101st Airborne and the First Cav were gearing up for a joint operation with the marines into the A Shau Valley. Some command and communications problems had turned up, so when my boss came back, he had some specific orders to get some single-sideband radios up there to help straighten things out.

"I told him that since I needed to go up to Dong Ha, I could take the radios and batteries on to the units at Quang Tri. He was very gracious and let me take his place."

O n the morning of February 8, I went down to Marble Mountain Airfield to hitch a ride on a Huey. Six Americans climbed aboard: the pilot, the copilot, the crew chief, a door gunner, a young PFC who was a reefer mechanic, and myself. We stopped at the Hue–Phu Bai airstrip on the way north to get a bite to eat, then continued over the coastline until turning inland over the Cua Viet River to make our approach to Dong Ha. While the reefer mechanic went into Quang Tri City to take care of his job, I worked on the communications problem and checked on my subordinate units at Dong Ha.

We had been gone about eight hours when we reassembled at the chopper pad for the flight back to Danang. A few minutes before we were to take off, the pilot told me he was having some problems with the instruments, which meant he couldn't fly above the clouds. He said he would fly nap-of-the-earth instead. That was fine with me. I soon noticed, though, that he had turned southeast toward the coast, rather than going back over the Cua Viet River—and he wasn't flying just above the tree-tops, either.

As we zipped along about three hundred feet up, I heard him yell over the intercom, "We're being fired on!"

He had taken a round in his leg. Turning his head to alert me and the others, he shouted, "We're on fire!" The fuel cell had taken the next hit and was blazing. I looked out the door and saw the muzzle flashes of three automatic weapons firing at us from a cemetery. The pilot made a wide swooping turn and came right down in the cemetery—a real pancake landing. He later told me he deliberately landed close to a big tombstone in order to clip off the rotor blades. It was a smart move that let us get out of the chopper without the risk of being hit by flying debris.

The reefer mechanic had put his M-14 on the floor between the two pilots. Instead of jumping straight out like the rest of us, he came through the passenger compartment to pick up his rifle and his uniform caught fire. We snuffed out the flames as he rolled in the sand. We also put a bandage on the wounded pilot's leg. But all the time we could hear the VC closing in on us, although we didn't know which direction they were coming from.

I asked the pilot, "Did you get a Mayday off?" Not enough time, he said. Machine-gun rounds on the Huey started to cook off like firecrackers. I didn't know at the time that an M-79 grenade launcher and a case of grenades were aboard, but if I had known, I would have gone after them. Fortunately, the crew chief had managed to pull off one of the M-60s and a belt of ammunition, and one of the pilots had grabbed the reefer mechanic's M-14. We decided to move to a nearby treeline for safety, but as soon as we got through it, we heard the VC right on our tails.

They came first to the burning Huey, then began to track us across the sand. By now we were in a hamlet, with curious women and children crowding all around. An old shell crater offered the promise of some protection, so we jumped into it as the VC closed within two hundred yards of us and started to spread out in a semicircle. Before long, we were almost eyeball to eyeball with them. Well, I had spotted a low place on the back side of the crater. I told the wounded pilot and the reefer mechanic to see if they could use it to escape. They did, but the VC captured the mechanic about thirty minutes later. The pilot was out for twenty-four hours.

I had a .38-caliber revolver loaded with only five rounds in the chamber for safety. I looked out at the VC and recognized an old army BAR, AK-47s, M-16s—there were about twelve of them and every one had some kind of automatic weapon. And I was standing there with a revolver.

The crew chief with the M-60 came up with some more bad news. "Sir," he said, "I've got a broken sear on my machine gun." I glanced at the five-round shot group he had loaded and saw sand all over it. With a broken sear and sand on the cartridges, the M-60 was going to jam for sure on the first round. That left the M-14 as our most powerful weapon. The copilot had it, but I could only wonder if he was really qualified on the M-14, if he even knew where the safety was. Our only other weapon was a

.45 pistol that one of the pilots had given to the door gunner. So that was it: a defective machine gun, an M-14 manned by someone who probably didn't know how to use it, and two pistols against twelve automatic weapons.

Nevertheless, it was nip and tuck for a while. The VC were hollering at us the whole time. Not a one of them spoke English, but we knew what they wanted from their sign language. Pretty soon, they followed up their demands by throwing a grenade in front of us.

"Fellows," I said, "if the next one comes in the hole, we're all gone."

I don't remember who suggested that we surrender, but I was the one who made the decision. As I saw it, we could either die there on the spot in a firefight or we could try to buy some time and escape later.

Moments after we raised our hands, the VC marched us into a bombed-out hut in the hamlet. A man in an olive-drab North Vietnamese uniform walked in and began telling the VC what to do with us. He was probably about forty-five and at least a lieutenant. The VC quickly stripped off our uniforms. Then they tied our hands and thumbs together behind our backs. It's amazing how effective a good, strong cord around your thumbs can be—you can't untie anything without your thumbs. Their next step was to take our boots before moving us out to a village. The sun was going down, but I guess they wanted it to get a little darker before they took us across the rice paddies.

In the village, the VC suddenly motioned to us to face a wall. This turn of events badly upset one of the enlisted men.

"Oh, they're going to kill us!" he cried. "They're going to kill us!"

"No," I assured him with as much conviction as I could muster, "we're worth more to them alive than dead." I said that with the thought that just a few days before, I had read about five marines who had been shot with their hands tied behind their backs not far from where we were.

The reefer mechanic, who had been captured by this time, was the only one of us who didn't have his hands tied. Out of an act of kindness, the VC let him lie down while the rest of us were facing the wall. They even gave him a cup of colored water that they indicated was tea. Maybe it was, but I'll never know because the rest of us didn't get any.

We moved out across the rice paddies after dark. Strangely, walking through them in my socks didn't bother me very much. When the mud pulled the socks off my feet, I had no desire to stop and pick them up, even if I could have done so. After a while, we came to a stream where two small boats were waiting. The VC loaded three men on the front boat. The reefer mechanic and I were directed into the second one.

"Colonel," he asked me, "are you a Christian?" "Yes," I replied. "Let's pray," he said, and we did so as we went down the stream.

I don't know how long we were in the boats, but it seemed only a short while. We then walked through more hamlets that were friendly to the VC. As we moved through these little places, which I knew were near the coast, the VC would stop us for a while and let the villagers come out to gawk at us. About four a.m., we crossed Highway 1 and moved onto small paths covered with pea-sized gravel. Perhaps the VC knew our feet were beginning to hurt by this time; they let us rest after four or five miles. As we did so, some two hundred men with bags of rice on their backs walked by us, heading into the mountains. I assumed they had offloaded the rice on the beach.

"Where are our people now?" I thought. "How can the VC march two hundred people loaded with rice down a path undetected?"

The VC roused us at first light. We hadn't walked very far before the trail began rising into the mountains.

I heard the reefer mechanic say, "I can't see to walk because my eyes are swollen shut." Up to that time, in the darkness, none of us could tell where we were going; the mechanic wasn't aware that he couldn't see.

The VC told him to sit down on the side of the trail while the rest of us walked on. I figured they would give him some medical treatment.

We had moved up the trail about five hundred yards when I heard a pistol shot. I thought, "Lord, they've executed that young soldier."

A couple of months later, when I was in the midst of an interrogation that lasted several days, I found his dog tag, as well as my own, in a trash pile. Not until I came home five years later did I learn—from his mother, in fact—that he had been killed. His gravesite was found near the place we had to leave him.

We walked for five days through very rugged terrain. Some of the hills were so steep we had to crawl up them on our hands and knees and slide down the other side on our rear ends. By the third day, the bottoms of our feet were raw. Some of the VC gave us their sandals, but the ones I got were so small they cut into the tops of my feet. Soon, I was suffering from raw soles and tops.

I had no clear thoughts during this ordeal except to stay alive. We were given very little water. If we slowed down to get so much as a drop of water off a leaf, a VC would put a round in the chamber of his rifle and say, "Go! Go!" in Vietnamese. And every time I fell behind, a guard would threaten to shoot me.

On February 13, we came to a small wooden cabin somewhere in the mountains near Khe Sanh. The cabin was about twelve by twenty feet and inside it was a bed made out of woven sticks the diameter of a finger. This was to be the bed for the four of us. An old Montagnard who lived there also had a cot of his own and a chicken—it seemed that almost every VC had a chicken. I also noticed that he had a bin of rice reserved for VC who passed his way.

The next day, a VC interrogator showed up. We had been prisoners for a week and they were just now asking us our names. The interrogator handed us a piece of paper that had twelve questions on it, starting out with name, rank, service number, date of birth, father's name, what kind of work he was in, why we had come to Vietnam, and so on. We answered the appropriate questions—name, rank, service number, and date of birth—and then I said, "Fellows, this is it."

We all handed the papers back to the interrogator, who got so upset he ordered a guard to come in and march one of the helicopter crewmen outside. I waited with the others for the gunshot, but it never came. Then another crewman was marched outside. Still no gunshot—the VC were bluffing. I later learned that the crewmen were held overnight in nearby cabins with some South Vietnamese prisoners.

As for me, the interrogator told me to get down into a small dugout about three by three feet in the dirt floor of the cabin. This was painful because I'd evidently cracked or broken a rib in the chopper crash. My feet were still hurting, too. I was cold, hungry, and despondent—and all of a sudden I remembered it was my fortieth birthday. The little adage that life begins at forty came to me.

"Lord," I said, "let me stay thirty-nine."

After dark, I crawled out of the hole to go to the toilet. I didn't ask permission to go; I simply did it. As I came back into the cabin, I picked up an egg laid by the Montagnard's hen on a two-foot-high ledge made of mud and bamboo. I handed the egg to the interrogator. Then I sat down on the dirt floor by a fire and dozed off.

I remember the helicopter crew chief, the fourth prisoner, shaking me awake and saying, "Colonel, supper's ready." In the week since I had been captured, I had been given two handfuls of boiled rice and a cup or two of water. I looked up to see the interrogator holding a saucer.

"It's a custom of the Vietnamese people to remember the special days in the lives of guests in their homes," he said. "I know you're not a guest in this man's home, but he knows it's your birthday and he wants to honor it with the only thing he has to offer. Here's an egg for your supper."

I was twelve thousand miles from home and poles apart from the

Montagnard ideologically, socially, and educationally. Yet he showed me a side of humanity that has stuck with me to this day.

The interrogator wasn't very good with English. He had a Vietnamese-English dictionary that he tried to use for translating his language into ours. During my interrogation, I decided to go beyond the "big four" answers allowed by the Code of Conduct and give him Anne's name and address. The Geneva Agreements on the treatment of prisoners of war encourage communication between a prisoner and his family. My rationale was, how will Anne know what's happened to me if I don't put her name and address down? I didn't see that as a violation of the Code of Conduct.

The Vietnamese never notified Anne that I was alive, but thirteen months later, my interrogator was captured by the Americans and he had on him the papers that I had filled out. At that time, the army changed my status from MIA to POW.

From the mountain cabin, I was taken by litter to another camp, where my group of prisoners stayed for thirty days. It was here that the chopper pilot who had evaded capture for twenty-four hours joined us, as did a black soldier who had been captured in Hue City in May of 1967.

After leaving this camp, we walked for nine days into the upper reaches of the A Shau Valley, suffering fifteen to twenty leech bites every day. Each one produced an open sore. It was cold, my weight was dropping, and I was developing serious infections from the leech bites. We spent a week there in a temporary holding area before starting up the Ho Chi Minh Trail for ten nights in the back of six-wheel trucks—the roughest ride I've ever experienced. We heard a lot of American aircraft during the trip, and one night we saw one get shot down.

We met other prisoners on the way north. Two of them were Filipino civilians captured in Hue and the others were ARVN soldiers. We had a total of thirteen prisoners in the back of a truck going along the trail in eastern Laos. Each day, the truck stopped at dawn and we'd be marched about a half a mile off the trail to a lean-to, where the North Vietnamese gave us two balls of rice and some water. Come dark, we'd return to the trail and catch another truck.

It was amazing to me how many trucks we met going up and down that trail, which in places was hardly wide enough for them to squeeze between the trees. All the trucks drove without lights. Every mile or so we'd come to an inspection station with a small blackout lantern. The driver had to identify himself at each station before moving on.

During this time, I was convinced that we were being taken to Hanoi to be released. The big operation in the A Shau Valley, along with a sweep north of the seventeenth parallel, and then the war was going to end: that shows you the mindset of a prisoner. I *wanted* to think optimistically.

In the back of the truck with us were two guards. Three North Vietnamese were in the cab of the truck: the driver, the assistant driver, and another guard. It would have been so easy for the thirteen of us to overpower the two guards in the back. We could have then banged on the truck to get the attention of the men in the cab, clubbing them when they came out. After that, we could have pulled off the road and set the truck afire when we heard an American plane.

Incredibly, that plan didn't occur to me until three years later. I was simply convinced that we were going north to be released. That's why I tell military people today in survival courses: *think escape*. Every moment, think escape and be ready.

I think we could have succeeded in taking over the truck because one of the guards went to sleep with his rifle sticking in my side one night. Just for the hell of it, I unscrewed the gas port plug on his weapon. The guards were just out of it. For three days, we Americans even carried walking sticks, but they were so much trouble on that bouncing truck that we all threw them away. We could have clubbed the guards with those sticks.

We stopped near Vinh for about three months before going on to the Hanoi area. Here I had my first serious interrogation. I was separated from the other guys at a camp I called Bao Cao and locked in a three-by-seven-foot cubicle. The interrogators quickly made it clear they had no food, clothes, or medicine for prisoners who refused to answer their questions. As sick as I was, I had to find an alternative to name, rank, service number, and date of birth. Most of us did.

While I still had the presence of mind to know what I was doing, I decided to answer all the interrogators' questions except those relating to my family with lies. I thus departed from my lifelong ethic of always telling the truth to a deliberate policy of lying to the enemy. The interrogators at Vinh spoke fluent English and most of them knew what they were looking for, but they apparently became convinced from what I told them that I knew nothing about operations on the battlefield.

I was still apprehensive and fearful for my life; anybody in such a situation who tells you otherwise would be stretching the truth. Not until August, when I was in a prison camp near Hanoi, did I really become convinced the Vietnamese weren't going to kill me. It was then that I went on the psychological offensive. I went after them. I didn't spit in their eye or double up my fist or strike at them, but anything I could to upset the apple cart for them, I did.

The North Vietnamese interrogators were very stern and matter-of-fact. They made me sit on a stool and would not let me cross my legs—to do so was a sign of disrespect. They, on the other hand, made quite a show of sitting at a table while they smoked cigarettes and drank hot tea. I'd sit on that stool for hours and hours at a time, always thinking about a way to fool them on the next question. One of my favorite ways to harass them involved answering a question before they finished asking it.

Slamming his fist down on the table, the interrogator would yell, "Wait until I finish asking the question before you answer!"

They liked to talk about the Americans violating the agreements on Laos, because in 1962 all the sides said they would have no forces in that country.

"Don't tell me that because you brought me through Laos and I saw your troops there," I said. When I could catch them in such a lie or half-truth, I'd just needle them a bit and they'd shut it off.

They would also demand that the United States recognize the sovereignty of East Berlin. I said that was a dichotomy.

"Here, you want Vietnam to be one, but you want Germany to be two," I'd tell them. "How do you rationalize that?" More often than not, the interrogator would bang on his desk. "Go back to your cell!"

They had a very rigid program. If I could get them off it, they usually didn't know what to do except send me back to my cell.

I nicknamed one of my Hanoi interrogators Crisco, because he was a slick character and more decent than most of the other North Vietnamese. I liked to play intellectual games with him. One day, I took a pencil and a wrapper from a cigarette package. In the center of the package, I drew a rectangle. In the other spots around the rectangle, I drew a wedge, a half-moon, and a thin line, all options of what the third dimension of that object might be.

"Let me show you this," I said to Crisco after one of our sessions. I had folded the cigarette package an inch square.

"Now, this is a three-dimensional object, but you see only two dimensions. Can you tell what it is by seeing the two dimensions?"

He didn't buy into that, so I said, "We've been talking about the war, about my changing my thinking, coming over to your view. You know one side. I know my side and I know your side because you have told me your side. But the truth lies beyond either one of us. There's a third dimension."

As I started to unfold the corners of the package, another interrogator came in and began whispering something to Crisco. He called off the interrogation, and I later found out that Ho Chi Minh had just died. It was September 2, 1969.

Three years later, Crisco and I were sitting in another interrogation. He had a teacup in his hand. He turned it around and said, "Now, you've got to look at this side, and at that side, you've got to look at all sides in order to tell the truth."

"Crisco," I said, "I told you that three years ago."

On another occasion, I saw a copy of *Time* magazine on a table. I asked Crisco if I could read it.

"No."

"Can the average Vietnamese read it?" I asked.

"No, we officials read the news and tell the people what we want them to know, because a lot of the news is poison."

"Sometimes poison makes an effective medicine," I said. "It'll cure a lot of ills." It was my way of criticizing their closed society.

The interrogators talked a lot about events in the United States. They especially liked to focus on riots, protests, and war resisters coming to North Vietnam in support of their effort. I was convinced then and now that Americans may have had the legal right to visit North Vietnam, but not the moral right because they prolonged the war by encouraging the Vietnamese to think American society was being torn asunder.

For most of my time in prison, the North Vietnamese kept me in isolation, away from other prisoners, because I was so uncooperative. I also earned a reputation for going on hunger strikes to protest almost anything. Every time they'd talk about how humane and lenient the Vietnamese people were toward prisoners of war, I'd throw it back at them.

"Don't tell me that. You've kept me in solitary for three years and when I quit taking my food, you take away my drinking water, you won't let me write letters to my wife, you won't let me talk to another prisoner—what's humane and lenient about that?"

The North Vietnamese didn't push Marxist-Leninist theory, although most of the books I got to read after the peace talks began in January of 1969 were of Russian authorship. I read the *Communist Manifesto* for the first time in my life, as well as a book on Karl Marx. That was it so far as Communist theory was concerned. Of course, they wouldn't let me have a Bible, but I was given a copy of Shakespeare's complete works for two weeks. I relished it.

When I was sick, the most common medicine I got was a little vial of what smelled like mentholatum. If I had a headache, I was told to rub it on my forehead; if I had a stuffy nose, I was to put it under my nose; and if I had a sore throat, I was to rub it on my throat. I suffered from beri-beri at one point and had kidney stones a couple of times. I couldn't urinate more than a tablespoon for three days during the first kidney-stone attack. Of course, I was given a vial of mentholatum to clear up the problem. Finally the stone passed on its own accord. I had demanded to see a doctor, but he didn't show up until a week later.

I stayed sane in prison by putting my mind in neutral and thinking about positive subjects: the trades I'd made in automobiles, the dogs I'd had, my family, my job, the house I wanted to build back in Georgia. In fact, I designed every detail of this house in my mind. I'd think about a subject intensely for two or three hours. Then I'd get up from my bunk, get some exercise, eat lunch, take a nap, and put my mind in neutral again.

I worked out a very detailed structure for my days. In fact, they became so structured that when the interrogators took me out for a session, my whole day's plan would be interrupted. When I returned to my cell, I'd continue thinking into the night. I had to finish my program for the day.

I quietly studied every move the North Vietnamese made, especially the guards and their habits. The detailed knowledge I gained from this kind of day-after-day observation allowed me to escape twice when I was in the Hanoi area.

I made my first escape in 1969 from a camp I call K-77. The bottom part of my cell door in this camp was made of solid, inch-thick wood panels set tongue-in-groove within a heavy, two-by-four-inch wooden frame. Having done some woodworking in my day, I knew that if I could somehow rip off the inside flange, I could move a panel out of the way and get into the prison compound at night.

Yet, what good would that do me? I would be surrounded by a wall fourteen feet high and a guard walking around inside the compound. But I knew that if I could evade the guard and get over that wall, I might find my way to Hanoi to the French consulate and ask for political asylum.

This plan got its start when one of the guards, a buck-toothed private, became my friend. Every day at noon, while almost everybody else was taking a nap, we'd chat for a while, each trying to teach the other a few words of our respective languages. We got to know each other well enough that he'd climb a fruit tree in the compound and pick some fruit for me.

One day, he came bounding up to my cell and said, "Today, I go Hanoi, see movie."

"Oh," I said, "which way?"

He pointed and I asked him how far he had to go.

"Ten clicks."

Ten kilometers—my prison was located six miles southwest of Hanoi. Now I knew where I was. Even though I was moved to a new cell, I was able to get a piece of wire out of the wall and fashion a small twist drill for boring holes in the door panel. I concealed the holes by plugging them with a mixture of bread, soot from my kerosene lamp, and toothpaste.

One day the private brought me a piece of aluminum from a downed American aircraft and asked me to make him a ring. One of the leg stocks in my cell had a three-quarter-inch bolt sticking out of it. I bent the aluminum around the bolt, ground it smooth on the concrete floor, and polished it with fine sand. Pleased with what I had made for him, the private then asked me to engrave the ring. For that, I said, I'd need a nail.

He brought me one.

I fashioned the nail into a chisel by flattening the head into a square and sharpening the point. I made the handle by baking layers of bread around the nail and its square head over the kerosene lamp, night after night. As I used my new chisel to chip off pieces from off the door panel, I threw them into my toilet bucket for disposal. I could take the panel out of position after three weeks of work.

On December 7, 1969, Pearl Harbor Day, after everybody else had gone to bed and the lights were out, I got up and rumpled my blanket to make it look like I was still asleep. I quietly moved the door panel out of the way, slipped out of my cell, and went out into the darkness. I had fixed the panel so that I could put it back into place from the outside, which I did quickly.

I scurried around the compound—only to stumble over a toilet bucket. A guard swept the area with his flashlight; luckily, the beam missed me. I now knew where he was, but he couldn't see me. I cautiously made my way into the administrative wing of the prison and went over an eight-foot wall, using a canvas ladder that I had made from an old duffel bag.

I had on my tan prison uniform, which I had turned inside out so the stripes wouldn't show, and a blue padded jacket like the peasants in China wore. In addition to the ladder, I had fashioned a fatigue hat and a map case out of the duffel bag. All Vietnamese officers carried map cases, but I used mine to carry some bread that I had stashed away. From a distance, I appeared as just another peasant walking on the road.

I walked up and down the road that went by the prison three times, trying desperately to find the railroad tracks that would lead me into Hanoi. I never found them. Still on the road at dawn, I asked a man standing beside his bicycle for directions into the city. Shortly after I began walking in the direction he pointed to, he pedaled by and offered me a ride. I got on his bicycle and rode into Hanoi with him. When he stopped at a precinct police station, I politely got off and started walking down the road.

A few minutes later, a policeman stopped me and asked to see my papers. Of course, I didn't have any. The policeman gently took me by the elbow and escorted me back to the precinct station.

I pretended to be a Frenchman who had lost his papers. The police rang up the French Embassy and by ten a.m., a small man wearing a beret and carrying an attaché case was standing near me in the station. Two Vietnamese interrogators also arrived about the same time as the Frenchman. One of them asked me a few questions in French, but I couldn't respond; I had no idea what he had asked me.

"You pilot?" he finally said in English.

"No, I'm Ben Purcell," I told him. "I was shot down in South Vietnam and your soldiers brought me north. I've been a prisoner of war in isolation for two years."

I said it loud enough for the Frenchman, if he understood English, to hear me.

Within an hour or so, the prison director arrived to take me back to K-77, where I was locked in leg stocks in my cell for two weeks. I lay flat on a wooden board for twenty-three hours and thirty minutes of every day, my ankles held firmly in place by the stocks. The guards released me for fifteen minutes every morning and afternoon to go to the toilet and pick up my meal.

The lieutenant in charge of the guards at K-77 was relieved as a result of my escape, as was a turnkey who had opened my cell and inspected it only three days earlier. Six months later, the turnkey returned to K-77; I never saw the lieutenant again. On the turnkey's second day back, he stormed into my cell and tore it apart. Maybe he had been away for six months learning how to inspect a prisoner's cell. Although my escape was a great embarrassment to them, I believe the North Vietnamese respected me for escaping—even if they could never bring themselves to admit it.

In December of 1971, a number of other prisoners and I were moved to a new camp somewhere north of Hanoi. This camp, which I called K-49, had walls eighteen inches thick. Each cell had steel doors rather than wood, and they opened into small enclosures I called cages. Barbed wire had been strung across the top of each cage to discourage escape.

My cell at K-49 was about ten by ten feet, larger than the one I had at K-77. It even had a primitive toilet in the rear. It also had a concrete reservoir that held about a cubic meter of water, as well as a rubber bucket to dip out the water for washing clothes and flushing the toilet.

Although I was still isolated from the other prisoners, I was allowed at K-49 to go into my cage and get fresh air every morning. After lunch, the guards would lock me up and let out the prisoners in adjoining cells. We were never in our cages at the same time, except for a few minutes during meals.

Still, we found ways to communicate with each other. Gene Weaver, a CIA agent in the cell next to me, had been a B-17 pilot in World War II and knew some Morse code. We were able to slip a few notes through a drainage hole between our cages and start work on a code.

Most American pilots had training in the Matrix code, which consisted of five lines of five letters. But I didn't know the Matrix code or Morse code, so Weaver and I had to work out a way to get a dash through the wall that separated us. I finally suggested two quick dots for one dash. *A*, which is dot–dash in Morse code, became dot–dot-dot. Weaver and I were the only two people in the world who knew that code. I have since been told it was one of the safest, most secure codes we had in Vietnam.

The first time I went into my cage, I looked at the barbed wire above me and figured I could get through it. Another escape wasn't a question of how, but when.

During the day, the guards kept an inspection hole in my cage door open so they could see what I was doing when I was in the cage. But more than that, they left my cell door unlocked during the meal hour, which gave me access to the cage late in the afternoons. The guards would return thirty minutes later to pick up the dishes.

I soon discovered that if I was standing on the toilet urinating when they came back for the dishes, they'd just lock the cell door, then the cage door, and not show up again until eight a.m. the next day. Whether they were just naive or respecting my privacy, I don't know, but their pattern gave me an idea. I started to exercise very strenuously, running barefoot on the concrete to get my feet tough in case I lost my Ho Chi Minh sandals during my escape. A week before I planned to break out on March 18, 1972, I was always on the toilet when the guards came to retrieve the supper dishes.

If my plan was to work, I had to have some realistic sound effects. I punched a small hole in the rubber bucket, so that it would take about twenty-five minutes to empty. Some dried leaves in the bottom of the toilet would make a loud sound when the stream of water hit them.

I had managed to get two nails from another part of the prison. I drove them into the wall and hung the bucket over the center of the toilet with a string. Then I took a piece of bamboo and put it over the top of the bucket. This allowed me to drape one of my extra prison jackets around the bucket. Next, I used a bone needle that I had made to stitch a pair of pants to the back side of the jacket. Bamboo around the pants cuffs made the legs look larger. Luckily, the toilet platform was three feet high, so a guard standing at the front of my cell couldn't see that my dummy had no head.

I assumed that when the guards looked in the cell, they would get nothing more than a glimpse of the uniform, lock the door, and turn around and leave. And that's exactly what happened.

Gene Weaver saw me leave during the meal hour. In fact, I had asked him to go with me, but he said, "No, I'm too old." I think he was fifty at the time. He gave me the V sign as I threaded my way through the barbed wire and scrambled over his cage wall. Once on the ground, I crawled through a drainage ditch in the camp perimeter and headed east into the woods. This time, I intended to "borrow" some fisherman's boat and set adrift in the Gulf of Tonkin.

I stayed out for thirty hours before getting caught the second night. The North Vietnamese put guardposts on all the major roads, which forced me to go cross-country. Shortly before I was recaptured, I was sitting on a rock beside a stream when a Vietnamese came down the bank on the other side—he looked right at me from twenty-five feet away and never saw me dressed in my black prison uniform. When he turned his back, I did a crab crawl very quietly and got out of his line of vision. I decided the best thing to do was get out of there. I came to a road and started moving lickety-split, going as fast as I could. I got less cautious. Suddenly, a soldier shined a flashlight right in my eye and starting shooting in the air. And that was it for the second escape.

Weaver later told me pandemonium broke loose at K-49 on the morning after my escape. He said the Vietnamese started screaming and hollering and slamming doors, locking everybody up. I figured they would clamp down hard on me, but I was surprised when they only gave me thirty days in my cell, didn't allow me to go into my cage, and put me on short rations.

When the guard brought me my evening meal, which by this time often consisted of cabbage, a boiled slice of pumpkin, some soya bean cake, and a loaf of bread, he would rake half of it off into the dirt and hand me the remainder. I went on a hunger strike to protest that kind of abuse. I'd just lie down on my bunk and drink a cup of water without eating anything. In response, the guard who was on duty the night I escaped began to cut my hot water ration down to three-fourths of a cup at meal time. The next day I only got two-thirds of a cup. On the day I received only a quarter of a cup, I was nervous and upset and threw the water at him.

Well, you don't throw hot water on a prison guard. I didn't want to hit him and I didn't want to miss him, so I threw it on the wall near the cage door and some of the water splashed on him. He turned around and shook his finger at me.

"That's not good," was all he said.

I started yelling for more water, saying I was Ben Purcell and that I had escaped and been recaptured. I said the camp director had told me I would be on short rations for thirty days, but he said nothing about short water. I was really telling Weaver and the others that I was alive. Within five minutes, the sergeant of the guard came running down with a pitcher of hot water.

"Be quiet," he pleaded. "Be quiet."

In late December of 1972, I started another hunger strike, this one for thirteen days, because I was still not allowed to write home. On January 6, Crisco promised he would take my request for permission to write a letter to the authorities in Hanoi. I was sitting in my cell late on January 26 when a guard brought me a pencil and a piece of paper and said I could write to Anne. I looked at that piece of paper long into the night. What do you say after five years? I just couldn't sort out all the things that I wanted to say.

When I got up the next morning, I started to write in words so small I could hardly read them myself. I covered both sides of that paper and gave it to a guard who came by my cell around lunchtime. Later that same afternoon, all of us Americans at K-49 were escorted out of our cells and taken to camp headquarters, where we were told the war was over. After the evening meal, we were to be taken to Hanoi in preparation for our release. We left about dark and were driven to the Hanoi Hilton, where I was put into a cell with other Americans for the first time in fifty-eight months.

In early February, a guard returned my letter of January 27 to me. He said it was too long, that I could write only a few lines. I condensed what I had put on two pages into six lines and gave it to him on February 9. I don't know what the Vietnamese did with it, but Anne never received that letter. Consequently, there was no direct communication between Anne and me for sixty-two months.

I believe three intangible things helped me survive in prison. One was my faith in America; the second was my hope that every day the sun came up, it would be the day I was going home; and the third was love, the love that I knew Anne had for me and our children, and the love that I knew Christ had for both of us. That was what kept me going, the knowledge that somebody cared.

March 27, 1973, was the day of our release. The North Vietnamese had given each of us a small AWOL bag to carry personal items in. In my bag, I had stuffed a bar of soap, a tube of toothpaste, some bone buttons, a hat, and a pair of undershorts that I had made from a worn-out pair of prison uniform trousers. I had worn the shorts on my second escape. In one of the pockets, carefully wrapped in cellophane, was a small American flag that I had also made, as well as an information card containing my name, rank, service number, date of birth, and blood type. I had carried these items so that I wouldn't be considered a spy if I were recaptured.

I especially wanted to bring the shorts and the flag home with me. As luck would have it, a young guard saw me reaching into my AWOL bag to get out a belt that I had forgotten to put on. He, too, reached down into the bag—and pulled out my shorts. When the flag and ID card came to light, he demanded that I give both items to him. I refused. Before that little incident was over, another guard and Crisco were called in.

"Purcell," said Crisco, "you're always causing trouble."

Taking that as a compliment, I gave him the flag and ID card. I still managed to get out with the hat and a couple of other items.

When I walked out of the Hanoi Hilton that March morning to go to the airport with a group of thirty-one other Americans, I didn't feel a sense of triumph, just a great, good feeling. I had expected to be released for a long time.

Everybody let out a joyous yell when our C-141 left Vietnamese soil. Since I was the senior American aboard, the public affairs officer accompanying us asked if I would say a few words to the press when we landed at Clark Air Force Base in the Philippines. While the other fellows were having fun drinking coffee, smoking cigars, and hugging the nurses, I was preparing my remarks. The thought occurred to me then that man's most precious possession, second only to life, is freedom, and that's what I said when we got off the plane at Clark.

I met Anne, the children, my mother, and several other members of my family at Bush Field in Augusta, Georgia, on March 30, 1973. I was asked again to make a few remarks. After thanking the president and the American people for keeping faith with us, another thought came to me in the glare of the floodlights.

"Anne," I said, "praise God that at this precious moment, my years of loneliness and your long vigil have come to a happy end."

I wasn't through with my remarks when Anne burst forward and embraced me. Why I said what I did, I have no idea. . . . I guess I just had in my mind certain things to say and I proceeded to say them. After the airport ceremony, we had our real family reunion at a nearby service club, a reunion that is still going on after fifteen years.

We went into Vietnam in an era when we felt we needed to stop the spread of Communism through Indochina. I think our long-term strategic goal was worthwhile, but we went at it piecemeal and with civilians making decisions on military operations. When you ask a man to lay his life on the line, you shouldn't call him on the radio from a helicopter and say, "Somebody back in Washington doesn't want you to fire that shot," and then he dies as a result. To me, it's immoral to send a man into combat without a clear mission to win.

There was also a generational difference among our soldiers in Vietnam. A lot of them were too much for "me" and not enough for the welfare of the majority. Many of them had no idea what they were doing in Vietnam or why they were there. Of the eight American POWs who were charged with misconduct, only one had a high-school education. They were easily duped when the North Vietnamese said, "If you'll just do this, you'll get to live with another person, you'll get more food and get to write your family." My answer to that was always no. Regardless of what was best for me, I simply believed the country's interest had to come first.

We paid a terrible price in Vietnam in lives and resources. So did the Vietnamese. Yet the war was not without some benefits. It raised the sensitivity of all the people of America to the horrors of war; they saw it on their television screens day after day, and they realized that war is not a way to settle international disputes. I also like to think that the seeds of democracy were sown in the hearts and minds of a lot of the people of South Vietnam during the war. They experienced a semblance of democracy for a while, and perhaps those seeds will germinate in the years to come. Maybe it won't happen in my lifetime, but someday all of Vietnam may be a more democratic society, more progressive, than if the war had never occurred.

I sometimes think about Crisco and some of the other North Vietnamese whom I knew while in prison. He was not a vicious person and I would be happy to visit with him today, to talk about the experiences we had and to gain an insight into some of his frustrations, not only with me but with other American prisoners. I'd like to know what he thought of us. And then there's the guard at K-77, the one who brought me fruit and wanted to learn English. I knew him for three years and would like very much to see him again. Today, he would be as welcome in my home as any other friend.

John S. Candler, Jr.

Atlanta, Georgia

Army platoon leader, 1968–69

●

I drove up to Jack Candler's brick home in Atlanta's exclusive Peachtree Hills section at last light. His wife Laura greeted me at the door. "Jack will be down in a minute," she said. "He's just returned from a run." As I waited for him in a small sunroom, I noticed a bookshelf laden with titles on the Vietnam War. Scion of one of Atlanta's First Families—patriarch Asa Candler developed the original formula for Coca-Cola—Jack was a platoon leader in the 196th Light Infantry Brigade during 1968–69. Today he is a mortgage banker in Atlanta.

A tall, slim man with full, black hair, Jack soon joined me in the sunroom. "I come from a conservative, flag-waving family," he said as we sat down for a conversation that would dwell on some of the hard moral choices Vietnam forced on commanders. "My grandfather was a commander of the Georgia National Guard, and my father served in the Army Air Corps in the Pacific during World War II. In addition, one of my uncles was a brigadier general in the Air Force Reserve."

Jack told me he was something of an exception to that tradition when he was a student at the University of Georgia in the mid-sixties.

"I was one of those who thought ROTC was interesting in parts, but largely just an unnecessary burden. I would say half my friends were active in ROTC and the other half, while not against it, were willing to get out of it if they could. I really didn't have any feelings about Vietnam one way or the other at the time, but by failing to take ROTC or other reserve training, I laid myself wide open for the draft."

I played the draft game in 1965 and lost it fairly. Of course, that doesn't mean I was happy to see my draft notice. Far from it. I had just finished college, gotten married, and was barely a year into my first real job. I was beginning to settle down.

I tried briefly to get into the Air Force Reserve as a navigator, which would have required a year in Texas for training after an instant commissioning as a second lieutenant. That would have been marvelous. I was almost through the testing and the air force was ready to sign me up when I had to take the eye test. Unfortunately, the test required perfect near vision for reading maps and symbols. I tested out 100 percent in one eye and something like 95 percent in the other because of astigmatism. It didn't amount to much, but it was enough to keep me out of the air force.

The week before I was to report for induction into the army, my brother-in-law introduced me to the commanding general of the Third Army. We met at a social club in which we were both up for membership. My brother-in-law said, "Jack's been drafted. He'd like to know where he's going for basic training." Don't worry about it, the general said. All I had to do was call his sergeant-major at Fort McPherson and he would tell me where I was going to be sent.

Not long after that, I went out to the induction center on Ponce de Leon Avenue one afternoon to take the army tests. The general's office had just told me that I would not have to leave for basic training until the next day. There was no problem with anything until 4:30 p.m., when one of the sergeants at the induction center told everybody there to listen up. "All right, you can go down the street and get a beer," he bellowed. "Be back here in thirty minutes, the bus is going to leave." I didn't even have a toothbrush. In fact, I didn't have anything except a company car from Georgia's largest mortgage banking firm. Talk about major stress—I was almost in tears. To make things worse, my wife and I were planning a quiet little dinner at home that night before she saw Soldier Boy off the next day.

I told the people at the induction center what my situation was. One of the sergeants was understanding enough to let me leave with the warning that I had to be back within one hour. "That's when the bus is really going to leave," he said. "Make it, or you're in trouble from day one." I was surprised he let me go because he'd undoubtedly heard all kinds of excuses. I drove the company car to my apartment about six miles across town and called Mother. I called Mother, not my wife—I guess I was a southern boy going home to Mama—and she took me back to the induction center. When we drove up, the other draftees were getting on the bus.

I spent that first miserable night at Fort Benning. The army wouldn't even let me make a phone call. I wasn't in the army; I was in prison. I laid up on that bunk, and I've got to tell you that big ol' tears welled up in my eyes for a moment. I was frustrated that night because I really did feel like a prisoner. But once basic training got under way, it turned out to be a very interesting experience—guys from all walks of life were there. I decided to work hard at basic because if I had to do it, I was going to do it right, gung-ho, and make everybody back home proud. I really got interested in that hodgepodge of American humanity. Most of the guys were very decent.

I got selected as the top trainee in my company and applied for OCS at the first opportunity. Now, the army didn't try to make me an Einstein in OCS, but it didn't teach to the lowest common denominator, either. I think I was very well trained. I learned a lot about leadership and small unit tactics. I also learned how to adjust mortar fire and read a map and compass, skills that really paid off in Vietnam. There was quite a bit of talk about the war when I was in OCS in early 1967. A lot of the instructors were captains and senior NCOs who had just come back from Vietnam. They were very good teachers. One day, we were told to look to our left and our right and remember that one of the men in those seats wouldn't come back alive. It was an effective attention-getter. Most of our training was directed toward the nature of the enemy and his tactics. There was very little emphasis on dealing with civilians in a war zone. I don't think I was properly prepared for that, but then I'm not sure how anybody could have prepared for it.

After OCS, I was stationed at Fort Gordon, which trained people for the Signal Corps, as the post reenlistment officer. I had a staff of senior and very experienced NCOs who basically ran the program, and, of course, they taught me what I was supposed to do: keep my boots shined and inspect the companies. It was a job with a lot of command emphasis, and yet it was repetitive, really pretty boring. Almost every year, Fort Gordon won the Continental Army Command trophy for the highest reenlistment rate, but the truth was, a lot of people re-upped for Germany and good duty elsewhere just to get away from the place.

I got orders to Vietnam in January of 1968. I was going to the 196th Light Infantry Brigade, which had just been hit very hard in Vietnam. I went to my supervisor, a major who was the assistant adjutant general of the post, to tell him what had happened. "Major Gillespie," I said, "I've just got orders for Vietnam and I'd like to request out of this duty and put in for a training company. I'm going to the 196th Light Infantry and I don't think they're going to need a lot of reenlistment officers. I need some troop duty."

He said, "Well, Lieutenant, not so fast. I think you're making a mistake.

You're doing a good job. You'd be a fool to get out of this. You ought to go to Vietnam and show that you've never had a training company, that you've never been with the troops—that you're a paper-pusher and a good one. You go training troops and they'll send you right to the field." I don't know if the major really believed what he told me or not. Maybe he did, that with no troop duty the army surely wouldn't send me to the bush.

When I got to the American Division headquarters at Chu Lai, the 196th was under operational control of the division as a maneuver brigade. The word at division was that I was going to be a platoon leader in the 196th. "If you last six months," one of the officers said, "then you'll get to push some papers around." I really raised Cain. "Wait a minute," I said. "How about letting me get a little more acclimated? I'm really not wired up for this mentally right now." I admit I tried to beg out of it a little bit. It didn't work. A week later, I was in the bush with the 3/21st Infantry. Before I went out to my company, though, the battalion commander ask me to have lunch with him at his bunker at LZ Center, up in the Que Son Mountains. "Let me give you three pieces of advice," he said. "Don't be a hero, keep your mind on what you're doing at all times, and be a good manager of your men." He told me to use my men wisely and never abuse them.

The Huey that flew me out to Alpha Company drew fire from a sniper as we came in. The copilot took a round in one of his legs. With what had just happened to him on my mind, I hit the ground convinced I wouldn't live through the day. All the other guys were standing around writing letters and opening their C-rations. It was another day in the war for them, nothing to get very excited about. Alpha Company had just come back from the DMZ, along with Charlie Company. They had been helping out the marines north of Dong Ha, near the Cua Viet River. Somebody told me my company had gone up with ninety-six guys and lost sixteen killed up there, which was fairly heavy for two weeks—one out of every six guys dead. I took over a platoon of eighteen men; it would have been full-strength at forty-two. Some of my men, including my platoon sergeant, seemed dazed by their experiences along the DMZ. I was new, scared, and ineffective.

The captain, a sharp young guy from California, had just been promoted from first lieutenant. He said I would get oriented to the area and what was going on during my first three or four days. Naturally, I hadn't been there two hours when we got orders to move up to one of the grassy little hills in our area. I looked down from the hilltop and, believe it or not, I saw some NVA, a squad of eight or ten of them in green fatigues and pith helmets. They were meandering down the hillside about three hundred yards away. I'm not convinced anybody ever really believed me, but the NVA were exfiltrating westward in small groups from a big battle that Delta and Bravo companies had just fought on a spur of Hill 488, where a marine gunnery sergeant had won the Medal of Honor in 1966. The captain suggested that I needed to lead a squad on line down the hillside while the rest of the company set up a perimeter for the night. We didn't see anybody down the hill, but the next day we got sniped at while we were moving into a laager at noon. I had to take another squad out to find the sniper. I think the NVA or VC were just letting us know they were still around. We called in artillery, but I don't know if the sniper was killed or not. At least he did stop shooting.

I never felt command pressure to hold down casualties in the 196th, but I think all of us had a natural, strong desire to protect our men. In mid-1968, there still wasn't a lot of disillusionment about the war, but I could clearly detect what the guys in my platoon were thinking: they were going to win the war single-handedly. They also believed Washington was playing politics with strategy by ordering the bombing halts. I said, "Look, our goal is to come back alive and yet not be derelict in our duty. Let's try to do what they ask us to do, but do it with some caution." The guys in my platoon liked me, I think, because I was a draftee and they could see that I wasn't out to build a record. We got along fine. They were basically kids who six months earlier might have been clerks, kids who went home after work to tinker with an old car and make out with their girlfriends. The next thing they knew, they had to choose whether to kill Vietnamese civilians or not. I've never believed many of them wanted to see people die.

So, we weren't fools. We did our duty, but we generally were not very gung-ho. We did what we were told to do in a very conservative manner. That's why the artillery was called in on that sniper: we'd spend ten thousand dollars on artillery rounds before we'd take a chance on losing somebody, and I'll never apologize for that. Maybe that wasn't a very bravado way of doing it, but we did begin to think we were in a kind of holding action. There was very little of the charge-a-hill-at-any-cost mentality. Yet, I believe that under different conditions these guys would have been as dedicated and motivated as any this country has ever sent to war.

I only had one guy in my platoon who really wanted to kill, and that was because he supposedly had a brother who had been disfigured a year or so earlier in another part of Vietnam. This guy was a fearless combat soldier. He loved to walk point and go on ambushes at night. Of course, we needed a few guys like that, but I was torn between reining him in and using him for what he did best because he had been involved in a nasty incident that resulted in the death of a Vietnamese woman. It happened while he was leading a small patrol of four or five guys in a free-fire zone near Tam Ky. What he did was wrong, but how much worse was he than so many other soldiers, who, when in doubt, killed Vietnamese? I let the incident pass without taking any punitive action against him, but I made it clear that if he ever did something like that again, I'd court-martial him. Did I handle it well? Who knows? But whether I made the right moral choice or not, this guy has to look at himself in the mirror every morning and live with what he did.

In our area of operations, almost everything involved civilians. That's the single thing I remember most about the war—the terrible plight of the civilians. These people and their ancestors had lived in the area where we were for hundreds of years, and now we had turned it into a free-fire zone. All they wanted was to be left alone by us, the NVA, and the VC so they could farm their rice.

I'll tell you what haunts me. We had to become hard. I'm not talking about My Lai or anything like that, but when we took fire from a village, we went on line and brought a lot of firepower down on it. Artillery almost every time. We had to fire into the villages because that's where the bunkers were, along the tree lines and at the edge of the rice paddies. When we went in, we would usually see civilian casualties, and at first it really bothered me. I became depressed. I didn't feel very proud of what we were doing. But I realized that I hadn't asked to be there and that if I was going to be at all effective as a leader, I had to get hard. It happened very fast, maybe within two weeks after I got to the bush, but it still scared me when I saw the guys chasing pigs around and hacking them up with machetes. Sometimes they'd shoot water buffalo. Only the day before we might see a little kid riding a water buffalo and here we were killing the animal, supposedly to keep the NVA from eating it or using it for transport. If you had the upbringing that most of us did, you couldn't do that and not feel some guilt or remorse.

God, those poor people were caught right in the middle. The VC came in at night and threatened them for cooperating with us. We'd come in the next day and want to know how many mortar tubes came through the village the night before, how many men. If a villager told us anything, the next night his child got his leg cut off. I saw some of that. Given our job, what we did wasn't so terrible. This is no apologia for the individual infantryman in Vietnam, but it was just a bad situation to be in and I don't think many of us were prepared for it.

We lost so many guys to booby traps. The VC booby trap of choice in our area was the M-26 fragmentation grenade, though we encountered some bouncing betties, too. Charlie would replace the time fuze of an M-26 with a blasting cap. Then he would put the grenade in a C-ration can, just slide it in there, a perfect fit, and hook monofilament fishing line to the fuze. He strung the line at ankle height across a trail so a trooper couldn't see it. Along comes a guy who hits the line and trips the blasting cap. Another casualty.

I was lucky in a way because I went to the 196th at an optimum time. Not much happened in our area until February of 1969, when we got some real heavy stuff and the 101st Airborne came down to help us. But by then the pipeline was full of lieutenants craving to get out in the field. When I left the bush after almost six months, I had lost only two men, one to rifle fire and the other to a booby trap. I say "only" not because I saw the loss of two men as any kind of statistic to be proud of, but because many other units had it much worse at other times and places.

I shifted over to battalion forward as the duty officer at a firebase on an isolated hilltop. The work consisted of pulling a daily twelve-hour shift, midnight to noon, clearing fire missions and keeping up with the troops. Later, I went to brigade forward as the executive officer of the headquarters company—very boring. It wasn't long before some of us without enough to do were hanging out at the officers' club, drinking too much hot gin. One night, after putting down one or two too many, I called the S-3 of my old battalion, a major from North Carolina, and told him I wanted to go back up there. "Come on home," he said. When I woke up the next day, I didn't follow through. I've always wondered what would have happened if I had.

I came back to the States in late May of 1969, got out of the army, and went back to my old job at the mortgage company. Although I didn't come back to protests in Atlanta, it was still a bit of a culture shock to see how the country had changed. I've read a lot about the guys who had a harder go of it in other parts of the country, the ones who were spit on, and I can only say that it makes me sick. I wish we'd all had more time for decompression.

I was well received back at my old job. Some people asked me about Vietnam, but I don't think they had any real point of reference about it, and I didn't have a lot of real big war stories to tell them. In August, though, my old unit at the 196th, Alpha Company, made the national TV news for refusing to fight. As luck would have it, I had to entertain an investor from a New York savings bank that night. I was itching to see my old company on the news, but all he wanted to do was have a drink and a good time. I read not long ago that the incident in Alpha Company had racial overtones. Apparently five black guys decided not to go up a hill after the company had taken some heavy losses in earlier attempts to take it. I remember some racial polarization of blacks and whites beginning to show up in early '69, somewhat as depicted in *Platoon*. Some groups of black soldiers that tended to stick to themselves made it clear they didn't want to associate with white guys.

Now that I think about it, one of the most dramatic events I witnessed in Vietnam involved a racial incident. We were on standdown in Chu Lai for three or four days of basically getting drunk and watching movies and Filipino music shows. A black guy suddenly started running around crazily during one of these shows, screaming and yelling that he was going to kill somebody. Somehow he found an M-16. We were able to throw him to the ground when he tried to run back into the music show with the rifle. A couple of medics gave him morphine or something—whatever the drug was, it knocked him out. We learned that some of the black power guys were making fun of him and threatening him for hanging around with white guys, rather than joining them. They had made him so mad he decided to do something about it.

One of my guys who got killed was a black. He was a very smart young guy who tended to be a bit of a renegade, but that didn't keep me from liking him. Another black in my platoon, a guy from South Carolina named Jackson, had come into the army through Project 100,000. He was a great big guy, very loyal and courageous—one of my favorite troops. I often read his letters from home to him and once helped him write a letter to his girlfriend. I remember people like Jackson. Individual days and moments come back and I think about the guys and the funny things they said. Some of them were wise guys and others sort of quiet. . . . It's very touching, very sad, to go to the Wall and see the names of the ones who didn't make it back, to remember them as they were.

At one point in Vietnam, I made a promise that if I got back in one piece, I would make a donation to the church. The amount I gave seems like chicken feed now, so I must not have put much value on getting back. The truth is, I found myself slipping away from the church after Vietnam because I had seen so many young Americans, eighteen and nineteen years old, have their lives taken from them, and I was wondering whether there was any reason or worth in their loss. I guess we've answered that by now. We started something in Vietnam that we didn't finish. Our intentions were good, in my opinion just as good as they've been in most other wars.

It seems that morally, there was a substantial historical precedent for our involvement there, but I think we basically blew it. The press largely turned Tet into a defeat, even though the enemy lost tens of thousands of men and didn't achieve his objective. At that point, had the country made a commitment to win, I think we could have done it. Whether the price would have been worth it, or how long it would have taken, I don't know.

I guess I just hate to think that we lost fifty-eight thousand Americans and then basically turned tail and ran, knowing there would be no "peace with honor," knowing that the South Vietnamese were going to be overcome. It was just a question of when it was going to happen. It think that's a shame, a dark moment in our country's history.

I've had nightmares about the war on rare occasions, but I think I've put it behind me for the most part. Yet, there is something that continues to trouble me: I can't fully forgive the guys who got out of it. What right did they have to decide not to go over there? On the other hand, if the war was a wasted effort, and if the American people were not behind it, you've got to wonder, are the guys who went to Canada the smart ones? Jimmy Carter may have had a point when he pardoned them. He said he was trying to put the bitterness of Vietnam behind us and heal the nation. Still, it galls me that they got off scot-free, even though in retrospect they may look like they made the right moral decision because of the way we conducted the war and let it be lost. They're not noble by any definition, but as you can see, I'm very ambivalent about what they did. If I'm not ready to forgive them, at least I'm ready to forget.

Gayden M. Roux

Metairie, Louisiana

Marine rifleman, 1968–69

•

"I went to the seventh grade at T. H. Harris Junior High in Metairie and quit," Gayden Roux told me at the office of psychologist Spencer Campbell, a former marine in LaPlace, Louisiana, who counsels Vietnam veterans. "I was brought up in an alcoholic home where a lot of fighting went on between my father and my mother. I figured the only person who was going to wind up hurt was my mother, and I didn't want to see that, so I left home in 1965 to live with one of my sisters in Fort Riley, Kansas.

"I came home to Metairie in November of that year when my mother went into a coma. Her liver enlarged and split from cirrhosis. She was only forty-two when she died, still a young woman, but despite everything she loved my father so much that if it took drinking to excess to be with him, she was willing to do it."

Gayden is small and compact, hardly more than five feet tall. He has a neatly trimmed mustache and reddish-blond hair. He was a marine rifleman and—thanks to his size—a sometime tunnel rat in Vietnam from June 1968 until April 1969. As we talked, he made frequent references to his father, a carpenter who had died several months earlier. Whether by default or design, the elder Roux had exerted enormous influence on his son's life.

"I could never do anything right in his eyes," Gayden finally said. "It seems I was always the one cut out of the floor act. I think the reason I joined the marines in December of 1967 was because my father always told me, 'You can never make it in the marines.' I've got his papers at the house showing the army tried to draft him in 1942 and 1943, but he was turned down every time because he was too short.

"I think that bothered him and he just passed it on to me. I only realized a couple of years ago that I wanted to go into the marines to prove myself to him."

I was working as a plumber's helper and going to trade school at night when I decided to sign up. I was making $3.75 an hour, which was pretty good money back then, and I was living at home. "If you want to go, you can go," my father told me. "If you want to stay, you can stay. You make the decision and don't ever hold it against me." At first, I tried to join the navy. I went down to the Customs House on Canal Street, near the river, and I took the physical exam and the mental test. After the test was over, the navy recruiter gave me a book.

"Just go home, study this book, and come back. I guarantee you'll get in the navy because you only missed by two or three points," he said. I walked out the door and looked down the hallway. At the very end was the Marine Corps recruiting office. I had a few friends who had been in the marines, and one of 'em was already in Vietnam. I liked the idea of being a marine. I walked into the recruiting office and told the man I wanted to see about joining up.

"Well," he said, "you have to take a test and do a few other things." I told him I had already done that for the navy. He gets up and goes down to the navy office. Five minutes later, he comes back, sits down at his desk and asks me if I wanted to go to Marine Corps boot camp that night. *That night.*

I said, "No, I want to wait until after the first of the year." I wanted to be home for Christmas because that was family time. I took the oath in December but I didn't go to boot camp at San Diego until the first of February, 1968.

I spent two weeks in a holding company before I started boot camp. My platoon had enough people, but two other platoons had to be assembled for our training company. That gave the Marine Corps two weeks to mess with us, to start tearing us down, before anything really happened. Once training started, one of the DIs who wasn't much bigger than me decided he liked to punch me in the solar plexus. I looked at him eyeball to eyeball and I don't think he liked that. He called me names like "scumbag," but that was just part of basic training where the marines tear you down and then build you into what they think a marine should be.

The only guy who talked about Vietnam very much at boot camp was a chief drill instructor who had worked in a morgue there during his first tour. He said he had seen the bodies of a lot of the marines he had trained. I think it had affected him because this man really wanted to keep us alive.

We could tell what kind of a day we was going to have by checking to see if he was carrying his Bible. When he had it, he was kind of mellow. But when he didn't have it, we were in for hell—much more exercise than usual. Well, he got so bad he wound up putting a lot of people in the hospital and was relieved of duty.

I went to Camp Pendleton for advanced training as a rifleman and secondary training in antitank, recoilless rifle, and flame thrower. I got to know a training sergeant in my battalion who was getting ready to go back to Vietnam for a second tour. I guess he liked me because he would buy beer for me even though I was only nineteen. You had to be twenty-one to buy beer in California. He never said much about the war. He just wanted to drink a lot.

On the way to Vietnam, we had a very lively bunch of people on the airplane. I asked one of the stewardesses how many trips she had made, and it was quite a few. Then she said something I've remembered ever since.

"I'd rather fly with the marines," she said. "They're more active. They talk more. The army guys are more quiet, like they're doomed."

My own feeling was that I was going to Vietnam and that I was going to come home alive. Maybe not in one piece, but alive. Nothing else mattered. We stopped on Guam, where we was supposed to get some shots, but I didn't want to get the one in the hip, the one that really hurt, so I copied what was written on another guy's shot card and put it on mine. I figured, so what? I'm going to a place where people are going to be shooting at me and I'm going to worry about a shot?

We landed at Danang, but I was sitting in an inside seat and didn't get a chance to look out the window as we came in. When the door opened, I was hit right in the face by all that humidity and the smell—diesel fuel and shit. The smell of diesel fuel bothers me to this day. I spent the night in a barracks at Danang and flew out the next day on a C-130, sitting the whole way on my sea bag and feeling butterflies in my stomach. I was going to Khe Sanh to join the 3/26th Marines, which had just come off Hill 861.

I remember my first night on guard duty at Khe Sanh. I was sitting on the ground, looking at the barbed wire and perimeter in front of me, that wide-open killing range out there. The moon was out and it was fairly light, and I could see the sergeant of the guard coming. I didn't move. I just sat super still.

"You were sleeping," he said when he got up to me.

"No, I wasn't sleeping," I said. "I saw you coming."

He asked, "Why didn't you halt me?"

"'Cause nobody told me to halt you."

He said to stand up and when I did, he hit me in the gut and knocked me seven feet.

"I could have been a gook and killed you," he said.

"If you'd been a gook," I said, "I'd have shot your ass when I saw you by the fence." He never believed I wasn't sleeping. I had to throw sandbags during the day as extra duty.

Three or four days later I went down to India Company, which had its headquarters in what looked like an old railroad station near Highway 1, south of Hue. I was there for a month before I pulled my first operation. We left the railroad station and went up in the mountains along there to make a sweep. We was taking a lot of sniper fire on Highway 1 and that was holding up convoys. I was on the highway when I saw my first guy get killed. His name was Waters, but he got stuck with the nickname "Muddy" Waters because the song was popular about that time. A sniper got Waters and I remember the CH-46 coming in to pick him up, and the sniper shot the chopper down. It came over us making circles and hit the South China Sea with a big explosion. Nobody got out of it.

The day before, we'd played games with the sniper. I'd put my hat on a stick and let him shoot at it, hoping the guy next to me would get a lead on where the sniper was shooting from. He missed the hat five or six times. I didn't know any fucking better. But you never forget getting shot at.

I was the smallest man in India Company and had a reputation as a crazy Cajun son of a bitch. The guys nicknamed me "Short Round" because I'm five foot two inches tall and at the time I weighed 110 pounds. That's how I got to be a tunnel rat. Most of the times when I went down, the tunnel would be clean. It really wasn't too bad. I carried a flashlight and a .45 pistol. The sergeant would say, "Go check it out," and I kind of enjoyed it. I always went down feet first because the tunnels branched off from the shaft. I held the flashlight high and to the side while I crawled, figuring Charlie would have a chance of missing me if he started shooting.

The first tunnel I went in was about three feet high and three feet wide, and it was about 150 feet long. It was very damp, but not muddy. I guess it took me twenty minutes to cover 150 feet. It was just a little tunnel that the VC probably used to get out of the area after firing a couple of shots at us. Toward the end of my tour, I went in another tunnel and brought three VC out. That was the first time I was ever in a tunnel with anybody. We had been told we wasn't taking no prisoners and so we was supposed to get some. We was sweeping an area and stumbled across three packs at the entrance to a tunnel. We put a grappling hook on one of the packs and backed off far enough to pull on the rope and see if the pack was booby-trapped. It didn't go off, so I dropped my gear and got my .45 and flashlight.

"Don't get trigger happy," I told the rest of the guys. "If you see anybody coming out the other end, make sure it ain't me." I didn't want anybody getting nervous because nobody knew where the hell I was going to come out.

I dropped down the shaft and started through the tunnel. I was easing my way through a turn with the flashlight in my left hand and my .45 in the other one, and I put the light up and I had it right in a guy's eyes. He was three feet from me and just sitting there. He was wearing green utilities, and the only weapon I could see was a knife. I could hear my heart thumping. Some of the other guys said they could hear the VC breathing when they went through tunnels, but I never heard anything except my own heartbeat.

I said to myself, "Well, I can shoot this motherfucker or I can bring him out alive. But if I shoot him, I'll have to drag him out."

I could speak enough Vietnamese to tell the VC to move. I started to back out. He started to come towards me but he never got no closer than three feet. He had to be scared because he was blind from the light and couldn't see a thing. All he could do was go by my voice. When I got back to the entrance, I yelled to the guys, "I've got a gook and I'm bringing him out."

Everybody was excited. I came out of the hole first and grabbed the gook by the back of the neck and yanked him out. And then came this body, and then another body. They was behind him in the tunnel, but I had seen only one. It was weird: I knew they had weapons. It was three to one down there, but I guess they ditched their weapons in the tunnel. I took a handmade belt and a knife off one of 'em. The knife was better than the one I had. I don't know if anything else was found in the tunnel because we moved on after that.

I wasn't scared while I was in the tunnel, but after three of them came out, I kind of got the shakes a little bit. I thought, "Well, that's life, you know. Sometimes you win and sometimes you lose. This time I won."

I got close to only two guys in Vietnam and both of them got killed. The first one was a navy corpsman who got it while we was sweeping an area and came up on a village. My fireteam was at the end of the platoon line. I looked at the village and had a feeling something wasn't right. After a while, I could look at a village and know. You noticed how the people was acting. I passed the word to the squad leader: "These sons of bitches ain't acting right. Something ain't copasectic here." Like I say, it was just a feeling.

About the time I talked to the squad leader, two snipers across a draw outside the village opened up and knocked down a machinegunner. The fighting was away from us, but I told the guys, "Watch them villagers. Anybody that comes toward you, blow him away."

We had a new lieutenant and he called for a couple of guys with experience. I was one of 'em. He had already sent the second squad down to get the machinegunner, and the snipers had wounded three or four more guys, just picking them off. We couldn't see the snipers because they was probably in spider traps.

A friend of mine who was the M-79 man in the second squad came running up to me. One of the snipers had blown his thumb off. He was holding up the bloody nub and hollering, "I'm going home!" A few minutes later, a Huey gunship came in and started working over the area across the draw. I ran down to look for the machinegunner. All I knew was that he was in the draw and had a sucking chest wound. I knew he was dead as soon as I saw him. Another marine was already there trying to carry him out, so I grabbed one of the machinegunner's arms and yelled to the other guy to take the other arm, and we dragged him out. We couldn't hurt him more than he'd been hurt. By the time we got him back, the snipers had knocked down eight or nine other guys.

A grunt who was carrying our bazooka threw off his gear and started to go down and get a man and a sniper nailed him, just like that. He was down a little draw, maybe four feet from me and Doc. Doc was ready to go to him.

"Doc, wait," I said. "I'll get him." But Doc wouldn't wait and when he reached down to get the guy, the sniper got him. Doc fell back in my arms and I was holding him and he told me, "Man, he's killed me." He was bleeding internally from a hit in the lung and I held him in my arms and I couldn't do a damn thing for him.

He went comatose and lived for maybe three minutes. His eyes was looking directly at me when he died.

"I told you not to go!" I screamed. "I told you I'd get him!" Doc didn't listen and he died in my arms and there wasn't a damn thing I could do for him. If he'd listened to me, he'd have made it.

I turned around and looked up and saw this guy going over the side of the hill about fifty yards away. He was wearing camouflage and my first thought was that he was marine recon. But he was the fucking sniper, so I opened up on him and he went down. Then I saw the other sniper and the lieutenant almost took the back of my head off, shooting his rifle from the rear of me. The guy I shot got up and started to move again and I nailed him with two rounds.

I kind of blocked out all the hollering and screaming. I was the type of guy who would try to patch you up, try to save you as much as I could. And I guess one of the problems I had for a long time after I came back from Nam was the fear of holding people and letting people hold me. Doc's death affected me very deeply. In a way, I loved the guy. He liked to call me Short Round. I could talk to him. But now I can't even remember his name; there's a black hole in my subconscious and I can't pull his name out of it.

Doc died when I had six months to go. My attitude by then was one of kill the gooks and keep my friends alive. We never messed with villages very much, but I remember one day we called in artillery after we saw seven NVA with full combat gear walk into a village. This place had maybe three hundred people and we called for fire for effect, which kind of flattened everything. I don't even know where we was, but we used to get a lot of contact in the area. It was spooky.

After the artillery stopped, women and kids came running up to us, bleeding and hurt, and we brought in medevac choppers to carry them out. That was the policy at the time—a real bummer, if you ask me. I mean, nothing really made sense to me. Five of us set up an ambush one night in the mountains. We knew the NVA was around somewhere, so we positioned ourselves near a stream and a trail that they had been using. We figured they would try to get water there. They did and we radioed the company that we had gooks coming in and we was going to open up on them. But it was some kind of holiday and we was told we couldn't do it, that a ceasefire was in effect.

I asked my sergeant, "What the hell am I doing out here? If I can't open up on them, what the hell am I doing here?"

We watched six or seven NVA walk through our ambush site to the stream, fill up their canteens and walk back out. They was maybe thirty yards from us. We had a Claymore set up that would have took them out. I was mad. The next morning I asked the lieutenant what I was doing out there if I couldn't kill the enemy. I told him I had been in a situation in which my fire superiority, my element of surprise, had been taken away. "If we had been in the place of the NVA," I told him, "they would have opened up on us."

In April of 1969, we was out in the bush on an operation when my time for R&R came up. At first, I decided not to go, but then I realized I was getting so close to the end of my tour. A friend of mine named Melrose Melnick was going if I didn't, but I had more time in-country, so I bumped him down the list and went.

When I got back, I saw my platoon leader at the base camp and he said our outfit was still in the mountains and had stumbled on a big NVA camp and hospital, even a school. He said the camp had bunkers like you wouldn't believe, that they could take a direct hit and nothing would happen. Then he told me Melnick had gotten killed when the NVA opened up. Him and me was so close. Somewhere I have a picture of me and him and another guy, and Melnick has his fingers over my head, you know, the two fingers sticking up. I feel responsible for his death because I knocked him off of R&R. I don't know what happened to the picture, but I want to find it and put it on the Wall, because when I see Melnick's name there all these feelings come up and I don't cry just for Melnick but for all the ones who got killed and whose names I can't remember. I remember their faces but not their names. As much as I knew Doc and cared for him, I don't think I'll ever remember his name again.

When I got back to my platoon, the whole company had moved in and set up a perimeter on two hills near the NVA camp where Melnick got killed. I remember it was about three o'clock on a Sunday afternoon and we'd just been resupplied with ice cream and letters from home. We was sitting around shooting the bull. Things was kind of quiet until the bastards started shooting at us. I grabbed my M-16 and jumped behind a bush. I saw the one who was shooting at me, but I guess I took too long to sight in. I switched to automatic and on the first burst my rifle fell out of my hands. I felt a burning sensation in my foot and saw leaves flying up in my face. I fell back and he fired again. My rifle hit the bush and he probably figured that's where I was. If he'd raised up to look, he most probably would have hit me again.

I looked down and saw this hole in my boot. I could see part of my sock in my foot. So I pulled the boot off and was looking for a battle dressing—I always carried three or four because my biggest fear was bleeding to death. It felt like something was in my foot. Finally, I found a dressing and wrapped up the foot. I crawled up to the corpsman, who redid it and gave me some pills for the pain. I guess I was going into shock. About that time the squad leader came up with my boot.

"Here, you might want this," he said. I told him I didn't want that bloody old boot, so he gave me the bullet that had hit me. Now I had a round with my name on it. I put it in my pocket.

Since I weighed only 110 pounds and the pain medicine was starting to take effect, the lieutenant told me to get on his back and he carried me down the hill to the LZ to get on a medevac chopper. It was maybe four feet off the ground when the NVA opened up on it, and all I could do was just sit there laughing my ass off. There goes my ride, you know. Somebody knocked me over because I was sitting out there in the open; I thought I'd been shot in the back.

It was starting to get dark, so I was put up with the corpsmen for the night. I was laying there with a guy who had got shot in the arm when I heard a rifle clink against the rocks. I knew something was getting ready to break loose, and it did. A guy somewhere was hollering for a corpsman and one of them took off to find him. The guy that was shot in the arm was scared and started to scream. I kept telling him to shut up because the NVA would shoot where they heard noise. He kept hollering, so I just grabbed a rock and smacked him on the side of the head with it. I knocked his ass out. I didn't want to take a chance on getting shot again.

A sergeant got hit behind the ear and the officers were trying to get a medevac in. The guy with the arm wound was supposed to help carry the sergeant to the chopper and get on it himself. As for me, I was supposed to be carried on. But if the chopper came under fire, it was just to pick up the sergeant, who had the critical wound, and the guy with the arm wound. Then the clouds started moving in and the chopper couldn't find us.

Early the next morning, another chopper was supposed to come in and if the NVA opened up on it, all three of us would be moved to the other hill to be taken out by basket. The chopper came in about nine o'clock and the NVA didn't shoot at it. We got on it and I was headed home to the States. I was operated on in Danang and then spent two months at a hospital in Japan. From there I went to the naval hospital in Pensacola.

I stayed in the marines a month and a half longer than I was supposed to because they put me on a medical hold. I got out in March of 1970 and went straight to work in a glass factory in Metairie that made bottles for hot sauce, cooking oil, and root beer, stuff like that. I went in as a relief operator making $6.15 an hour.

I learned right away that talking about the war wasn't a very good idea. Nobody wanted to hear about it.

I was drinking in a bar in Metairie one night, though, and I did mention that I had been in Vietnam. Some guy wearing jeans, a real smartass, accused me of being a babykiller, of playing God. He tried to start some trouble with me.

"Forget it, man," I said. "I'm leaving."

I didn't want to take him on in the bar—I wanted him outside, out there on his turf. I made sure I antagonized him just enough to make him follow me out. I had a .357 Magnum in my car. I was sitting there in the front seat and had the door about half open and he came over and grabbed it the way people do when they think they're big and bad. I laid the .357 on the window frame and pulled back the hammer.

"Now I'm going to play God with you," I said. "You've got a choice. Move the car door and I'll cut you in half. Let go and back away and I'll let you live. It's up to you." He backed off. I didn't talk about Vietnam after that.

I worked in the glass factory for six months. It was 130 degrees in there, just like being back in Vietnam. I finally quit and went to school under the GI Bill to study plumbing. About that time, I fell in love with the girl who lived next door. She was a little younger than me—she was sixteen and I was twenty-one—but I really did love her. Her and her family moved up to Memphis, but we wrote back and forth and after a while her parents gave permission for her to marry, and that's what we did in December of 1972. We got married by a justice of the peace in Hancock County, Mississippi.

We lived in Metairie in the house her parents had. I loved her, but like she says, I never told her. She could never feel that I loved her; she thought I was cold. It's hard for me to get close to people, very hard. I mean, I didn't even hold my daughter when she was a baby. The marriage lasted seven years, but we've come a long way since then. We've been divorced for nine years and we're the best of friends. I guess the one who suffered the most out of it was my oldest daughter. It put a lot of strain on her.

I went back to living at my daddy's house and finally got thrown out. My sister and brother-in-law was living there, too, and they said I was a bad influence on their kids. I lived on the streets of Metairie for about six months. I could usually find a place to sleep because I was working as a plumber at the time and had passkeys to houses that we was putting plumbing in.

Nobody really hassled me. I stayed away from people as much as I could. The only thing I wanted to do was work. Finally I got tired of waking up and not knowing where I was, so I said, "Fuck it, I ain't going to do it anymore." I quit drinking, smoking, and taking drugs. It was tough, and I got the shakes, but I wouldn't go back to them. That was eight years ago and I haven't touched anything since.

I met another woman—her second husband had been a marine in Vietnam, too—and I fell in love with her. We lived together for four and a half years, but I still couldn't bring myself to say how I felt about her.

When she would put her arms around me, I'd just pick her up and put her aside.

"Don't touch me. Just don't touch me," I'd say.

I figure that maybe half of the trouble I have relating to people comes from Vietnam. I still didn't understand why I didn't like to hold people or let people hold me. I don't blame her for getting rid of me. I'd have done the same damned thing. All I knew was that I was very unhappy, hurt, and I didn't want people to know what I felt inside of me.

I still have a lot of dreams about Vietnam. I don't remember much about them because of the medicine I take, but when I wake up, I know I've been dreaming because the bed's a complete mess. If I forget to take my medicine, I see a lot of violence and blood—things I want to forget about. I deal with Vietnam this way: I was just doing my job. You know, that's the only thing I can say to you. Just doing my job, paying the price. I lost my youth in Vietnam but I'm not bitter about it. I can't be. It's just something that happened. You know, it don't do any good to be bitter about it; all that's going to do is get you fucked up.

I'm going to school now, taking up electronics, and everybody says, "That's great, you'll make good money at it," but they don't realize I'm really going to school because right now that's all I want to do. I wasted my youth but I know now that I'm more intelligent than I ever thought I was. Knowing that has helped a lot.

My father died in May of 1988 and I've sorted out a lot of things about him, too. I'm dealing with everything now a little bit at a time. A piece here, a piece there, and eventually it all falls into place.

Mary Laraine Young Hines

Raleigh, North Carolina

Red Cross "Donut Dolly,"

1968–69

●

Mary Laraine Hines—everybody calls her Larry—didn't have to go to Vietnam in 1968. She volunteered to go as one of the more than six hundred civilian Red Cross women who served in the combat zone from 1965 to 1972. On the day we talked, she was wearing a powder blue T-shirt with the words "Donut Dolly—I Never Sold Donuts, Coffee, Kool-Aid or Anything Else" on the front. Larry was a Donut Dolly, by all accounts one of the best. In the twenty-one years since her tour in Vietnam, she has received many honors from the Raleigh community for her Junior League volunteer work with abused children and other at-risk groups.

A friendly, attractive woman in her early forties, Larry wears her brown hair short. She and her husband, Tom, who flew missions over Vietnam as a navy carrier pilot, live in a large, comfortable, neo-Georgian house in Raleigh's tony Hayes-Barton district. They are the parents of three children.

Sitting on a sofa in her spacious living room, Larry and I talked all morning about the Vietnam she knew. Her most vivid memories centered on her Red Cross service with the army's American Division in southern I Corps, the scene of bitter fighting in 1969. At first, she tried to hold back the tears as she recalled the people and events of that time. It was finally too much for her, and she whispered an apology for the outbreak of emotion. There was nothing to apologize for, I said. As much as any soldier, Larry Hines still feels the pain and emptiness of loss.

"I remember hearing about Vietnam while I was in high school in Lexington, North Carolina," she said, "but it wasn't until I entered the University of Georgia in 1964 that I began to see it was going to be my generation's war.

"I became very aware of Vietnam during my junior and senior years, when I was a fraternity sweetheart at Sigma Nu and heard a lot of the fellows talk about being scared of the draft. Sometimes I would go into a classroom and there would be virtually no men in it because a rumor was going around Athens that a reserve unit somewhere in Georgia needed forty or fifty people. As soon as the guys heard that, they jumped in their cars and drove all night to Valdosta or Macon or wherever the reserve unit was supposed to be."

Some male students at Georgia tried to get a doctor's excuse from the draft, or took medication that would raise their blood pressure, Larry told me. A few rushed into marriage because, in the mid-sixties, that was still an exemption from the draft. "Then," she said, "you had to have children to get an exemption, and finally after 1968 there were few exemptions and almost everybody was getting drafted."

I come from a family that's always stressed volunteer service. I guess you could say I came by my inclination honestly, but I didn't quite know how to translate good intentions into helping the young men who were being sent to Vietnam. I was an English major at Georgia, I had no medical training, and I couldn't pass a military physical because of poor eyesight.

I felt a strong pull to go back to North Carolina, so before graduation I arranged for interviews at the university placement office with Wachovia Bank and Trust Company, North Carolina National Bank, and First Union Bank. I felt they would hire me as a customer service representative because of my interest in people and their problems. While I was waiting for my first interview, which was with Wachovia Bank, a Red Cross recruiter named Hazel Breland walked into the lobby of the placement office. There must have been twenty other people in that room. Hazel glanced at all of them and came over to me.

"Do you have a minute to talk?" she asked. I said I did. She took me to an office and started showing me brochures about the Red Cross SRAO Program, which means Supplemental Recreation Activities Overseas. This was the "Donut Dollies" program and the more she told me about it, the more it seemed like a perfect blind date. I mean, it was an exact match for what I wanted to do. I didn't even want to go to my bank interview or any other interview after that.

I think Hazel picked me because the Red Cross was looking for a certain type of girl, one who could work well with people. In addition, I'd been around a lot of young men as a fraternity sweetheart, had worked as a camp counselor for three summers in Wisconsin, and had traveled in the Bahamas, Europe, Mexico, and Canada. Hazel warned me, though, that the Red Cross usually had twenty-five applicants for each person chosen from the Southeast. And she said they would do very extensive background checks. She didn't raise my hopes very high at that point, but I was genuinely excited about the program.

Two weeks later I was told that I had been selected for more interviews at the regional Red Cross office in Atlanta. As I went through the selection process, the Red Cross people talked about the physical dangers in Vietnam—Tet had just happened—and the ways men relate to women in a war zone. I also had to go down to the Athens Police Department to get fingerprinted, just like a criminal. I found out that the Red Cross even went back into my elementary school records to make sure I was a truthful person and someone who would make the recreation program strong.

I was told the Southeast had not only the most applicants for the program, but also the best-qualified ones because the girls could take the heat and humidity in Vietnam and seemed to have the deepest feelings about supporting the men who were fighting the war. I was accepted into the program in March, which gave me three months to get ready to go to Vietnam.

I got very different reactions about my decision from people. Some of my friends were thrilled that I was going, but a few of the guys that I dated were really turned off and didn't want to talk about it. Maybe it was threatening to them, that I was volunteering and doing all I could to go over there, and they were doing as much as they could not to go. The Kappa Alphas, for example, were very gung-ho about the South's military tradition—Robert E. Lee and the Lost Cause—but Vietnam was different. I knew a lot of them were feeling conflict inside because they weren't living up to the heritage of our region.

I got most of my shots for Vietnam at the Naval Supply Officers School in Athens. The typhoid shot made me very sick. I got it on April 4, 1968, which turned out to be the day Martin Luther King, Jr., was assassinated. I was running a fever and was only half-awake when I heard the news; I just couldn't comprehend what was going on. This country seemed to be so strife-ridden and coming apart at the seams. And, then, a few weeks later, my clock radio woke me up at four o'clock in the morning—I had set it early to do some last-minute cramming for my last final exam—and I heard the news that Robert Kennedy had been shot. I ran up and down the sorority house halls, waking up everybody, and we all went down to the living room to watch those surrealistic images on television.

I graduated from Georgia on June 8, 1968, the day Bobby Kennedy was buried. It was a dreary, drizzly day. It should have been a wonderful, happy time in my life, but all I could think about was what had happened to another Kennedy. The week just seemed to be full of death.

I went up to Washington, D.C., a month later for two weeks of Red Cross training, some of it from SRAO girls who had just come back from Vietnam. This was a time of street riots, burned-out buildings, and people camping out on the Mall. The Red Cross put us up at a hotel and ordered us to observe a curfew. It was unsafe to be out at night because of all the racial tension.

The Vietnam and Korea recruits stayed together at the hotel. My roommate was a Korea recruit from Nebraska, so I got to know a lot of the Korea-bound girls. For the whole two weeks of training, they tried to talk me out of going to Vietnam. "You've still got a choice," they would say. "Come on and go with us to Korea. Nothing'll happen to you there." I never wavered. The last night we were all together, we went to see *The Graduate* and they gave me a pair of black pearl earrings for a going-away present.

"We don't think you're going to come back," they told me. I really think to this day that they expected something terrible to happen to me.

I had my first real exposure to the military at Travis Air Force Base in California. I saw hundreds of GIs when I walked into the terminal. I decided to try to talk to some of them, but most of them didn't want to say anything. They were so glum I began to think my job was going to be harder than I had thought. Many of the guys had already served a tour in Vietnam and they knew exactly what they were going back to when we left California.

It took twenty-four hours to get across the Pacific. There were eleven of us girls on the plane, and the guys were really nice to us on the way over. Some of them bought leis for us in Hawaii and I wore mine all the way to Vietnam. But most of them still were not talking much at all. They seemed very scared and very young to me. We had been told that we would be older than many of the soldiers because their average age was nineteen, and we were all college graduates who had to be between twenty-two and twenty-seven. In a way, we probably looked like their big sisters.

"I want everybody in your seats," the captain said over the PA system when the coast of Vietnam came into sight. "I want your seat belts on. We are going to make a very steep descent. It will be very quick." And it was. We got over Saigon and he just went down and in. As we made our approach to land, I could see all these bombed-out places and a lot of small craters from mortars and rockets. On the side of the runway at Tan Son Nhut were trashed-out F-4s and C-130s.

The captain said he was going to take the plane as close as possible to the terminal. He also said we would walk down the steps single file, we would be met by American soldiers carrying M-16s. We could not stop or take pictures. The heat was just unbelievable when I walked through the aircraft door. I don't know why Vietnam's heat seemed so different from the Philippines or anywhere else. The smell was overpowering, too. It all hit me then that I was getting ready to face something terrible. I walked into the terminal and, like all the other civilians, signed a big log book. It was the first time I had ever used military time. I signed in at 0600 hours, 24 July 1968.

We Red Cross girls were taken to the Massachusetts BOQ in Saigon to get some sleep, two to a room. The rooms were very French, with the hand-held showers and tiles everywhere, and a crazy-looking little lamp with no shade. The windows were partially covered up with masking tape. Nobody had to tell me why. The Red Cross people in Saigon warned us not to stand on street corners, not just because of danger from bombs or being shot, but also because of the "Saigon Cowboys." These hoodlums would come down the street on their mopeds and rip off your purse, watch, and even rings. We were told to never go out in groups of more than three and to be in the BOQ by ten p.m. One thing we could never do was take flash pictures in public places like restaurants. Somebody forgot that rule once when I was eating dinner at an officers' mess with a group of girls, and the whole table was escorted out immediately—I mean, the first flash and the MPs were over there. The girl who took the flash picture just didn't realize the seriousness of what she had done.

We had three days of training in Saigon, and I got very sick while I was there. We had been told to avoid the water, something I had been very careful to do. But my group was invited to an officers' club for a social hour, and I had a gin and tonic—the "proper" tropical drink, I thought. It didn't taste very good to me, though, so I held the drink for two hours. Of course, the ice melted, and I think that's how I ingested something very bad. We were supposed to leave for our assignments the next day, but I woke up about two in the morning, and, truly, I have never been so sick in my life. Never. I spent the night on the toilet and vomiting. "What's the matter?" one of the other girls said. "Can't you hold your liquor?" It was not that I'd had too much to drink. That was not my problem. I should have had several drinks instead of holding that one for two hours.

The Red Cross arranged for a jeep to take me to the Third Field

Hospital just down the street. I was told it wasn't dysentery, just something in the water that the medical people called "Ho Chi Minh's Revenge." I would just have to wait it out. That meant two days alone in the BOQ, since the other girls had gone on to their units. I soon had a real problem with the Filipino manager of the BOQ. He kept trying to get too familiar. I couldn't lock him out of my room because he had a key, of course. Fortunately, he left me alone to recuperate once I threatened to report him to the military and Red Cross authorities.

I had orders for Dong Ba Tinh, which was the headquarters for the Eighteenth Engineer Brigade and several helicopter companies. I was slightly disappointed with my assignment. I think all of us wanted to be with a combat unit from the first day. The Eighteenth Engineers was a small outfit that had only six girls assigned to it. The main focus was recreation center work, but the brigade did have a couple of forward runs to base camps at Ban Me Thuot and Bao Loc. The rec center was open from ten in the morning until ten at night, plenty of time for the guys to come in and get a cup of coffee or Kool-Aid, read a book, play cards and board games, or just talk to us. We improvised a lot, like writing to DJs back in the states and getting them to send us Top Forty tapes for the troops. A Red Cross support chapter in Minneapolis sent us popcorn, balloons, pens, and puzzles. We constantly tried to come up with new ideas, even things that sound crazy, like fashion shows and paper airplane contests. But the guys loved our programs because they were such a diversion for them.

People frequently ask me about drugs in Vietnam. I think the closest I ever got to them was at that center. The guys knew they could not consume any kind of alcohol or drugs in our centers, but occasionally somebody would say, "Do you smell that? That's marijuana." It was a sweet smell coming through the screens, maybe from some guys leaning against the hootch. I don't know because I didn't look. It wasn't my job to police that. My job was to show these guys a little bit of home, how to just get away from the war for a while.

I soon realized that the enlisted guys fell into two categories. Some of them worshipped the ground we walked on. They couldn't talk to us enough, they brought us presents, they wrote us notes and letters—they treated us like princesses. And then there were those who treated us normally. We got a lot of flak from them for dating officers. "You girls are here for us during the day, but when you go out at night, it's always with the officers," they'd tell us. There was something to what they said, because the officers were closer to our age and educational level. Furthermore, our Geneva Convention cards said we were supposed to have the privileges of a captain. For other purposes, such as transportation, we had the same priority as a GS-12 civilian.

I'll never forget the first memorial service we girls went to at Dong Ba Tinh, walking into that little chapel, seeing those sad faces, hearing the hymns played on the piano, and there in front of me were these boots and four steel helmets. A helicopter had gone down. I didn't know the guys who got killed and I'm glad I didn't. It was very difficult to stand up and read a Bible verse, and I remember thinking for the first time, "What am I doing here?"

I had so much trouble with sickness at Dong Ba Tinh that I used up my two weeks of sick leave in only five weeks. To make it worse, I picked up some skin rashes that nobody could figure out. One of the Red Cross people told me, "You're not going to make it. You were sick in Saigon, you've been sick here. Some people just can't make it in Vietnam." My response was exactly opposite from that of a GI, who would have said, "Oh, well, sorry about that. Let me go home." I went absolutely wild. I screamed and cried, "You can't send me home!" A lot of my reaction came from a growing feeling of being needed; I felt special and important in Vietnam. And, I'd been given a wonderful send-off in the states, so I wasn't about to go home and say, "Well, I got sick. I couldn't make it."

The Red Cross supervisors in Saigon finally said they would give me a probationary period at Cam Rahn Bay Air Force Base, where there was a big hospital. "We're going to figure out what's wrong with you," they said. Fortunately, my health problems disappeared there.

Cam Ranh was a very interesting place. The navy had an air station next door to the air base. Some of the guys there invited three of us girls to go with them one Saturday on a medcap run to a village. I was fascinated by that because, even though I saw Vietnamese workers on the base, I had never seen where they lived. I could not believe the poverty and primitive living conditions. I had seen terrible poverty in Mexico and parts of Spain, but never the equal of Vietnam. We gave out toothbrushes and toothpaste to people who had never seen such things. They were fascinated by toothpaste and even tried to cook with it.

Pigs and chickens walked in and out of hootches in the village, and there was no sewerage, of course. People walked over to a filthy pond to bathe. There were no young men in the village, just old men, young mothers, and babies in long shirts. We weren't supposed to pat the children on the head or take pictures of people in groups of three, because that was an unlucky number. A lot of the people were afraid of cameras; they thought their spirit would be captured and kept inside our little black boxes.

I stayed at Cam Ranh about five months. We had two recreation centers and a staff of eight girls there. The base was big and modern, well kept with paved sidewalks, palm trees, a beautiful beach, air conditioning, and movies. Believe it or not, the most depression I saw in Vietnam was there, among the enlisted men. Cam Ranh was an incredibly quiet place because nothing life-threatening ever happened there. There were no heroes except for the F-4 and Caribou pilots. The GIs would get well-intentioned letters from Girl Scout troops or church circles saying, "I'm praying for you. You're so brave and we thank you for defending our country." These guys didn't feel they were brave or defending the country; they weren't even issued weapons. It was like being locked up at Fort Bragg for a year with no family or social life.

My last assignment was at Chu Lai, the base camp for the Americal Division. I went up there in February of 1969 as the program director, which was a promotion. When we went out to LZs and firebases, we didn't take just Kool-Aid packets and cookies. We lugged big canvas bags that held short-timers' calendars, books, and props for a thirty-minute program, usually an audience-participation game that we made ourselves. My job at Chu Lai required me to coordinate the program schedule and line up transportation for the girls going out to units in the field.

The Americal had three infantry brigades—the 11th, the 196th, and the 198th—and there were six of us assigned to the division. Two girls would go out to each of the brigades every day. I soon got to know where we could and couldn't go, because every night when I called for helicopters, I might be told, "You girls shouldn't be going in that area this week. It's going to be real hot out there."

Chu Lai was in Quang Ngai Province, the least pacified province in Vietnam. When we had rocket and mortar attacks, the Red Cross girls had to go to a communal bunker with majors and lieutenant colonels who were old enough to be our fathers. We'd go running out there at night with our steel pots, raincoats, flak jackets, flashlights, and tennis shoes. Some nights we stayed in the bunker, which was just a big steel culvert covered with sandbags, for hours, listening to the rockets whistle overhead and to the sound of rifle and machine-gun fire on the perimeter. If the rockets were coming in too close to our trailers for us to make it to the bunker, all we could do was roll out of our bunks and pull our mattresses over ourselves for protection.

I think it's amazing that of 627 girls who served in Vietnam over a seven-year period, only three died. One died from fever. Another one, Hannah Crews, who was from my home county in North Carolina, died in a jeep accident, and the third one was raped and murdered in her bed by a GI in Cu Chi.

We always caught our helicopters at Graves Registration in Chu Lai about 5:30 in the morning. The choppers that had been out all night picking up body bags landed there. All we could do was stand and watch while the guys pulled those green plastic bags off the choppers, maybe twenty-five or thirty of them some mornings. I think I dealt with what I saw by not allowing myself to believe GIs were inside those bags. I know this sounds callous, but the bags were stacked up like cordwood, and I had to think of them as cordwood, not as somebody's husband or father or boyfriend or brother.

The Hueys usually had to be hosed out before we could take off because they were so littered with mud and blood and even bone fragments. We always went to the field early in the morning because the cloud cover was over the valleys and it was safer to fly over them. After half an hour or forty-five minutes, we'd get to our first LZ or firebase and serve breakfast to the troops. We spent our whole day going from hill to hill, making maybe six stops before getting back to Chu Lai about supper time.

I was in one Huey that took a hit. My reaction to it reminded me of the truth in Winston Churchill's observation that the greatest feeling in the world is to be shot at without result. I felt exhilaration rather than fear. The bullet came right through the passenger compartment—I was sitting on the floor—and went out the roof, leaving a big, jagged hole. I mean, here I was in my baby blue Red Cross dress, and I almost got shot by a .51-caliber machine gun. The picture I have from that day shows me standing next to that Huey with a genuine smile on my face!

I dreaded to fly on the big twin-rotor Chinook choppers. They were huge and noisy. The first time I flew on a Chinook, we went out to an LZ to serve a supper of rice and country-style steak. Because of our schedule, we were supposed to eat ours on the Chinook. Somebody handed me my supper on a Styrofoam plate just before I walked up the cargo ramp of the chopper. The rotor wash was so strong that the plate flew up in my face: I was suddenly covered with rice and gravy and country-style steak. All I could do was laugh about it.

The main reason I didn't like Chinooks came from seeing what had happened to one that had landed on an LZ. For some reason, it started rolling downhill after it cut its engines. About thirty GIs were inside when the chopper rolled right through some concertina wire, hit a mine and blew up in flames. Although I was depressed to see the shell of this burned-out, horrible tragedy, the guys at the LZ could joke about it. They called the ones who got killed "crispy critters." It was black humor, but how else could they deal with such things?

The 196th Light Infantry was my favorite brigade. I had certain of its

LZs that I loved to visit. One was on a hill called LZ East. Even though it had fourteen men on it, the program director before me hadn't scheduled visits to East very often. I went out there a couple of times not long after getting to Chu Lai, and I found the guys very appreciative. They could watch us through binoculars as we flew into LZ Center and, of course, wanted to know why we didn't come over to East as often.

I started to make a very determined effort to see those fellows whenever I could. Just like the army, we had to keep program statistics—how many men we saw a day, how many miles we traveled. I really racked up some stats getting out to East. I got on a first-name basis with the guys, but only their first names; I almost never knew the last names of the people on those hills.

May of 1969 was a terrible month for the Americal Division. The fighting was so bad we didn't get out of Chu Lai for two weeks. We made a lot of hospital visits during this period and, when things settled down some, I went up to the 101st at Phu Bai for a week. I was aware during this period that a lot of bad stuff was going on around LZs East, West, and Center. When I got back from Phu Bai and started scheduling our routes again, I asked to make a stop at East.

"You won't be going to East anymore," one of the Americal officers told me on the phone.

My first thought was, "Well, they've shut down LZ East," but I asked him, "Why not?"

"LZ East isn't there anymore," he said. "While you were gone, they were overrun at night by sappers with flame throwers and all those guys died."

I just could not believe it. If I missed a stop there, one soldier in particular would always say, "We didn't have Tuesday last week." I think the Donut Dollies were the only thing good that happened in that guy's life while he was in Vietnam. To be told over the phone that he and the others were all dead was just awful and unreal. The next time I flew out to LZ Center, I told the pilot I wanted to go by LZ East.

"I don't think you want to see that," he said.

"Yes, I do," I told him. "I do want to see it."

It still was not real to me. We flew by East and there was nothing left; it was just blasted and charred. I have a color slide of the men who were lost there and I always try to show it when I give talks about Vietnam. They're all standing there waving good-bye. . . . I show it to people because I can't let the memory of those men die.

Everywhere I was in Vietnam, I found myself gravitating toward people from North Carolina and Georgia. Maybe it's because they could dance and talk like I did and they knew what grits were. There just seemed to be an instant bond between people from the South because of our common cultural heritage. I'm sure that people from Michigan and Alaska did the same thing, but people from the South really found each other in a hurry. In fact, I ran into five or six guys that I had known at home in North Carolina; the 312th Evacuation Hospital in Winston-Salem had been called up and stationed in some Quonset huts near our compound at Chu Lai. Those fellows had thought they were getting out of Vietnam by joining a reserve unit. But it was always fun to visit with them and share news from home.

I learned during my first week at Chu Lai that you didn't make hospital visits by starting at Ward One. You started by going on the high-numbered wards, where the malaria and VD patients were. We took around calendars, ballpoint pens, and things like that, but mainly we went just to talk to the guys. A lot of them in the last three wards, One, Two, and Three, were dying. We would go first to the nurses' station, where one of them told us about the beds we needed to visit most. The nurses were so overwhelmed with just trying to keep people alive that they didn't have time to sit by a soldier's bedside and read *Stars and Stripes* or the Bible to him, or write a letter to his mother or girlfriend, or read his mail to him.

Many of these men had been horribly burned and maimed. I didn't know you could be hurt that badly and still be alive. I mean quadruple amputations, blindness. The stumps of their legs would be in what looked like peach baskets held up by wires connected to little pulleys on the ceiling of the Quonset hut wards. God, these guys were so brave. A lot of them had worried when they got to Vietnam that they weren't going to come back whole. And to make it all worse, some of them had been wounded by short rounds fired by our own artillery.

Here I was, an English major on the hospital wards of Vietnam. I had no training in medicine, grief counseling, therapy, or psychology. But I learned to listen and to hold the hands of soldiers, because I realized they were horrified not only by what had happened to them, but what was *going* to happen to them if they survived. They sometimes asked me how they looked. A lot of them couldn't see.

"What do you think my wife is going to say when she sees me?" they would ask. Or, "I can't go home like this. My girlfriend won't love me like this."

I couldn't minimize their fears. I couldn't say, "Don't be silly," or "Don't worry about it." I just had to let them open up and say whatever they felt and just hold on to them and cry with them.

It wasn't a good idea to develop serious relationships in Vietnam, but I did that with an infantry lieutenant from Georgia while I was at Chu Lai. When it came time for him to go home in May of 1969, he said he didn't want to go, that he would extend his tour so we could go home together in August. I really think that's what he intended to do, but I couldn't handle that responsibility. It was hard because I wanted very much for him to stay with me, yet I didn't want him to stay and get killed. And I knew that he had to go back to the life he had in the states, that it was not really going to work out for us. Just before his DEROS, he had his CIB and a religious medal he wore on his dogtag chain engraved with our initials. He gave them to me in the field, saying they represented good luck, courage, and love.

After he left, I went through the motions of the job, but inside I felt confused, abandoned, and sad, even though he wrote me a letter every day. We weren't supposed to fall in love with anybody over there—that's one reason the Red Cross moved us around every few months—but I had done it. The intensity of that romance will always be a bittersweet memory.

It was a bad time. On the night of June 8, we were sound asleep when we were jolted out of our beds by something really heavy. A rocket sounds very different from a mortar; it sounds a lot more powerful coming in and it makes a big thud when it explodes. This thud sounded fairly close, and we all knew it was bad. I told the girls to go to the bunker. While we huddled there, I remember thinking that exactly one year before I had graduated from college.

The rocket hit the Vietnamese ward at the 312th Evac, about a quarter of a mile from where we were, and it killed Sharon Lane, a nurse from Ohio. A lot of nurses didn't like being assigned to the Vietnamese ward. For one thing, you didn't know if half the people in there were for us or against us. Some of them were prisoners. Sometimes you'd see families in there and that was very depressing, because they usually had been hit by our own fire. Sharon, though, was a very warm person who liked her Vietnamese patients. She saw them as a special calling, one that most people didn't want.

After the sun came up, I went outside and took a picture of the sunrise and that was one of the most beautiful pictures I took in Vietnam. A cloudbank reflected the sun in all sorts of purples and yellows. I thought again about walking down an aisle and graduation and then walking out in the middle of all this death, about what a journey I had made in a year. Our jeep driver, a young Spec 4, took us over to the hospital to see what had happened. The rocket had hit Ward 8, which was in a Quonset hut, and had just blown it to pieces: the whole roof was gone, beds, everything.

When she heard the rockets starting to come in, Sharon evidently had put mattresses on top of a lot of her patients, but I think they took a direct hit. I only hope she never knew what hit her.

We were all really upset because, even though we knew the enemy was always aiming at the hospital, they finally had hit it. It was just like when we heard they were always trying to shoot down the medevacs. I mean, it was just such an unfair, cruel war with no decent rules. I don't think we realized the uniqueness of Sharon's death at the time. I guess we thought there was never going to be an end to it all, and we figured that like the GIs, she was one of many who were going to die.

It really hit me—I had been right there in that very ward. I had known Sharon; she was a sister, a blonde, very attractive and very professional. And yet it was not real to me, just like it was not real to me that people were in those body bags I saw. The attitude among the military was that such things were to be expected in a war zone, and in a way, I guess we all got to thinking Sharon's death was a very noble thing. I wrote my mother the next day and told her that if I died like that, it was all right because I was serving my country, I was happy, and I felt fulfilled in my job.

This all happened when I was about ten months into my tour. The truth is, I was getting really tired. I can look through my photo albums and see the bright-eyed "Girl Scout" who arrived in Vietnam in July of 1968 and who looked so different by April of 1969. The emotional drain and the psychological traumas had taken their toll. I still thought, "Once I get back to the real world, I'll be fine." I had a lot of confidence that life was going to work out for me, and yet in my heart of hearts I wasn't that secure or excited about leaving Vietnam.

I stopped for a few days in Bangkok, Singapore, and Japan on the way home. I landed at Travis, proudly wearing my Red Cross uniform, and took a flight from San Francisco to Los Angeles. While I was waiting in the San Francisco airport for my flight to leave, I heard two women sitting behind me bitterly bitching and moaning about a cigarette machine at the airport that didn't have Marlboros. They'd had to settle for Winstons. The pettiness and stupidity of what they were saying—I just felt rage inside me. I wanted to turn around and say, "Who really cares? I mean, do you give a damn that at this minute people in Vietnam are getting killed, 150 to 200 a week, and you're sitting here worrying about the cigarette machine being out of Marlboros?"

I had never had that kind of reaction to complete strangers. I suddenly felt that I didn't fit in, that I couldn't stand to be around people like that. Still, I went on down to the La Jolla area to see some old friends before flying on to North Carolina on the day of the Charles Manson murders.

The country had changed and I could sense it. Maybe California was just the wrong place to start getting back into American life. I realized that public opinion about the war and the people who were fighting it had become decidedly negative. And I was shocked by such obvious cultural changes as the casual acceptance of recreational drugs, Woodstock, and miniskirts.

My life in Vietnam had been so intense that I really didn't care what my friends in La Jolla were talking about or doing. One of them had gone through the Navy Supply Officers' School in Athens and he told me he had lied to get there. He convinced the navy he was colorblind so he couldn't be a line officer; he knew supply officers didn't get assigned to river boats. In a way, I was happy for him, but in another way I was disgusted. I thought, "I'm going to be back with a whole lot of people like this and I have got to learn that they did what they felt they had to, and I did what I had to."

When I got home, my mother was very tolerant and let me do my own thing, which at that time involved sending letters, tapes, and packages to my buddies still in Vietnam. I thought about Vietnam and dreamed about Vietnam, staying up half the night and sleeping half the day. I lived at home and my mother didn't hassle me, something I am thankful for to this day. We never talked very much about what I saw and did in Vietnam. I found that to be true with a lot of my friends, too. We just didn't talk about it very much. If we did, it was on the level of talking about a trip to Bermuda: the land, the climate, very superficial things.

I had trouble settling down because I was looking for the same intensity at home that I had known in Vietnam. It took me a long time to realize that I would never find the thrill, the high, the adrenalin rush or whatever you want to call it, of life in a combat zone. It's really true that until you have fought for it, life has a flavor the protected will never know.

I took a car trip alone to New Orleans to see some college friends, but I know I was not myself during our visit. Still unsettled, I came back to North Carolina and took a plane out to George Air Force Base in California to see some F-4 pilots that I had known at Cam Ranh Bay. I stopped by Fort Sam Houston in Texas and Fort Polk in Louisiana on the way back to see other friends. I just couldn't seem to find a niche; I kept gravitating toward people I had known in Vietnam. After six months of indecision, I decided I had to get on with it. I fought against going back to Vietnam with the USO or Special Services. I decided to help people, I think, by enrolling at the University of North Carolina at Chapel Hill in 1970 to earn a master's degree in special education.

My first semester at Carolina coincided with the Kent State shootings, which polarized people even more against the war and the military. Once, some people who found out I had been in Vietnam said, "You supported the babykillers and are just as guilty as the people who held the gun." They were the kind ones. Others called me a war whore. These people were not really interested in listening to me, so I would just say, "I didn't go to Vietnam because I support the war effort. I went there because I cared about the people who were fighting and dying there. That's really all I have to say."

A lot of Vietnam veteran reunions are going on now, and they're bringing people closer together. When I was at Cam Ranh Bay, for example, the Red Cross girls lived in a Quonset hut next to the nurses and we didn't get along very well with them. Maybe I understand why now. A couple of months ago, I talked to a nurse about the war. "Can I really tell you how I felt about the Donut Dollies?" she said. "I thought you were the silliest things I had ever seen. You were in my way. You didn't have a serious thought about you." She thought we were just cheerleaders, nothing more than donut brains who were messing up the guys' heads. We seemed like sorority girls to her because we wore those little short dresses and had a curfew, and the nurses didn't care for that. Their lives were so traumatic and so serious that we appeared giggly to them.

"It took me a long time to understand what your role was and why you were there," the nurse said, "but now I do appreciate you and I'm sorry we didn't talk in Vietnam."

Of course, we resented having a midnight curfew. We couldn't even frost our hair, because that was considered really loose, nor could we hold a beer or a cigarette or a weapon while we were in uniform. We were supposed to be incredibly wholesome, all-American girls. Even our medications were checked because nobody was supposed to take birth control pills.

I went to a big reunion in Houston in 1987. I was out walking in Hermann Park by myself with my "Donut Dolly" T-shirt on when I saw a man coming toward me. A lot of the veterans at reunions wear fatigue jackets and hats, but this one was nicely dressed in khaki pants and a polo shirt. He had on big sunglasses that prevented me from seeing his eyes, but the closer he got to me, the more aware I became that he was crying. He was so choked up he could hardly say more than "Excuse me, excuse me." He stopped me and stood there and cried, tears just rolling down his face and onto his shirt.

"I just feel so bad," he said. I told him that one of the reasons we were together was to get our feelings out, to talk about them.

"What is it you want to say?" I asked him.

"I never told you girls thank you," he sobbed. "I never said thank you." He had been at Lai Khe with the Big Red One. He remembered the Red Cross girls in those bright blue dresses jumping off the resupply choppers.

"God," he said, "I can't tell you how it felt. You smelled good and you were laughing. We'd been out there for weeks and were really down. You made us feel so good when you left us a calendar or a paperback book, or maybe just a pencil. It just felt great because we had to be gentlemen when you were there. We weren't animals, we weren't killers, we were people again. When you got on the chopper to leave, we all said out loud or to ourselves, 'That's what I'm going home for. That's who's waiting for me when I get home.'"

Perfect strangers come up to me at reunions and just talk and talk and talk. It doesn't matter if I was in Vietnam at the same time or place they were. What matters is that I was there at all. They'll say, "You came to my bedside and you held my hand and you wrote my mother, or you came out to visit my unit." They don't mean me specifically. They mean the collective me. Me, the Red Cross girl.

I still get letters from veterans who had really bad experiences in Vietnam. One in particular, an Americal Division company commander from Louisiana, writes and calls me now and then. He lost sixty-eight people in his company in one night. He's been divorced three times and just can't seem to get it together, but he knows I understand his pain and he trusts me with his feelings and memories.

I knew when I came back that I probably could never marry somebody who had not been in Vietnam. I met Tom on a blind date arranged by mutual friends who thought we both needed to talk about Vietnam. I can talk to Tom about the war; he understands there are times when I just have to dwell on it. He's not threatened by that. But I think it's been hard for a lot of other veterans to find someone who can let them deal with their Vietnam experiences in whatever way they need to.

Was the war worth it? In a personal sense, it was for me. I learned a lot about myself and about life and commitment to others, but it was different for the nation. If we ever get ourselves into anything that stupid again, Vietnam was worth nothing. I would not ever want my sons to be in such a futile situation. Vietnam truly drained the youth out of so many people whose lives are never going to be the same. A lot of veterans lost their friends and part of themselves there, and I think they know they will never recapture what was left behind.

S. Ernest Peoples

Beaumont, Texas

Army helicopter pilot,

1969

•

Thousands of army warrant officers—many of them hardly beyond high school—flew helicopters in Vietnam. Despite their youth, they enjoyed the respect of every combat soldier, and never more so than when they went into a landing zone under fire to pick up casualties. But these pilots enjoyed no immunity from enemy fire. Ernie Peoples is one who became a casualty himself.

We talked for several hours on a warm summer evening in Beaumont, where Ernie operates a welding and machine shop. At forty, with his full head of black hair and faded cutoff shorts, he could have been mistaken for someone in his mid-twenties. "I tried to be a college student for a while after high school," he said. "I entered Lamar University here in Beaumont in the fall of 1965, intending to study engineering, but I changed my major to having a good time and only lasted three semesters. I wasn't thinking about Vietnam at the time. I realized a war was going on over there, but it was a long way from home—a long way from Beaumont, Texas. While I was at Lamar, though, I had several friends who went to Vietnam and one of them got badly wounded. He was paralyzed when he got home and died about a year later, when I was in the military myself."

Ernie quit college in January 1967 and went to southern Louisiana to work as a roustabout on oil platforms fifty miles offshore. Servicing the rigs required a lot of flying back and forth in Huey and JetRanger helicopters.

"That looked like a glamorous occupation to me," he said. "Since I knew it was only a matter of time until I got drafted, I got to thinking that if I had to go in the army, I might as well be a helicopter pilot. After a few months on the oil rigs, I decided to sign up for a two-year enlistment and try for warrant officer flight school. I got my draft notice on the very day I enlisted."

I went through basic training at Fort Polk, Louisiana, and from there went to Fort Wolters, about fifty miles west of Fort Worth, for flight school as a warrant officer candidate. I think flight school, or at least that part of it at Fort Wolters, was tougher than basic training. I mean, we had inspections every day, spit and polish. We went to classes part of the day and flew part of the day. And we still had physical training, though not as much as in basic.

When I first got to Fort Wolters, the army put me on medical hold. I had some kind of kidney disease when I was a child and there was some question about me being physically able to be a pilot. So I was at Fort Wolters for about eight weeks before I actually went up in a chopper. Everybody had four weeks of ground school before flight training, and because of my medical hold, I had to wait for another instruction cycle to start. Until then, I just did odds and ends around the school, hanging around most of the time. Whenever somebody crashed a helicopter, me and a few other guys would have to go out and stand watch over the chopper. Other than that, not much happened.

Once I started my instruction cycle, which consisted of two phases called basic and primary flight training, I was busy at least ten hours a day. Most of the academic part of flight school could be done during the day, in the classroom. Flight training itself was done on the little bubble helicopters that the army had then, the OH-13, OH-23, and TH-55. The TH-55 was a strange little machine that resembled an apple with a toothpick stuck in it. After fifteen hours of basic training, we moved up to primary training, which gave us seventy-five hours of time in takeoffs, landings, cross-country flying, formation flying, and night flying.

I didn't have any particular problems with the instructors at Fort Wolters. Some of them seemed very nervous, though. My first instructor was like that. He was a captain who like to scream and carry on. "Goddamn, Peoples!" he would yell, "are you trying to kill us?" Just typical army harassment, but looking back on it, I think he was trying to get me accustomed to operating under pressure.

There was quite a bit of talk about Vietnam at Fort Wolters. We liked to sing "I Want to Fly a Huey Cobra" to the tune of the Oscar Mayer wiener jingle and boast about going to Vietnam as a one-man army to end the war. By this time, I think I really wanted to go over there. Certainly, I knew that by becoming a helicopter pilot I had a very, very good chance of going. And if I had to go, I sure wanted to go as a pilot versus going as a grunt.

After Fort Wolters, I went to Fort Rucker, Alabama, for fifty hours of instrument flight training in OH-13s before moving into Hueys. We spent our last week of training in the field to simulate conditions in Vietnam, even to the point of having mock rocket and mortar attacks at night. Near the end of training at Rucker, things began to ease up. Flying was becoming a job, and I basically knew how to fly a helicopter, or so I thought. The Huey was one fine piece of equipment. Compared to the piston-powered trainers, the Huey was much more stable and powerful because it had a very smooth thirteen hundred horsepower turbine engine. I felt like I had traded in a Chevrolet for a Cadillac.

I finished training at Fort Rucker on the day before Thanksgiving of 1968. I made my last flight and took the holiday off. In early December I went through two graduation ceremonies at Rucker. In the first ceremony, I got my commission as a warrant officer; in another one the next day, I got my wings. I also had my orders for Vietnam by this time. Of the thirty-five or so guys who went through Fort Rucker with me, I think only three didn't get orders for Vietnam.

I spent most of December at home on leave. I remember a few people making comments about the war and me being a helicopter pilot. "Hell, a helicopter pilot. All he is is a glorified truck driver," one guy said. Another one tossed off something about me being nothing more than cannon fodder in Vietnam. I didn't pay much attention to that sort of talk, though.

I left Beaumont on New Year's Eve and flew to Seattle to catch a civilian airliner going to Vietnam. Several of my classmates from flight school were on the plane with me. We talked quite a bit during the flight, but I don't remember that we talked very much about the war. We came into Cam Ranh Bay at night. When we got on the ground, it was hot, dark as hell, and flares were being shot up. I spent the night there and flew out by chopper the next day to Nha Trang. After a couple of days there, I went up to Pleiku, home of the Fifty-second Aviation Battalion.

Art Papale, a guy from Biloxi, Mississippi, who had been my roommate all through flight school, went with me. We reported in to Major Ted Kerns. "Well, you two fellows are going to Kontum, to the Fifty-seventh Assault Helicopter Company," Kerns said. That didn't come as good news. The Fifty-seventh was known as "The Gladiators." We'd heard stories about them ever since we'd been in-country. People would say, "Whatever you do, don't go to Kontum. That's rocket city."

We told Kerns, "Oh, hell, major, we don't want to go there. We've already heard the stories about Kontum. That's rocket city, a bad place to go."

"Well, it might be," he said. "But in a couple of weeks I'm going to transfer up there to be the CO. Y'all be there when I get there." He was ready for us. So we said "Okay," as if we had a choice, and went on to Kontum.

Late in the afternoon of the day we got there, Art and I were standing around with some pilots who had been a class or two ahead of us in flight school. We were talking about being the new guys on the block, about all the stories we'd heard about Kontum. "Yeah, we do have rocket attacks," one of the guys said. "We have them frequently. They sound like—"

Just as he puckered his lips and whistled, the real thing came over. Everybody had enough sense to hit the deck but Art and me. And then all of a sudden the biggest goddam explosion I ever heard went off not far away. We got a rocket attack within a hour of getting to Kontum. It hit the POL dump and made a pretty fire with a lot of black smoke. We went to the officers' club that night and got drunker than skunks—beer, whiskey, it didn't make any difference what we were drinking.

I started flying a couple of days later. My company had three airlift platoons equipped with D-model Hueys. My platoon leader was the one who assigned my missions from day to day. One of the first things he told me was that when I got out of flight school, I knew how to drive a helicopter—not how to fly it. I had to fly as what we called the Peter pilot for about three hundred hours before I could become an aircraft commander. For one thing, being stationed in Kontum meant a lot of mountain flying. Most of the LZs that I went into were single-ship LZs; in fact, I'll say 99.9 percent of them were. A single-ship LZ had room for only one Huey at a time. Sometimes these clearings were made in the forest with explosives and sometimes they were just small open areas covered with elephant grass.

The first day I flew in Vietnam, I spent ten hours in the air on an ash-and-trash mission for the Second ARVN Rangers. They had found an NVA base camp in the jungle and my company spent all day hauling out rice and weapons. My Huey drew some small-arms fire and I remember how easily I could hear it because I had become accustomed to all the various noises that a helicopter makes. By the end of that day, I was exhausted, too tired to even think very much about coming under fire on my first mission. I may have thought something like, "Golly, is every day going to be like this?" or "When is my day off going to be?" But mostly I was just out of it.

Flying helicopters in Vietnam quickly got to be routine. A lot of people still ask me what it was like. "Well, I got up the morning," I say. "I had a cup of coffee and strapped my helicopter to my ass. Then I went out and flew all day long and came in at night and unstrapped it from my ass and got drunk." We drank a lot to relieve the stress. Some guys would fly with hangovers. Being in a helicopter for hours at a time is tiring as hell. If I was flying straight and level, it wasn't too bad. It was the takeoffs and landings that demanded so much concentration. You know, ten hours of flying in one day is probably as stressful as driving from Beaumont to Canada on the back roads.

My company's ships took hits once in a while. It had lost very few people, maybe only two, when I joined it. The Hueys stood up well to ground fire unless they were hit in a vital area, and by that I mean the engine or the pilot. But you know, I don't think Charlie really aimed at us most of the time; I think he just started shooting and hoped for the best. There was no armor plating around the engine, but we had some on the pilots' seats. We also had something called the chicken plate, which was armor that helped shield us on the door side of the aircraft.

I got shot down five times. The first and worst time came when I had been in-country three months and was still a Peter pilot.

My battalion was flying in support of the Special Forces' clandestine missions against the Ho Chi Minh Trail in eastern Laos; these were some of the SOG operations that you've probably heard about. Some of us got fairly close with these guys at Kontum. We'd meet at night and drink and talk about the war. I was told that a lot of the information they picked up was on the president's desk in Washington within twenty-four hours. Maybe so, maybe not, but I do know that my battalion once put an entire company of Americans and Montagnards into Laos, almost on top of the Ho Chi Minh Trail. We took them out after a week there.

In fact, on the day I first got shot down, my ship was one of four Hueys on a mission to drop off a team of Americans and Montagnards in a valley about twenty miles inside Laos. One of the Americans on my ship had "Fuck You, Ho Chi Minh" written on his jungle fatigues. I don't remember if he or the other Americans had name tapes on their fatigue blouses, but I'm sure they had dog tags.

The rule of thumb for safety from ground fire in a helicopter was stay below fifty feet and above fifteen hundred. Everything in between was very risky. I think we had just cleared fifteen hundred feet on our way out of the valley and were heaving a sigh of relief when some bastard with a .50-caliber machine gun opened up on us. He hit us in the engine because the flame went right out and we started losing power.

We had to autorotate in a fast descent to the jungle. Fortunately, I had a lot of confidence in the pilot, who got right on the radio and told the guys in the chase ships that we had been hit and were going in. The crew chief and the door gunner seemed to take everything in stride. For them, it was just another bad day at the office. I say that in jest, but that's really what it had become for those guys. Flying helicopters and going down in them was just another job in Vietnam.

The pilot and I talked the whole way down. The first thing we said was, "Where are we going to go?" We started looking for light green growth. This would be an area of new or small vegetation, much safer to go down in than trees. Luckily, we did find some light green growth, which turned out to be short trees. As the pilot flared the ship and set it down right into the top of them, I noticed that our forward air speed had dropped to zero. We were falling out of the sky by the time we made it to the trees. The Huey rolled over on its side and the blades broke off with a lot of noise and commotion, then it just dropped to the ground with a big jolt.

The Huey came to rest on its left side. The pilot's arm was broken in two places and the crew chief, who sat on the left side, was pinned in. The door gunner was all right and so was I. I opened my door and quickly climbed out of the wreckage; the first thought that had come to my mind when we hit the ground was, "The ship is going to catch on fire." I yelled to the door gunner to get the fire extinguisher and spray the engine. While he did that, I started getting the pilot and crew chief out, which wasn't as hard as I thought it was going to be. The ship hadn't rolled completely on its side, just at sort of a forty-five-degree angle.

A strange thing about the crash still sticks in my mind. I had an M-16 beside me and a cigarette lighter in my flight suit pocket. When we hit the ground, the M-16 went through the windshield. But I don't know to this day what happened to that cigarette lighter. It was gone from my pocket and I never saw it again.

We stayed in contact with the rescue chopper, another Huey brought in from Kontum, with a survival radio. The rescue Huey had a McGuire rig, a kind of web seat that could be lowered to the ground with a 150-foot nylon rope. At the end of the rope was a two-inch strap about eight feet long, and the person being picked up assembled his seat out of it.

We knew the NVA were near us because we could hear them while all this was going on, even though the jungle was very thick. For a while, it seemed like we would all get out in one piece, but when the crew chief was being pulled up to the Huey, the NVA shot him in the head. He was a specialist four or five and I don't even remember his name. That's one of the worst things about Vietnam—not remembering the names.

The bastards got lucky and shot me on September 26, 1969. It happened while I was the aircraft commander on what we called a "people sniffer" mission. In the passenger compartment, we had a guy with a map and an operator for the instrument, which was connected by a flat tube to a nozzle mounted on one of the skids. The people sniffer was sensitive enough to pick up ammonia from urine, and I guess, perspiration. It was a way to look for Charlie when he was hiding in the jungle.

We were less than fifty feet off the ground when somebody below opened up with a whole clip. I could hear the rounds slamming into the chopper and then felt something happen to my left leg. You know, you read stories of searing, hot pain and that sort of thing, but I didn't feel that. I just knew I had been shot.

The round that hit me came through my cyclic control stick and cut all the wires in it. In the short amount of time it took me to recover from being shot, I looked at the instrument panel and saw warning lights flashing. We were losing RPM and flying in a peculiar attitude, going forward and backing up.

My Peter pilot had grabbed the controls and was shouting, "My pilot's been hit! My pilot's been hit!"

He was new in-country and had panicked when Charlie started shooting. I guess it was his first time under fire. I couldn't talk to him on the intercom because of the cut wires, so I slapped him on his helmet and yelled that I had the aircraft, to leave it alone. I was pretty sure we didn't have any critical damage. We were still in the air and nobody else on the aircraft was hurt. After the Peter pilot got his composure back, I gave the controls to him and we flew to the Special Forces camp at Duc Co, near the border with Laos, to set down.

I had my million-dollar wound, my ticket home. I was flown to the hospital at Pleiku for an operation, but I really had nothing more than a big flesh wound. There was no nerve damage or anything like that. I guess the worst thing that came out of it was a big scar almost the length of my left thigh. I went on to the Seventh Field Hospital in Japan and stayed there a couple of weeks for physical therapy, then came home to Beaumont on convalescent leave for a month.

I still had two years left in the army. I wanted to go back to Fort Wolters as a basic flight instructor, but when I called the Department of the Army about a slot there, the personnel officer suggested another assignment.

"How about Fort Polk?" he asked.

I said that was close to home, but in God's name, who wants to go to Fort Polk? He said check it out and call him back. So I went over to the airfield at Polk one day and took a look around. I liked what I saw—the place was small, just a few officers and warrants, so I called the guy in Washington and said I'd take the assignment.

After a while, I was selected to be the junior aide to the general who ran the post. He was an aviator, and general officers who were aviators were required to have a rated aviator on their personal staff. It was a good job, but it didn't change my mind about staying in the army, nor did a new regulation that said warrants who had served a tour in Vietnam could apply for direct commission to first lieutenant. I didn't want to go back to Vietnam. I'd had all of it I could physically take.

I wasn't thinking about the moral worth of the war at the time. I was thinking about all the violence I had seen, the friends that I had lost. Art Papale was one of them. I told people that I wasn't a cat, I didn't have nine lives, and that I would rather lose my life in a whorehouse in the United States or to some irate husband than to a slant-eyed son of a bitch in Vietnam.

I got out of the army in 1971 and came back to Beaumont. I grew up here and if nothing happens to change it, I guess I'll die here. I got married to a Beaumont girl about a year after getting back from Vietnam, so this was the logical place to come back to. I worked for a while after leaving the army before starting school again at Lamar University to earn my degree in business administration.

Sure, I've thought a lot about the war since coming back home. I still have dreams about it and used to have nightmares, though none recently. These were "what if" nightmares—the ones where you get to the point of getting killed and then wake up.

It's hard to say what Vietnam took from me because I don't know what kind of person I'd have become if I hadn't gone. Yet I do know that I underwent some change over there. I'm still majoring in a good time, but I do believe the war left me rather hard and cold. I have compassion for other people, but it's probably not as strong as it was before I went to Vietnam. I mean, a person cannot go through a war, regardless of which war it was, and live with death every day and not be affected by it.

I guess through the years I've become somewhat bitter about the war because people don't seem to understand it. One time I saw a guy wearing a cap that had an outline of Vietnam on it. The writing on the cap said, "If you ain't been there, shut the fuck up." And that's just the way I felt about it when I started thinking about the peace-hippie-love-waterbed generation of the 1960s.

Vietnam veterans get treated like second-class veterans. My dad and I had a big confrontation about this not too long ago. He and I were watching a *60 Minutes* segment on Vietnam veterans. Some of them were hugging each other and saying, "Welcome home, brother."

My dad made a comment about it: "Well, nobody welcomed me home from the Second World War."

I said, "People weren't demonstrating in the streets when you came home. You fought a war that was the thing to do. The whole country was behind you. I fought in Vietnam and the country was divided. Half of the people were saying 'Go for it' and the other half was saying 'Get the killers back home.'" I'm proud to be a Vietnam veteran. Whenever I hear a Huey go over, I'll stop what I'm doing and go look at it. Oh, man, even the way they smell, that JP-4 exhaust, brings back memories. There's nothing in the world like it.

Charlie Earl Bodiford

Atmore, Alabama

Marine machinegunner,

1969–70

●

Charlie Earl Bodiford is the deputy warden at Holman Prison, a three-story concrete fortress surrounded by a high chain-link fence laced with concertina wire along the top. Like a huge cresting wave, the wire spills into the prison yard to foil escape; an inmate bent on getting out must first survive passage through a thicket of razor-like barbs, then confront the main fence itself. Holman is Alabama's maximum security prison. On the day I stopped there to talk to Charlie, the institution housed 644 inmates. One in ten was on death row.

At the entrance to the prison parking lot was a carefully tended flower garden, its yellow marigolds a stark contrast to the drabness of the prison grounds. A sign at the gate instructed visitors to push a button for admittance. When I did, an electrical lock snapped open and I walked through the gate toward the administration building where Charlie works.

Between telephone calls and occasional interruptions by inmates clad in spotless white shirts and pants, Charlie talked about his tour as a Third Marine Division grunt on the DMZ in 1969–70. He is a small man, about five and a half feet tall, with a quick smile and a ruddy face.

"I spent my teenage years in Selma, Alabama," Charlie told me. "My father was a mechanic and my mother was a machine operator at a cigar factory. A lot of racial trouble was going on in Selma during the sixties, and it was a difficult time to be there. The blacks lived in one part of the town and we lived in the other. Our school was on the other side of the black project, and we had to go through it. Needless to say, if we didn't go in a group of ten or twenty in the morning to school, we just didn't go. If there was just a single guy or maybe two or three, the blacks would harass us and try to beat us up. They'd call us 'soda cracker' and cuss us and throw dirt clods and rocks at us. Of course, we did the same things to them.

"At the time, I was raised to think blacks was inferior to whites. I was considered an average, normal white kid in Selma: I didn't like blacks, period. Naturally, when Martin Luther King marched on the Edmund Pettus Bridge in 1965, I went down to see what was going on. I was curious. I wasn't involved in any way, but it was a spectator sport, you might say, because Sheriff Jim Clark was not the type of man that was going to back down. So I knew for a fact that if King pushed the issue and came over the bridge, there would be some violence, and there was. That time was a very closed aspect of my life. I can see back now what a narrow point of view it was."

I quit high school in 1967, when I was in the eleventh grade, and went up to an Oldsmobile factory in Michigan to work. One of my uncles was working there and he told me how much money I could make and that he would help me get a job. So I went to Lansing and started making pretty good money, six or seven dollars an hour. I chromed bumpers. The bumpers came down a rack and I operated a machine that dropped 'em in the chroming vat and then took 'em out.

I liked the job and stayed there about a year, but I got discontented with being up North. All my family and friends was down South. I had a '55 Chevrolet, so I just told my uncle, "I think I'm going back South."

"Well," he said, "what are you gonna do when you get back down South, Earl? You know they not going to pay you anything. Why don't 'cha go in the military and make a career of it?" His brother Doug happened to be in the marines and he was home on leave at the time. Doug and me got to talking about the marines and he got me so fired up—shoot, I went right down to the recruiting station and signed up. At first, the recruiter was going to sign me up for only two years to see if I liked it.

"Hell, no," I said. "Give me the whole four years."

He did, but I signed up for the 120-day delay program because I wanted to come back home to Selma and tell my mama and daddy that I had joined the marines. Both of 'em thought it was a good idea. In fact, I don't think any of us really thought much about the war in Vietnam. I remember hanging around the house, though, getting bored waiting for my 120 days to run out.

One day my mother told me to take out the garbage and do this and that, and I said, "Shoot, man, I'm going to go some place where everybody's going to quit telling me what to do." Of course, I had already joined the marines, where everybody told you what to do twenty-four hours a day. I went on to Parris Island in September of 1968 for boot camp. It lasted eight weeks at that time and was pure hell. We had some pretty tough drill instructors. I mean, they was running us through there for Vietnam.

I got in big trouble with my DI, a staff sergeant who had just come back from Vietnam, because I tried to read a letter from an old girlfriend after lights out at nine o'clock. I was damn sure determined to see what that letter said, so I got up under my blanket and turned on my flashlight. I was reading the letter when all hell broke loose. The DI snatched them covers off and kicked me out of the bunk. Oh, man, he got on my case bad. He was mad.

He screamed, "You scum of the earth, can't you follow orders? Get to my office, you maggot!"

I'll never forget it. I was standing in his office and he hit me in the stomach. Of course, marines aren't supposed to fall down, so I just stood there and took it—twenty-five licks. He was yelling and raising hell. About the twentieth lick, I got to thinking, "Something's got to give here. This man's about to kill me." He saw me look over at his NCO sword in the corner.

He yelled, "Go for it, maggot, and I'll kill your ass before you get to it!"

I didn't go for it because I knew the big guy meant what he said. He was a pretty tough guy. But I think he knew I was fixing to defend myself if he kept hitting me. After that, he got off my case. He recognized me as somebody in that platoon that he could push only so damn far, and I think I earned a little respect from him. He started to treat me better, even gave me little positions of responsibility in my platoon.

I think the DI figured 80 percent of his platoon was headed to Vietnam. Just before graduation, he called out orders. I was naive as hell. He called out one guy's name and said, "Washington. Bremerton, Washington."

Everybody said, "Yeah!"

I didn't know where the hell Bremerton, Washington, was. He called out a couple more places and then said to one of the guys, "WestPac."

Everybody said, "Well, damn." Where the hell was WestPac? Then he called out my name and said, "WestPac." I thought, "WestPac, that's west. I must be going to Camp Pendleton, California." I got to thinking about all those girls, all those surfers, and I said to this kid sitting next to me, "Man, I'm going to California."

He said, "Yeah, I know you are. They cross everybody to Vietnam through California."

"Are you for real?" I said. "What the hell do you mean, Vietnam?" And he told me that's what WestPac really meant.

I went to Camp Geiger, North Carolina, for infantry training, and then on to Camp Pendleton to learn how to use the 3.5-inch rocket launcher, flame thrower, and 106mm recoilless rifle. Nobody had enough time to go home after finishing the training at Pendleton because we was shipping out to Okinawa in a couple of days, so some of us went down to Tijuana for a last fling. We had a ball and really didn't care how we felt before catching that plane to Okinawa. Talk about hangovers—you could have led the whole bunch of us off to hell and nobody would have cared.

I stayed on Okinawa for a couple of months, I guess. It was a staging area for Vietnam. I'd get ready to ship out and a sergeant would start calling names and telling people when to board the airplane for Vietnam, but my name never was called. I believe I'd still be on Okinawa if I hadn't just went and asked one of the sergeants, "When the hell am I going? I'm in no rush, understand, but I ain't no chicken, either." The truth is, I was tired of walking around picking up cigarette butts every day.

"Wait a minute," the sergeant said. He walked in to see the first sergeant of the transient company and the next morning my butt was headed to Vietnam. I just asked for it.

When I got off the 707 in Danang, the heat and humidity just hit me like a lead weight. I stayed in a big wooden barracks at Danang for a couple of days, but I couldn't sleep very much because of the all-night shellings, flares, pom-pom guns, and mortars. I stayed up the biggest part of the night just watching it all.

Some old vets there really opened our eyes up a lot. They told us what to look for, how to survive. They said forget what the marines taught us in training, it was different in Vietnam. A sergeant who was fixing to rotate home called a bunch of us together and talked to us sort of like a father figure. "Listen, it's going to be hell when you get there. Don't let anybody bullshit you," he said. "The first thing you do, get a boonie hat and throw away them goddamn helmets before you die of heat exhaustion. Then get your ass down and keep it down." He was concerned about surviving in the bush—walking point, watching for booby traps, light and noise discipline, the things that made the difference between living and dying.

I got sent out the 1/9th Marines at Firebase Vandegrift, close to the DMZ. When I got there, I learned that the company had just lost some people on an ambush because the gooks had turned Claymores around on 'em. Needless to say, the gunny was upset. He lined us new guys up and told us what we was going to do. I was to be the M-60 man. I didn't say anything. I had laid down behind an M-60 in infantry training and pulled the trigger, but that was the extent of my training with it. The gunny was the type of fellow you didn't question; he was a very serious man.

The next guy in line was a cook. "You are an antitank man," the gunny said. "Hey, wait a minute. I'm a cook," this guy said. "No," the gunny said, "you was a cook. You're an antitank man now." The cook and me had got to be pretty good friends on the way to Vietnam. Not long after we got to Vandegrift, he was waiting with several other guys to get on a chopper to go out to LZ Foster to burn off fields of fire. Some 122mm rockets whistled over and landed right in the middle of those guys, about a quarter of a mile from where I was. I was supposed to be on that chopper, but the gunny had held me and an 81mm mortarman back to go out on another chopper the next morning because we was actually going to a company. If I'd gone down there, I'd be dead, too. That really hit me hard. It was the first realization for me that people got killed in Vietnam, that some guys didn't come back.

A lot of marines felt like being at a combat base gave 'em more security. Not me. The gooks constantly fired 122mm rockets and 82mm mortars—*pow! pow!*—and I was the one walking around inside that perimeter thinking, "Am I going to be in the wrong place today?" I've been close enough to 122s to hear 'em come in like a jet plane even when I was in a bunker, and being inside was the only thing that saved me. Sometimes I couldn't find a bunker and I'd just have to fall face down on the ground and hope to Jesus that rocket would hit somewhere else. If you could hear 'em, you was all right. It was the sons of bitches you didn't hear that you had to worry about.

A couple of days after I got to Vandegrift, I took a chopper out to LZ Russell, four or five clicks up toward the DMZ. My company was protecting army 105mm howitzers at the LZ. I got there about four o'clock in the afternoon, right before dark, and was sent to a gun emplacement with a 106mm recoilless rifle overlooking the trash chute. A M-60 machine gun was there, too. Every combat base on the DMZ had at least a M-60 on its trash chute, because that was a break in the line. About five o'clock, the gooks fired an 82mm mortar into our line there just to probe it. Well, the 106 guy, who was a Mexican, or at least looked Mexican, jumped straight up. He was going to fire back at the gooks because he saw the flash. He hollered for his crew to get up there on the gun, but everybody wanted to stay in the damn trench.

Nobody moved. I couldn't understand that, so I just jumped up there and grabbed a HEAT round and shoved that thing in the breech. It surprised the hell out of all of 'em. I slapped the Mexican on the helmet—that was the signal to fire—and *whoosh!* that 106 round hit dead ass on top of the gooks. Whooo, the first time! The other guys scrambled up out of that trench and jumped all over us.

"How in the hell did you know how to do that?" they asked me. "Well," I said, "I was a 106 man until I got this damn machine gun the other day." And I hit it off with 'em, just like that. They all wanted to know where I was from. Alabama, I said, and they started calling me Alabama after that. In fact, I liked to have forgot my real name over there.

We had a lot of blacks in my company. I had been brought up with that line between blacks and whites, but I noticed that the other guys didn't look at it that way. To them, Vietnam was a whole different ball game. Everybody was in it together.

Well, a couple of days after getting to LZ Russell, I was laying in a little tent, trying to keep the sun off and reading a Superman comic book that one of the guys had brought over with him. This guy named Teague and me got to talking and pretty soon we was good friends. A few minutes later, our squad leader, a black guy from New Jersey, came in the tent to get some rest. He just laid down and put his head on my stomach. I looked at the black guy and said, "What the hell is this? I'll tear your ass out of its frame!"

Ol' Teague, he just looked at me. He didn't say anything. I told the black guy, "Hey, why don't you move your goddamn head? I ain't your goddamn pillow!"

He said, "No problem, man, no problem." He probably didn't think about what he was doing and just got up and left. Teague said, "Hey, we don't have no problems with blacks here. That might be the same dude that saves your ass someday." And I got to looking at it that way. As the week went along, it became evident to me there was no racial trouble in the company. The black guy was going to eat the same C-rations I was, he was going to drink the same water, and we didn't have any room for trouble. We had too much other stuff pressing on our minds.

My company ran a lot of patrols and ambushes. It got to be more or less routine work and by my ninth month I had been in so many fire fights that I considered myself a seasoned grunt. I couldn't imagine doing anything else. I saw quite a few of the North Vietnamese—usually after we had shot 'em. You'd get glimpses of 'em during fire fights. If we was going to ambush 'em, we'd let 'em get as close to us as possible. Other times they would be thirty-five or forty yards away and we'd put 81mm mortars on 'em.

I walked into one ambush myself on a water run. We was coming off a hill and there was only one place to get water, a small stream. The gooks knew that sooner or later we was going to get some water there. I wasn't actually toting any canteens on the water run; I was along with my M-60 for security. I was the fourth man in the squad. The point man wasn't really looking for trouble, or else he would have seen the ambush. Sometimes we'd get those types. Charlie opened up with AK-47s and hit him first. And when they did, we knew what was coming down—they was going to hit us from both sides. They did and we immediately assaulted 'em. That flushed 'em out and put 'em on the run. They was very quick; they killed four of us and I think we killed six of them. They had a 82mm mortar that they was trying to fire into us, but it never was on target. We had twelve guys and they would have killed all of us if we hadn't known what to do. The whole thing lasted about 45 seconds.

Near the end of my tour, I moved over to Mike Company, 3/4th Marines. One of the other companies got its ass kicked up on Mutter's Ridge when it landed on a hot LZ and the gooks just ate 'em up. I was back at Vandegrift when the choppers brought in all those shot-up guys. Body bags was everywhere. My battalion commander at the time was a major. It hit him so damn hard that them gooks had chewed up a whole company that he saddled up two other companies and we went across the DMZ as a blocking force. Mike Company flew in ahead of the gooks moving back into North Vietnam and set up the blockade. The other company came in behind 'em and pushed 'em toward us and we killed their asses. I mean, we took every one of 'em out.

Well, we liked to have had a riot at Vandegrift after that because the major got busted from the field. He got court-martialed for going into North Vietnam without permission. And you know, we thought he was the greatest thing going because he showed us that he would stick up for his men regardless of the consequences. Man, they liked to have a mutiny up there. The only people who got the situation under control was the chaplains. A bunch of them came in and started talking to the guys and that sort of eased things.

I got put on convoy duty for a while and I probably wouldn't be here today if it hadn't been for a lance corporal we called Charlie Brown. He'd been over there two tours and he was good. He was a real Rambo, the type of individual that, if you was standing security at night, he'd slip through the damn wire and hunt him a gook to take out. You would never see him. Of course, he was in trouble all the time because of that, so a gunny put Charlie on my truck as a kind of punishment. He wanted Charlie to suck in all that dust and heat instead of being out in the bush where he belonged. My truck was a security truck. Several of 'em was always interspersed throughout a convoy in case we got hit. If that happened, the guys in the security trucks had to rush up to a truck that got hit or broke down and protect it until it got moving again.

Like most security trucks, mine had sandbags on the bottom for protection against mines, and it carried a bunch of ammo and grenades. Well, Americans are suckers for kids, you know. Whenever we stopped in a ville, the kids would run up and yell, "Chow! Chow! Chow!" and we'd give 'em our last can of C-rations. They'd get up on the truck and crawl all over it, and we'd pet 'em. Charlie had told us two or three times to keep the little bastards off our truck. We thought he was the meanest son of a bitch around and had a little problem—you know, not liking kids. In fact, the rest of us talked about whipping his ass because one of the kids got up on the truck and Charlie just grabbed him and threw him off.

"I've done told you sons of bitches to stay off this truck!" he hollered. He just sat over there in his corner and we continued to let the kids get on the truck. "Put your hands on one of these kids," we told him, "and we're going to whip your ass." He didn't say anything. A little piece on, a truck broke down for about thirty minutes and them kids was all over us again. All of a sudden, Charlie stood up with his M-16. Two of the little bastards had got a case of grenades and was running down the goddamn road with 'em. And Charlie blew the back of their heads off. Those kids had left us one grenade. Charlie scooped it up and threw it out of the truck: *ka-boom!*

"I told y'all not to let them son of a bitches up on this goddamn truck," Charlie said. Well, that taught me right there. The man knew what he was doing. I felt stupid as hell. I had let my compassion for other human beings override what I had been taught. It was not a mistake any of us on that truck ever made again.

I saw a lot of civilians get killed, but not by American fire. The gooks would kill 'em because the people in a village would patronize us or have something else to do with us. Charlie would drop mortar rounds on the hootches after we left a ville, and that was more or less to teach the people a lesson. He wouldn't kill 'em all, just enough to let them know he was around. It worked. We could go back in a ville the next day and the people wouldn't have anything to do with us. Of course, you couldn't blame 'em.

A lot of the marijuana that the guys smoked came from the villages. Nobody smoked pot in the bush—any marine who did was subject to pushing up daisies. But it was very prevalent on the combat bases. Guys would go in the bunkers when the CO wasn't around and smoke pot just to get rid of the stress. It was easier to get marijuana than alcohol. The marines passed out only two beers a day—how the hell was anybody going to get a buzz off two beers? The guys could give a gook a pack of C-rations and get a twenty-pack of marijuana already rolled, just like a pack of cigarettes.

Some guys in my battalion got killed smoking pot. They was on the trash chute with a M-60 and got to smoking that stuff, just got spaced out and didn't know what was going on. The gooks walked right up to that trash chute and opened up with AK-47s and bangalore torpedoes and those guys on the M-60 never knew what happened.

I had two years left in the marines when I got back to the states in March of 1970. I went to the Portsmouth Naval Disciplinary Command in New Hampshire as a corrections guard, which is how I ended up in penal work. We had about four hundred prisoners there in a building that looked like an old castle. A lot of marine and navy guys were there who had been in Vietnam, and it was kind of hard for me to come down on 'em because I knew what they had been through. One guy told me he was in for killing a hamlet chief's daughter who turned out to be a VC, but he was convicted of killing an unarmed civilian because the South Vietnamese government made a big issue out of it.

I got out of the marines in September of 1972 and came down here to Atmore because my first wife was from here. Her father worked for the prison system. At first, I got a job at a textile mill, but it was basically a menial job loading clothes in a hopper and giving 'em to some ladies to sew. I never would have worked out there because I had just got out of the marines, and, well, I was not going to have no lady boss. I stayed there two weeks and put in for work here at the prison.

I remember hearing Warden Potts say to the assistant warden, "I don't know if that guy can handle convicts around here. He's pretty small."

"Yeah, but he's feisty as hell," Warden Digman said. I figured that if I wanted a job, I'd better put my two cents in. I did, and I've been here ever since.

You know, in the last few years I've come to think there is such a thing as post-traumatic stress disorder. I can't explain it, but whenever I go to bed at night, I don't get up under the covers. I sleep with a little light blanket on top of me, like I did in Nam. I remember having a flashback on Okinawa, after I had left Vietnam. I didn't have another one until 1987, when my brother Allen and me was deer hunting up in Marengo County with a couple of our cousins.

I didn't know it at the time, but this sagebrush field went into an angle, and as we walked, we was getting closer and closer together. The sage-brush was chest high. One of my cousins was on the far left, I was in the middle, then there was Allen, and our other cousin was on the far right. I noticed that Allen and me was moving ahead of the others a little bit. Allen was about thirty yards away. "Let's all stay in line in case we see a deer when he jumps up," I called over to him.

My cousin on the left yelled that he saw a deer. I don't know if the boy did or not, but he cut loose with double-ought buckshot from forty yards away and hit Allen in the side of his neck. The other kid was standing next to my brother. He hollered "Man down!" just like in Nam. I go running like hell over there. And I see it's my brother bleeding and goddamn, I just—hell, I'm looking around for a radio to call a chopper.

"Earl, snap out of it!" Allen yelled. "Snap out of it! Goddamn it, help me, get me out of here!" I was still looking for a medevac and then the boy, he ran up there and saw what he had done and just went crazy. He turned and ran and fell on the ground, screaming "I killed Allen! I killed Allen!" I already had my shotgun on him, because I was thinking he was a damn gook. I was going to blow his shit away. Thank God, Allen kicked me in the stomach and snapped me out of it. I came that close to killing the boy. I guess it was just the trauma of seeing my brother shot down. I can't say that some Vietnam vets don't suffer flashbacks daily. I can only say that I haven't. But I know they exist because I've experienced 'em.

I've got a low boiling point, I guess you would say. It don't take a lot to set me off. I didn't used to be like that. I've already experienced one heart attack and I ain't but thirty-eight. Thirty-eight years old and already had one heart attack four years ago. Occasionally I have little pains in my chest, but heart attacks run in my family. My father died of a heart attack, my grandfather did, my uncles did; my brother, who's two years younger than me, he's had a heart attack. But then I've lived in some type of stressful environment from the time I was growing up in Selma to the marines, to Vietnam, to the prison here.

I don't talk to people much about the war unless they're Vietnam vets. I have a couple of buddies up around Frisco City who was in Vietnam and we all identify with each other. But I don't talk about it much with my wife. I tried two or three times to explain to her what took place over there, but like most people, she can't visualize Vietnam in its entirety and impact. I guess you just had to be there and see it to understand it.

Donald L. Whitfield

Eutaw, Alabama

Army machinegunner, 1969

•

I heard about Donald Whitfield from John Pippen, an Alabama veterans affairs officer stationed at the VA hospital in Tuscaloosa. On an August afternoon, we drove forty miles down Interstate 59 to Eutaw to find Whitfield. Inside the aging Greene County courthouse, John and I asked a couple of regulars passing time at the Coke machine how to find Whitfield's place. "You mean Fort Reagan?" one of the men said, winking at his friend. That's what Whitfield calls his two-thirds of an acre just outside town.

Whitfield wasn't home, so John and I didn't venture beyond the imposing bamboo fence that marks the perimeter of Fort Reagan. At the gate, John pointed to an ankle-height nylon tripwire connected to a car horn mounted on a twelve-volt battery. Donald Whitfield doesn't like unannounced visitors. Nearby, a huge, fading Confederate battle flag tacked over the front door of his mobile home flopped in the wind. We left a note in Whitfield's mailbox, saying I wanted to talk to him and would come back the next afternoon. When I did, I found a sweat-soaked Whitfield mowing the grass around a small vegetable patch at the rear of the mobile home. He struck me as a Walker Evans photograph come to life: lean, deep-eyed, and hungry. "Just call me Whit," he said with a wide grin.

We took refuge from the Alabama sun in the shade of a nearby oak tree. As we swilled iced-down Sprite, Whit talked about his 1969 tour as a machinegunner with the Third Brigade, Eighty-second Airborne Division on the western approaches to Saigon. Later, he proudly showed me Fort Reagan's "guard tower," a tiny shack perched atop a power pole he had gotten somewhere, and a twelve-foot-deep tornado tunnel pressed into use as a refrigerator. At the bottom was a single item: a jar of Kraft salad dressing that Whit raised and lowered with a thick string.

Whit's electric power and telephone service had been cut off for nonpayment after he lost his job as an auto mechanic. To get water for drinking and bathing, he had rigged up a gutter to tap runoff from the tin roof of his garage, where he planned to spend the winter. Inside were engine parts and tools arranged so neatly they might have been in a stockroom. Whit saw me glance at a fifty-five-gallon drum that had been converted into a heater. "I'll put a cot next to it," he said. "I'm gonna make it, Bubba."

Whit's family was living in a public housing project in Greensboro, Alabama—"the kind of place where you was lucky to have three shirts and two pairs of pants"—when he was drafted in September 1968. He had been out of high school for five months. "My family was always poor, very poor," he told me. "To make it worse, my father lost all sense of responsibility when I was three years old and ran off to Mobile. Like a lot of other men, he was crazy about women, I guess. He left my mama to raise five boys and seven girls."

I'm gonna be honest with you. I had heard some about Vietnam in 1968, but I was a poor fellow and I didn't keep up with it. I was working at a Standard Oil station making eight dollars a day. I pumped gas and tinkered a little with cars. I had a girl I saw every now and then, but I still spent most of my time with a car. When I got my letter from the draft lady, I appealed it on the reason it was just me and my sister at home. We were a poor family and they needed me at home, but it did no good. Once I got to Vietnam, my mother got my check; I didn't keep but ten or twenty dollars. I don't think she would have made it if I hadn't done that.

I went off to Fort Benning for basic training in the wintertime and almost froze to death. After that I went to advanced training at Fort McClellan to be a infantryman, 11B40. I knew a month before I graduated from AIT that I was going to Vietnam. Just about everybody was going to Vietnam, but once I got there, I never saw anybody that I went through basic and AIT with. That's what made it so bad over there: I didn't know nobody, not a soul.

Nobody at Fort McClellan told us much about Vietnam, except how to look for booby traps and that sort of thing. I guess they wanted us to find out for ourselves. Most of the DIs was E-5s and E-6s and they tried to scare us about some of the conditions over there. I reckon that was trying to make us mean as hell. I wish the drill sergeants had been a little easier, Bubba. They brainwashed us so much about that gonorrhea, I never touched a single Vietnamese woman.

I went over on a commercial 707 from Travis Air Force Base. While I was in the terminal, I noticed that most of the guys didn't talk very much. We just waited and kept the place clean until we heard our name called to get on the airplane. It's funny, we didn't never say, "Hey, man, we gonna get over there and kill 'em." I guess we mostly thought about home. When a airplane came in from Vietnam, I'd see a bunch of guys come off, all dirty and ragged, and boy, that would scare me. Good God, I got scared when I saw what they looked like.

My airplane landed at Tan Son Nhut air base and it must have been 115 degrees when I walked down that ramp. The first night in Vietnam was rough. It rained. I was in one of them little ol' hootches and crying, twelve thousand miles from home and didn't know a damn soul. The next day, everybody had to stand in a line—shit, further than that house up yonder—to find out what unit we was going to. When they called your name, you might as well get ready to get shipped out.

I wasn't a paratrooper, but I got assigned to the Eighty-second Airborne at Cu Chi anyway. I got orientated there, got my rucksack, grenades, canteens, boots; I stayed there about a day. I flew out to the damn field in a Huey and went to a squad with two blacks in it. I remember one of 'em was a dude from Birmingham named Scales. Most of the guys in the squad was eighteen or nineteen years old; I was twenty, but of course I was still like a damn kid. Since I was from Alabama, they nicknamed me that. Most of the guys turned out to be from Alabama and Tennessee. We got mortared that first night, and I cried like a dog again.

I hadn't been there very long before one of the sergeants handed me a M-60 machine gun. I had probably shot a hundred rounds from one in basic training, but I learned how to use that 60 and it kept me alive, Bubba. That gun could put out more firepower than a damn squad, and I always made sure I had a lot of tracers in the belts to help me close in on a target. I carried all twenty-five pounds of that M-60 on my shoulder for six months.

My company did a lot of patrolling. We got the roughest damn deal. Shit, I thought I was going to get killed every night. I was terrified the whole time. We'd get intelligence reports about Viet Cong in the area and have to go out to find 'em. Even if we could sneak up on the sons of bitches, it was still scary. I can look back now and how some of us lived through it is beyond me. We'd get to a village and lob some M-79s in and wait for the sons of bitches to come out and you're gonna open up and blow 'em away. People know where they're going in the daytime, but at night it's different. Like if night fell right now, you couldn't make your way through those oak trees over yonder. Same way in Vietnam. We didn't know what was out there at night, only that somewhere, somebody was going to try to kill us.

I remember we set up a ambush one night outside a village near Cu Chi. I remember it because we killed a water buffalo there that day and an old *papasan* with a gray beard came running over to us, yelling and crying. I thought something was up right there. Five of us set up in some grass about twenty yards from where the Viet Cong and NVA was meeting in a hootch. They couldn't see us, thank God, when we started shooting. We just opened up and one or two of 'em come flying out and started shooting back. It must have lasted fifteen or twenty minutes, but one of 'em still got away.

I'm gonna tell you, Bubba, it's hard to kill a human being. First you got to see him, then you got to try to hit him. It's harder than you think it is. I had four hundred rounds for my 60 that night. I got one Cong for sure. I was glad to kill the son of a bitch then, but if you ask me to reflect now . . . Well, they thought they was right and I thought I was right. They was representing Communism and I was representing America. We was fighting for freedom, fighting to retain something, and those people was going to retain nothing. Me and my buddies, we'd have destroyed the whole country if they'd let us. Now it bothers me a little bit, but I was doing what the government told me to do. It bothers me because I know we killed some innocent civilian people. If you like it, you don't mind it, especially if you have the kind of firepower I did. Most guys didn't talk much about killing, maybe because we spent most of our time running the Cong and NVA out of villages and trying to keep 'em away from Saigon. I come through villages where heads, arms, and legs had been severed from bodies. I saw women all cut up. Communism is brutal. I done seen it, Bubba.

We'd go out in helicopters fifteen or twenty miles from Cu Chi and jump off, sometimes in muddy water that came up to our waists. If we had ever got in a firefight in water, I do believe all of us would have been killed or wounded. The way it turned out, I got my Purple Heart when a booby trap blew up. Some of us had just jumped off a chopper and was starting to make some sweeps when a new sergeant—that was his first day and his last day in the field—told me to set up a machine-gun position. Well, anytime you go into a place where you've never been, you come out the same damn way. But he didn't. While me and three of my buddies was setting up the 60, he took three or four steps in a direction he'd never been in and set off a goddamn loud booby trap. Metal hit him everywhere and he started hollering. A few pieces hit me in my nose, ear, and leg—look real close and you'll see a cut place on my nose.

I hollered, "Medic! Medic!"

I was in pain. I hollered like a dog, blood running out of my nose. I thought I was going to die. Goddamn, I thought I was dying. Blood came out for a long time. I wasn't in real bad a shape, so I just walked around, jittery and nervous, until the medevac chopper got to us. The sergeant was a mess. The medics cut all his clothes off on the chopper and pumped him full of morphine. Then one of 'em took some gauze and wiped the blood off me.

I spent two weeks in the Third Field Hospital in Saigon, but I went back to my unit too damn quick, in my opinion. The truth is, I didn't want to go back; there's no point in lying about it. After you see what I did, you're scared. That shit was real. Anybody who hasn't been there just don't know, Bubba. My wounds wasn't healing very good, so the captain gave me a couple of days off when I got back to Cu Chi. And then it was right back to doing the same damn thing, search and destroy. We was still pulling missions all the time, trying to keep the Communists off balance.

I had to go on another night ambush. This time, a Viet Cong slipped through our trip flares and Claymores and liked to have killed us. If it hadn't been for the radioman, he would have. We had made a circle off a trail in some bushes. The radioman was the only one awake and he heard some noise. He was reaching down to get his rifle when he saw the Cong. A black guy was sleeping there and that Cong could have killed him, but he didn't. While the Cong was looking at the black guy, the radioman shot that VC three times in the right side. The Cong laid there and moaned "Ahhhh, ahhhh" for what must've been five minutes. I was so damn scared, and then we got attacked—the big stuff, mortars and rockets. The bullets was coming hard. I just knew we was going to get overrun that night. I was so scared, I hoped somebody would go ahead and kill me and get it over with.

Everything is fate or luck in a war zone, Bubba. You may walk point and not get shit and you might walk point and get blown away. I was walking point along a rice paddy dike when the last guy in line set off a booby trap. A few minutes later, I stepped on a mine and it didn't go off. I was walking across some sand when I heard a click. Maybe it didn't go off because it was the monsoon season and the mine was wet. That's all I can figure. The demolition team came in and blew it up. That son of a bitch would have split me up. I would have been blew slap to—they'd have come picked me up in a body bag.

I said to myself, "Good Lord, it wasn't my time. It wasn't time for me to die."

I dreaded the booby traps, but the mortars was the ones that kept me off balance. They kept hounding me, and it just bothered me because there was nothing I could do about it. Every time we was in the open, we dug a hole before we set down.

We worked the Mekong Delta a lot, which meant our feet hardly ever left the water. All of us got ringworm, especially those boys from the North. They just couldn't handle it like us boys from the South; we was used to it. Their feet would look like pieces of raw meat. When we got out of the water, we'd be stung by them goddamn ants. For some reason, they'd sting me right around the neck. I'd throw everything I had down to get them son of a bitches off me. That's when we found a lot of them old bodies that somebody had killed. You didn't know how many people you killed because they dragged 'em off. The Communists just do not want a body count. And then there was the snakes. Me and my buddy liked to get bit one day by a bamboo viper. It came right between our rucksacks while we was resting. I got my machete and killed that son of a bitch. If that snake would have bit me, it would have killed my ass dead. You had shit everywhere that could kill you. You didn't know what was out there, what with the mosquitoes trying to bite us and the leeches. Boy, I want to tell you it's a damn wonder we are alive. I bless the Good Lord—somebody was looking after me.

When my company came out of the bush to rest and refit, we'd go to Yellowstone National Park. That's what we called Cu Chi. We might have a movie and that was about it. I did go to the USO a couple of times, but I was strictly military when I went to town. I didn't mess with those women. And we didn't have no trouble with the blacks. I saw movies that said we done the blacks wrong, but it wasn't like that where I was. Let's put it like this: they make pretty good soldiers, but they're not what we are. White Americans, can't nobody whip our ass. We're the baddest son of a bitches on the face of this earth. You can take a hundred Russians and twenty-five Americans, and we'll whip their ass. I'll tell you what I hated most about going back to Cu Chi or a firebase: the shit detail. Damn, one day I had just got a haircut and was all cleaned up, and then the first sergeant, he was black, he put me on the shit detail. I had to mix it with diesel fuel and burn it.

I felt sorry for the Vietnamese people. Damn, the Cong was killin' 'em. They didn't eat much but rice and they was poverty-stricken and didn't mess with nobody. I said I was going to kick them goddamn Communists' ass to keep 'em off these civilian people. They worked so hard and had nothing to show for it except a black shirt and pants, some flip-flops, and a straw hat. But you know, they must be some of the strongest people in the world. I tell you, I was strong, but I stopped one of those *mamasans* one day and picked up her shoulder pole and I couldn't walk with it. I noticed there wasn't many dogs and cats over there. They eat 'em. And rats big as possums. I done seen it, Bubba. It's a damn shame.

I came home early when President Nixon started pulling troops out in 1969. You had to have seven months in-country to go home early. I made it by twenty days. If I'd only been there only six months, I'd have been sent to another unit. When I got back to Greensboro, my mother wanted me to go to church in my uniform and the preacher asked me to stand up. After the service, only one person, the man who ran the Western Auto store, came up to me and said thank you. Only one person—and I didn't even like him. You know, I didn't realize then that people thought we was over there killing kids. We killed the people who tried to kill us. The people back here didn't appreciate what we was trying to accomplish in Vietnam.

I still had some time left in the army after I got back, so I got assigned to help train the Rangers at Fort Benning. I'd been thinking about staying in because I was a sergeant by that time, but it was the blacks that changed my mind. Half the time, the blacks wouldn't get off the trucks for exercises. They didn't like to do police calls, but in the food line they all rushed forward. I couldn't stand the lack of discipline, so I got out of the army in 1970 and went back to pumping gas in Greensboro for eight dollars a day. I even went back to the same damn housing project to live. I'd read stories about veterans going back to the same job they had before going in the service, because they didn't know what else to do. I stayed at the gas station for about a year, until the man who ran it went out of business because people wouldn't pay him. Then I went on down to Demopolis and worked for a couple of years as an auto mechanic.

I like fast-assed cars. It's my way of getting kicks, the acceleration and the power. But I had a wreck about a year and a half ago when a man ran a stop sign and almost totalled my car. It scared me. I got real slow at work. I couldn't stand to be around noise after the wreck. Finally, I sued the man and his insurance company for twenty-five thousand dollars. When I went to court four months ago, I wore my army uniform with every goddamned ribbon on it and I acted as my own lawyer. I don't trust lawyers, see. That other lawyer, he didn't talk loud to me. Nothing has been settled yet, but I still hope to get something out of it.

Somebody would be abrasive to me at work and I'd be abrasive to him. I couldn't take orders from anybody but myself, so I walked away from my job. That's when the post-traumatic stress developed. I've been so fearful of society since then. You can see I'm big into bamboo. The fence around this place is Perry County bamboo, the biggest bamboo. I wish it was twice as big for protection. I'll tell you this: a Vietnam veteran ain't shit in this country. I'm living off a $500 refund check from the IRS and $450 in back money that I got from the VA when it gave me ten percent PTSD. I get $71 a month from the VA. I probably got the only fort in the United States like this, and I really got post-traumatic stress disorder. I pick up aluminum cans to make a few dollars. You get fifty cents a pound and there is twenty-four cans in a pound. I figure it costs me $6 a day to live. You wanna know what I lived off of last year? Crackers and biscuits.

I owe the bank about $2,000. I just lost my phone and my power's been cut off. I borrowed some money on my car, so I guess they can take the car and the place. I bought this place in 1980 while I was still working in Greensboro, driving fifty miles a day. I paid $315 a month for it and got down to eight payments left. I have a shotgun and a .22 rifle in the trailer, but it really ain't the firepower, it's the principle. Where would I go to live if they march me off this property, Bubba? To the woods?

I didn't drink whiskey before I went in the army. I had to move out of the housing project in Greensboro because I was making more than $90 a month. Too much money to stay there, so I moved in with a guy in Eutaw and he got me to drinking whiskey. I started smoking marijuana in 1981 because it helps calm my stomach and makes me creative. It picks me up. I research ants—believe it or not, there's ants that don't even sting. I'm into anything you can imagine on weed. I tried growing some, but a man down the road thought I killed his dog and he came down here and took some pictures of my plants. A narcotics man from Tuscaloosa and the chief of police drove right in here. They got out and pulled their badges and made a big deal of it. I'd never tried to hide the weed. After they went through the preliminaries and all this kind of shit and I showed them where all the plants was and they read me my rights, they didn't arrest me. About two months later they called me to come up there to Tuscaloosa to get fin- gerprinted. I got to talking to one of 'em and said, "Ain't it kind of funny that y'all come out there and bust a fucking Vietnam veteran for smoking weed?" And then he got to feeling sorry about it and told me to go see a judge. I'm gonna have that cleaned from my record before I die. That hurts my feelings to this day.

I fly the Rebel flag because this is the South, Bubba. The American flag represents the whole fifty states. That flag represents the southern part. I'm a Confederate, I'm a southerner. We're losing the fucking battle down here right now, Bubba. This right here is Nicaragua. The fucking Com- munists—we got so many Communists in this town. We just had one commissioner go to Nicaragua. He's a black, see. I don't go up there to the social services office and ask for no food stamps or nothing. I just don't want to ask. We Americans have too much pride, I guess. Aw, I could go up there and get food stamps and get the unemployment and the fucking check, but I'd have to answer questions. I think the people that owe me are the Veterans Administration and the man that damaged me. That's the only ones I'm asking money from.

I like to died last winter from the medication I was on. It was freezing, nineteen or twenty degrees. I was staying in my trailer all day in a little bitty room with a electric blanket that my sister gave me and a little electric heater that I cut wide on. This man right up here that died about six months ago went and cut a pine tree for me just to give me some wood. I've had more of my friends die in the last year or two, but my mother was the one who set me back, boy. I ain't over my mama yet. Me and my mama, we was close. I don't even go see her grave, it hurts me so bad. I don't want my brothers and sisters to help me. They do a little bit, but they ought to help me without asking.

Noises bother me at night. I like to set up. Ever since they cut my outside light off, I get out in my chair here. I saw twenty-seven meteors last night from nine-thirty to eleven o'clock. Lord, I have nightmares and a lot of 'em are about Vietnam. I go back to some of the villages and the night patrols we was on. I feel cheated about Vietnam, I sure do. Political restrictions—we won every goddamned battle we was in, but didn't win the whole goddam little country. It took eight years to mine a fucking harbor? It's a fucking shame! We was the sons of bitches who went over there and got into combat. No person who went into combat was the same. Before I die, the Democratic-controlled Congress of this country— and I blame it on 'em—they gonna goddamn apologize to the Vietnam veterans. All I want 'em to do is come forward and say they're sorry for not letting us win the war. I want it public. They sold us out in Vietnam, Bubba. We fought a war for ten years that we could have won in less than a year.

Paul L. Lieberman

McLean, Virginia

Army quartermaster officer,

1969–70

●

A cold wind toyed with the last leaves of autumn as I pulled into the driveway of Paul Lieberman's brick house in McLean, an upscale Virginia suburb of Washington, D.C. Paul was as friendly in person as he was on the telephone. "Come in," he said as he opened the front door, "we have a lot to talk about."

A man of trim build, his shock of black hair speckled with gray, Paul was wearing faded jeans and a red and blue western-style shirt with imitation pearl inlays in the buttons. He suggested that we go down to the basement family room to talk.

Paul went to the war in 1969, the year American troop strength peaked at 543,000 and then began to recede as the Nixon administration undertook the nation's long, agonizing withdrawal from Vietnam. By the time Paul arrived in-country as a quartermaster officer, the logistical apparatus supporting U.S. troops had spawned bases as large as medium-sized cities. The base Paul came to know, Long Binh, an installation that sprawled over twenty-five square miles north of Saigon, had a population of 43,000.

Paul grew up in Orlando, Florida, the son of a lay rabbi who worked in the convention/travel business; it was the same occupation that Paul himself would eventually drift into. In 1966, however, he was living in Leesburg, Florida, and attending Lake Sumter Junior College when he got a telephone call from the Lake County draft board. "The woman on the phone told me my name was second on the list," Paul told me as he took a drag on a cigarette. "I had graduated from high school in 1962, so my four-year deferment was almost up. Suddenly, I was facing a big change in my life."

When he went to the campus later that day, he talked to a woman army officer who was giving entrance tests for a new two-year ROTC program. Paul told her about his situation and she told him about ROTC. If he was accepted, he would have to go to ROTC summer camp that year.

"Naturally, I was thinking hard about the draft," he said. "During the noon hour, I went down to a little bar a couple of blocks away and had a liquid lunch. It was there that I decided to take the ROTC test. I took it under the influence of three Scotch-and-waters. I don't remember a single question, but I made a perfect score."

I never took ROTC very seriously because I didn't think anything was going to happen to me, not even when an instructor at Fort Bragg said that summer, "Half of you are going to Vietnam and half of you won't come back." I never let myself believe that.

In the fall of 1966, I transferred to the University of Florida for my last two years of college. I graduated in May of 1968 with a bachelor's degree in advertising and a commission as a second lieutenant. My orders for active duty said I had to go to the quartermaster school at Fort Lee, Virginia, and I'll admit I started to worry a bit then.

After quartermaster basic, the army in all its wisdom decided to put me in Graves Registration. For six weeks, I learned how to identify dead soldiers through their fingerprints and their dental records. I saw all the horror movies about death. The instructors threw death at us left and right. Slide shows were filled with the wreckage of automobiles and people. The major in charge of the course even brought in photos that he had taken of the dead in Vietnam—dead Vietnamese, dead Americans, every imaginable form of man-made death.

One day, my class went up to the Medical College of Virginia in Richmond to witness an autopsy. When we walked into the autopsy room, the first thing we saw was a body on a table. The man had fallen down a flight of stairs while running from the police. The pathologists were getting ready to saw the top of his head off so they could remove his brain. I couldn't stand to look at it. I turned my eyes toward a corner of the room, and there was the body of a newborn baby on another table. With Diane pregnant with our first daughter at the time, something just hit me and I walked out of that room.

One of my classmates followed me. "Paul," he said, "you've got to come back in."

"I'm not getting near that room again," I told him. "Forget it. There's nothing you can do that's going to force me back in there."

I had never seen a dead person before. The only funeral I'd ever been to was that of a next-door neighbor, and it was a closed-casket service. I heard later that more bodies were brought into the autopsy room and that one of them was a guy who had drowned. One of my classmates said the pathologists demonstrated how to cut the fingertips off a body and roll the skin around your own finger to make fingerprints. He said that's how it was done with "floaters."

The next week, we had to go up to the morgue at an air force base at Dover, Delaware, and that's where Vietnam came home to us. The bodies of East Coast soldiers who had been killed in the war were brought to Dover. We walked into a small one-story brick building. From the outside, nobody could tell what it was, but inside was a room that held about three hundred aluminum coffins. Somebody on the mortuary staff remarked that it was a slow day. We were told to stand in the middle of the room. The coffins were stacked up alongside the walls. And right there in the middle of the room, a mortician wearing a spotless white lab coat was standing over a body on a table. The body was encased in plastic that looked something like Saran Wrap.

One of my classmates had told me he wanted to be a mortician. He was standing behind me. I turned around and whispered, "Darrell, I don't know if I can handle this." When the mortician started to slowly unwrap the body, Darrell put both hands on my shoulders and said, "You're going to make it." I wasn't so sure. When the body was fully unwrapped, I could see it was an eighteen-year-old kid. He'd been shot through one of his eyes.

The mortician standing over the kid had a cigarette in his mouth. I became obsessed with the ash—it kept getting longer and longer, so long I was sure it was going to fall into the hole in the kid's head. I couldn't take my eyes off that trembling ash. Nothing else in the room seemed to have any importance except what was going to happen to the ash. Finally, the mortician threw the cigarette to the floor just before the ash fell; he hardly glanced away from what he was doing. He ground out the butt with his shoe and went on with his business.

The major in charge of our class was a stocky, gentle man who constantly impressed on us respect for the dead. He didn't like the civilian morticians. He told us they were overpaid at forty-five to fifty thousand dollars a year, and just as bad, in his opinion, waddled around like penguins in their little white coats. But for the morticians, it was all just a job. They had to figure out how to make the body of the eighteen-year-old kid viewable. Their attitude was, "What can we do for him before we send him home to mom and dad?" They talked about the kind of patch they could put on his forehead and about all the different mortician's tools—I guess that's what they were called—that they used.

While they worked on the boy, we moved to another room to see the body of a guy who went down in a helicopter. The body was simply burned to a black crisp and seemed to have shrunk. The man must have tried to put his head down and hold on to his knees as the chopper went down. All I remember is that it looked like a part of a body, and it was wrapped in plastic, too. The way the morticians embalmed it was to throw some kind of powder on it and wrap it in a white sheet.

After that, we went to still another room to see where the bodies were dressed. This room had the body of a black sailor who had tripped on a ship and cracked his skull. The morticians who worked here showed us how they put him in his navy whites. They did it by splitting the clothing up the back. Then they stapled his mouth together.

All of this must have taken half a day. Our last stop was the casket room, where we saw the eighteen-year-old kid again. There was no evidence that he had been shot, or that anything violent had happened to him—the morticians were very good. Then we were shown what they did with unviewable bodies. A board was put over them in the coffin, and on top of it was laid the man's uniform.

In a very real way, I was scared and uncomfortable that day, but there was also something so fascinating about the whole assembly-line process of making death presentable that I couldn't take my eyes off it. None of us talked about what we had seen during the bus ride back to Fort Lee. There was a lot of joking about the elections and everything else that was going on in the country, but no talk about death.

During quartermaster basic, we all had a chance to talk to the major about our assignments. I certainly wanted to talk to him about mine. When my time came, I walked into his office and said, "Why did you put me in Graves Registration? What is it in my background?"

"You've got a degree in advertising and the army didn't know where else to put you," he said. "You're not going to get out of it." He started telling me some war stories. In one of them, he was in a foxhole in Vietnam with his buddy during a firefight, and his buddy got blown away. "I got sick," he said. "I threw up all over the foxhole, but I survived it. And you will, too. But I'll tell you a secret: if you really don't want to do it, you don't have to, but you're going to have to go through this class. When you get to your next assignment, try to refuse it if you're put in Graves Registration. Chances are, you won't be assigned to it."

I took his advice and made up my mind to never serve in Graves

Registration. I would refuse to do it. I made it through the class, but to this day I still have an occasional nightmare about that kid on the table. I'll wake up and see that body wrapped in plastic with only the head sticking out, a bullet hole in it.

I think I lost a lot of my fear of death that day in Dover, but I also told myself that if I went to Vietnam, I was not coming back in an aluminum box. "If this is what death is in the army," I remember thinking, "I don't want to have anything to do with it."

And I didn't. I drew an assignment to Oakland Army Base, where I spent a year processing soldiers out of the service. It was a kind of warehouse operation, but rather interesting because of its enormous contrasts. When I went to work, usually at night, I'd walk in the front door where the guys were being processed to go to Vietnam. Then I'd saunter down to a big bay to see those who were coming back.

The kids going over were wearing fresh uniforms. They were innocent, nervous, and for the most part ready to go. The ones coming back after a year or two, or whatever time they'd spent in Vietnam—there wasn't a kid among them. These were grown men. It was among them that I saw my first thousand-yard stare. Some just sat in the bay and looked straight ahead, maybe finding it hard to believe that they were finally back in the states. We'd get two or three planeloads from Vietnam every night. Of course, there was a lot of "hurry up and wait," but we gave every returning soldier a ticket for a steak dinner to help make the process easier. It took about three hours to get a man paid and processed out of the army.

I delivered a standard speech every time a planeload came in. "Now, remember," I'd say. "You're going to be walking out of here with a lot of money. The cabbies know you're carrying a lot of money. A lot of times they'll roll you for it, so be careful. If you're smart, you'll take a bus to the airport. It's a very antiwar atmosphere out there in San Francisco. You're going to be spit at and you're going to be called names."

I used to sit and talk with the guys who'd come back. I'll bet I heard a hundred thousand different stories about Vietnam. It struck me as a highly individualized war, but one I still didn't believe I would ever see. When I signed in for duty at Oakland, some of the administrative people there said they were short-handed. That was good news to me. "The army doesn't send people who work here," they said. "You're safe."

My daughter Sara was born on March 7, 1969, and I took a week off to stay with Diane and her at our little rented house in Alameda. On my first morning back at work at the army base, one of my co-workers said, "Paul, you've got a letter at the post office." That really worried me because my mail didn't come through the army post office there. Sure enough, when I opened the envelope, I had orders for Vietnam. I was going in August. From March to August, I had a lot of time to sit there in Oakland and ponder my future. I really wish I had gotten orders in March to walk right onto a plane and get started on my year.

I took thirty days of leave at home before going over. It was a pleasant time; Diane and I took a cruise down to the Bahamas, and my family, which had gathered in Fort Myers, threw a birthday party for me when we got back. Later, Diane and I went up to Birmingham for a couple of days to find an apartment for her and Sara to live in while I was in Vietnam.

We stayed at my sister's house in Fort Myers during my leave. On the morning of August 11, my brother Eddie was supposed to drive me to the airport to catch a flight to Miami. From there, I was booked on a flight to San Francisco. My alarm didn't go off. I opened my eyes at seven a.m. and the flight was scheduled to leave thirty minutes later. In a state of sheer panic, I shaved and put on my dress greens in all of ten minutes. Then I saw Sara in my sister's guest bedroom. She was five months old, sleeping in a crib near the door. I picked up her to say goodbye and I don't care what people say, but that kid at that moment knew something big was happening. Our minds connected. I knew my life was changing and she knew her life was changing.

She looked at me and said, "Daddy." Five months old and she said "Daddy" for the first time that morning. I thought I was going to be strong, but it was all too much. I handed Sara to Diane, kissed my wife goodbye and walked out the door. In the car, I broke down and cried as we pulled away from the house.

Eddie got me to the airport in time. I remember telling him as I got out of the car, "If anything happens to me, take care of Sara and Diane." That's what they do in the movies, isn't it? I was feeling as emotionally empty as I've ever been in my life. I felt I was saying good-bye to everything that I had ever loved.

With two hours to kill at the Miami airport, I noticed that Air Canada had a reservations counter there. I spent the whole two hours walking back and forth in front of that counter. I had a change of clothes in my carry-on bag. A flight would soon be leaving for Montreal. I thought, "I'm going to Vietnam to be in a war. Do I go up and buy a ticket to Montreal and get out of this?" Finally, I told myself not to do it, that Vietnam was the major event in the life of my generation and I ought to go see what it was all about. I boarded the flight to San Francisco and never reconsidered my decision.

The flight to Vietnam left from Travis Air Force Base at three o'clock in the morning. Even though I slept most of the way, I do remember thinking that a jet airplane with stewardesses and steak dinners was a hell of a way to go to war. When I got to the Ninetieth Replacement Battalion at Bien Hoa, I spotted a guy I had served with at Oakland. "For God's sake," I told him, "get me a good assignment."

That first night in Vietnam, we took twenty-six rockets on the perimeter. I was sound asleep when I suddenly woke up to the sound of *boom! boom! boom!* I rolled off my bunk and pulled my mattress over me and asked God to take care of me. Welcome to Vietnam with twenty-six rockets. After three days of hanging around the Ninetieth, I got assigned to a supply and service detachment of the Saigon Support Command in Vung Tau, down on the coast of the South China Sea. Not a bad deal, I thought—Vung Tau was the in-country R&R center for the Americans, the South Vietnamese, and, some people swore, the North Vietnamese, too.

One of the administrative officers at the Ninetieth told me I was going to be the Class One officer at Vung Tau. "What's a Class One?" I said. I couldn't even remember what the term meant. "You're going to be in charge of distributing food from a warehouse," he said. "At least it's not Graves Registration," I told him. "I can handle that." The army put me in charge of four warehouses. One of them was filled with beer. I had no idea of what I was supposed to be doing, but I learned that to get along in Vietnam, I had to barter. Pretty soon I was trading steaks and beer for helicopter rides to different places in the Vung Tau area.

I hadn't been in Vung Tau very long before an officer I roomed with told the colonel that I'd been trained in Graves Registration. The colonel called me in. "All right, Lieberman," he said, "you're going to be my Graves Registration officer."

"Well, sir," I replied, "I work with food. I'm around food all the time and I have to go into the reefers and move stuff around. You're going to put me with dead people?" He thought about that for a few moments. "OK, all you'll have to do is sign your name on the papers. You don't actually have to get involved in it." Six weeks later, a sergeant who worked for me said an Australian had been killed at Can Tho, down in the Mekong Delta, and his body had been brought to the hospital at Vung Tau for identification. "I need an officer to come over and make the identification," the sergeant said. I went over to the hospital, sweating bullets the whole time. The Australian was in a body bag that had been placed on a table. It was the first body bag I'd seen in Vietnam. Two of his buddies were already there. I got up as much courage as I could, walked up to the table, and unzipped the body bag.

One of the Aussies said, "Yeah, that's his hand." "How do you know?" I asked him. "That's his ring on his finger," the man said. That was enough identification for me. My sergeant said he would get one of the doctors at the hospital to sign the papers. I reminded him in no uncertain terms that he had told me no other officers were available to sign them. "Sir," he said, "I just wanted to see if you'd come over and do it. You're my officer-in-charge and I wanted you to make the identification just to see if you had the balls to do it." I never made any identifications after that.

Later, my outfit moved up to Phu Bai, near Hue City. I got out of the food business there when a new colonel came up from Long Binh to inspect my warehouses. As luck would have it, he spotted some sacks of flour that had been ruined by rats. "Lieberman," he said, "I want you on the next plane to Long Binh." I was crushed—I had been relieved from my job. It took one of my enlisted men to put it in perspective. "What are they going to do to you, Lieutenant?" he said. "Send you to Vietnam?"

The colonel later called me into his office at Long Binh and apologized for what he had done. "I'm sorry I had to do it that way," he said. "But you should never have been there in the first place. I see you have a degree in advertising. I'm about to lose my information officer, and I want you in his job." He was very candid about what he wanted: his name in headlines. He was bucking for general. And that's what I did for the eight months I had left in Vietnam.

It was an easy job, maybe because it was unauthorized. I even had to go on R&R during an inspector general's visit so he wouldn't know I was at Long Binh. I wrote press releases and was responsible for several reports that were due periodically. The job also gave some opportunities to travel around Vietnam and do a few exotic things, like go up in Cobra helicopters. And I guess I did my part to get the colonel promoted to general.

Long Binh was a huge place in 1969, supposedly the largest army base in the world at the time. It even had swimming pools. It was also very boring. Some of us would go looking for new officers' clubs just to mark time, or maybe smoke dope. Although killing was going on all around us, our little twenty-five-square-mile world seemed almost unreal. I started to see the war as such a waste of lives and resources. Once, I had to do a Report of Survey on a petroleum laboratory that burned up when a rocket hit it. The office I was writing the report for kept sending it back for more information. Finally I said to hell with it and threw all the papers in a trash can. I never heard a word about it.

When I came home, I went through Oakland Army Base, the place where I had spent so many nights, and got out of the army. Diane and my family were in San Francisco for a convention, so we had a reunion right there during the breakfast hour at the St. Francis Hotel.

My mother was bursting with pride that I had made it back all right. "This is my son, who just got back from Vietnam," she said to one of the Japanese-American elevator operators. "Yes," said the woman. "My son came back in a box." Nobody spoke another word until we got out of the elevator.

I had written seventy-eight letters to prospective employers while I was in Vietnam. I got positive responses from two of them, Sears and Rich's Department Stores in Atlanta. Sears wanted to send me to Wyoming. Rich's wanted me in Atlanta, and that's where Diane and I wanted to be, too. But I sensed that something wasn't quite the same in me after I got back to the states. Two weeks after my return, one of Diane's uncles invited us to a party. One of his golfing partners started quizzing me about my feelings toward the war, and I said it was the most ridiculous thing I had ever seen. "All that's coming out of it is dead young Americans in body bags," I said. "We've got millions of dead Vietnamese over there. The whole thing is a waste." When he said he watched television and knew what was going on over there, I went over the table for his throat. A doctor at the party had to calm me down.

I worked at Rich's for a year. My job was so boring I couldn't stand it. Other jobs didn't work out much better. Day by day, I was withdrawing further into myself. Finally, Diane had to look for work. She had never worked a day in her life, but she landed a job with an actuarial firm that paid her enough for us to make it.

For the next seven years, my seven years of bad luck, as I call them, I was a dropout. I became so paranoid that I would look right and left before checking our mailbox. Nothing made sense to me anymore. It seemed as if everything I had been taught about patriotism, the family, the good of America, was collapsing in front of my eyes. And let me tell you, I had been a believer.

Diane and I had another daughter, Amber, in 1971. Don't ask me why I brought another kid into the world. Maybe it had something to do with a feeling that Sara wasn't mine. I felt like I had lost her while I was in Vietnam. She had become Diane's daughter, so to speak, so we had Amber—a kid for me. Diane probably should have given up on me during the seven years of bad luck because I stayed so much in my own little corner. I wasn't giving much of anything to her or the kids. But Diane saw something in me, enough worth to see me through the ordeal, and in that I was luckier than a lot of other vets.

I had come to think that Vietnam twisted my values. I didn't see any honor in the war: the whole thing just came down to dead and screwed-up young men. If I tried to talk about the war, people told me to forget it. They didn't want to hear anything about Vietnam. My thoughts kept going back to that morgue in Dover, Delaware. I felt a lot of guilt, personal guilt, for the war itself. It was as if I had become responsible for it all. I even started to believe that I was a babykiller because I hadn't had the moral courage to stand up and say "Enough!"

I came out of my shell very slowly. I started working again when Amber turned six and entered grade school. I think being around my kids so much made a big difference in my attitude toward the world; kids are open and honest, and I felt refreshed by their innocence. At first, I took a night job with an air freight company in Atlanta—I wanted to work at night because I didn't feel I was ready to face the daytime world. Later, as I gained more confidence, I enrolled at Georgia State University to work on a degree in hotel management. I went to my classes and then worked the graveyard shift at the air freight firm, everything still at night. I finally went back to the daytime world in a job at Ted Turner's television station, just before he started the Cable News Network. In the four years I was there, I worked my way up from the lowest-paying job at the station to a pretty decent job in the traffic department.

Diane and I came to the Washington area in 1985 when she had a chance to take an actuarial job at three times her salary in Atlanta. I figured I owed her a lot, so I quit my job at Turner Broadcasting and we moved up here.

We both went down to the Wall on a trip up here before we decided to make the move from Atlanta. I stood in front of it for the longest time with Diane next to me, and I broke down completely. I let all my feelings about the war run through me. My first job here was with the Vietnam Veterans Leadership Program because I wanted to make things happen for vets and that was where they were happening. I helped open the Washington office and that became one of the most stressed-out jobs I've ever had, working with vets on the streets. It was like being in Oakland all over again—the thousand-yard stare, war stories.

After that I went to work as a travel planner. The sister of one of my friends in Atlanta was working here in an agency, and she helped me get started. I had to learn the business from the ground up, but she made it easier because she knew that I wanted to continue to work with Vietnam vets. When we first sat down to discuss the job, we talked almost all night about Vietnam and how we could arrange for vets to go back there.

Leo Spooner, Jr.

Oldsmar, Florida

Army reconnaissance platoon member,

1970

•

Morning fog still hid Tampa Bay in a white shroud when Leo Spooner and I drove the few blocks from his mother's house to R. E. Olds Park. "It's a quiet there," he said. It was eight a.m. on a Saturday morning, and Leo had four hours before he had to punch a time clock at nearby Tampa Bay Downs, where he works as a pari-mutuel betting clerk.

Leo served with the First Cavalry Division in III Corps from March 1970 until December of that year. He arrived in-country two months before Vietnamese and American troops stormed across the Cambodian border in May 1970 to clean out enemy supply bases and staging areas.

As we talked under a picnic shelter, a paunchy, graying man strolled up and asked if we knew the site of a World War II airfield. Leo thought it was a couple of miles away, toward Tampa. "I don't recognize much here any more," the man said, looking at the green shoreline across the bay as it emerged from the fog. I wondered later what he would have said if he had known that Leo and I were veterans of quite a different war.

Thin and athletic, with a neatly trimmed mustache, Leo told me he was nineteen and in his second year at St. Petersburg Junior College in April 1969, when the mail brought a letter from his draft board. He was to go to Jacksonville for a pre-induction physical.

"I was sure I had passed the physical, so I ran down to the air force recruiting office to see what I could work out there. The air force wanted four years of my life, so I just said, 'Oh, the heck with it. I'll take my chances with the draft and see what happens.' A week later, I got my draft notice."

Leo was living at home and working part time at a Sears store in Clearwater, selling shoes. Although he watched television news reports on the war, Vietnam was not something he thought about very much.

"It all seemed so far away from me, even though a close high school friend of mine, a pretty good guy, had been killed over there. Then, too, President Nixon was talking about pulling out of Vietnam. He was going to stop the war and get everybody out. I believed him."

I went up to Fort Benning for basic training with a lot of reservists and National Guardsmen. I learned a real lesson there. A lot of the draftees had committed some kind of criminal act and were offered a choice of going into the army or going to jail. All my life I had been brought up to believe it's a privilege to serve your country. It was hard for me to think the courts were in effect sentencing criminals to serve in the United States Army.

Well, I had a very good DI who didn't take any nonsense off these people or anybody else. He was a Mexican-American with a big round face; he looked just like Smokey the Bear. Sergeant Quantero was a very fair man who taught me a lot about getting along in the army. Right from the beginning, he told my platoon that if we ever got to the point where we wanted to run away or do something else that might cause trouble for us, we should come talk to him. I did that one night when he was charge-of-quarters. I was tired of training, of being cooped up and getting up at four o'clock in the morning seven days a week. I had hit my low point, I guess, and I went out and got drunk. When I got back to my barracks, I walked into Sergeant Quantero's room and told him I was thinking about going AWOL.

"It took a lot of courage to come talk to me instead of leaving," he said.

I really appreciated his willingness to listen to me. I finished basic at Fort Benning and went straight from there to AIT at Fort Polk, Louisiana. I remember seeing a huge sign at the entrance to Fort Polk: "Welcome to Tigerland, Training Ground for Combat Infantrymen for Vietnam." I still wasn't very worried about going because of all the talk about pulling out. On the other hand, I decided to buy as much time as I could—just in case. I learned that Fort Polk had a course for squad leaders before AIT got under way, so I volunteered for it. The course only lasted a week, but it ate up one more week of my two-year obligation.

I also figured I could buy even more time by signing up for the NCO School back at Fort Benning. It would make me a three-striper, a sergeant E-5, so I went back to Benning the day after I finished AIT at Fort Polk. In ten months, I went from an E-1 to an E-5. Sometimes I wonder how much good it did me. Would you believe that everybody in my training company at the NCO School except me and two other guys got orders for Germany? I was handed orders for Vietnam and thirty days of leave.

I came back to Oldsmar and tried to learn as much about Vietnam as I could by studying maps and encyclopedias. I also got together with some high school buddies and went to a few parties. Most of the talk I heard about Vietnam from the people I knew was along the lines of "Well, I'm glad it's you and not me"—not very comforting, you know. Most of my friends were in college or about to get married, so I'm sure they saw me as a kind of stand-in for them so far as Vietnam was concerned.

When my 707 made its approach to Bien Hoa airfield, I looked out the window and saw huge potholes all over the countryside. These holes were bomb craters and they weren't very far from the Ninetieth Replacement Battalion, where I stayed two or three days—God, the heat and stench were awful. I was ready to get out of there by the time I got orders to the 2/5th Cavalry at the First Cavalry Division.

"Boy, this is nice," I thought. "I can ride around in all those helicopters instead of walking everywhere." I must have been living in fantasyland. I didn't know the reality of the situation in Vietnam, didn't have any idea of what to expect. But I could see after a couple of days of learning how to look for booby traps and other hazards that it wasn't going to be like those war games we played in basic training and AIT.

I hopped a ride on a C-130 to a 2/5th Cav base somewhere out in III Corps. I was supposed to get my assignment to an outfit there. When I walked into the company clerk's tent to sign in, I got my real introduction to the Vietnam War.

"We've got incoming wounded," he said. "We need you down on the helicopter pad to help get some guys off the choppers."

I asked him where the wounded guys were coming from. "They're coming from the reconnaissance platoon," he said. "And that's where you're going." What great news. I hustled down to the chopper pad, but I must have been pretty much of a blank to everybody else. All I wanted to do was help one guy, just do as little as I could, and get away from it. I tried to help a grunt in shock get off the chopper, but when I reached for his M-16 and rucksack it was like lock and load on me. He wouldn't let me take that rifle away from him, so I just grabbed his rucksack and another one that belonged to somebody else.

The recon platoon had lost one man killed and three or four wounded in an ambush. I was scared by what I saw at the chopper pad—very scared—and I remember thinking, "What the hell have I gotten into here?" The next day, I caught a ride on a Huey going out to a firebase, getting closer with each hop to joining the recon platoon. I spent one night at the firebase, loaded down with ammo, hand grenades, and Claymores. Even with all that ordnance hanging on me, I didn't feel very secure when we got mortared after sundown. Talk about being green . . . I huddled in a foxhole while everybody else stood up to watch the show. Later during that miserable night, the first sergeant told me to be at the chopper pad at six a.m.

"Jesus Christ," I thought. "How much farther out do I have to go?" I don't know where the resupply chopper took me. I only know that I got off at an LZ with a lot of jungle and bamboo around it. I was still carrying a Claymore in a green bag hanging around my neck when I checked in with the recon platoon.

The chopper was bringing them food and water and me, fresh meat. Everybody was pretty quiet because of what the platoon had gone through the day before, but the war was still on and I went out on my first patrol that very day. We moved out at ten a.m. and I don't remember how far we walked, only that I was hot and exhausted when we stopped at five p.m. to set up for the night.

"Since you're the new guy," my squad leader said, "I'm going to give you first watch."

"All right," I said. "How long does a watch last?"

"An hour and a half."

Everybody but me stretched out at six p.m. to get some sleep. I figured I would be off watch at seven-thirty p.m. so I could get some sleep myself until I went back on watch at eleven p.m. As luck would have it, I went to sleep after my first watch and slept until two a.m. the next morning. Did I ever catch it the next day from the squad leader. I never made that mistake again.

I was what the troops called a "shake-and-bake" noncom. I had gone through a school to become an E-5; most other NCOs had come up through the ranks. When I got out in the field with the 2/5th Cav, I was just another E-5 coming in who didn't know anything about combat in Vietnam. That didn't go over very well with PFCs who'd been in the bush for four to seven months. Some of them made little wisecracks about my rank and inexperience, but I didn't let them bother me. In fact, I was just another grunt for a while in a platoon that had only twelve men in it, with a second lieutenant and a staff sergeant in charge. I noticed that Lieutenant Smith treated his men well. In return, they respected him not only for his fairness, but for his courage. He had plenty of it.

The day after I joined the platoon, we killed five dinks. Again, we had walked almost all day. Nothing out of the ordinary had happened. While we were setting up our night position, somebody passed the word that some dinks were in an open space about a hundred yards from where I was. All of a sudden, the war broke loose. Some of the guys about fifteen feet from me cut loose with an M-60 and M-16s and killed the dinks just as the sun went down. It was over and done with before I really knew what was going on.

I was scared that Charlie would come down hard on us that night. Usually, we sent a party out to check bodies for maps and other documents, but Lieutenant Smith didn't want to risk having any of us get caught in the open. We waited until the next morning to check the bodies. That was the first time I had ever seen a dead person. One of the guys grabbed a gook's arm to turn him over, and the gook's arm came off—I mean, it came right out of his shirt sleeve. The GI started beating the dead gook with his own arm. The other guys got in the mood and pretty soon they had a little celebration going on. I'm sure their euphoria came from feeling they had made Charlie pay dearly for his ambush of the platoon a couple of days earlier.

The dead gooks weren't NVA. They were boys near our age, maybe nineteen or twenty. Most likely they were VC, and I say that because they were wearing old, raggedy pajamas and straw hats. They were armed with AK-47s, SKS rifles, and a few hand grenades. The other guys in the platoon took the weapons and some personal articles off the bodies for souvenirs. There was no mutilation of the bodies, other than the arm that came out of its socket. All I wanted to do was get away from there.

As a reconnaissance outfit, we weren't really supposed to mix it up with Charlie. We were sort of like the old Indian scouts, looking but not fighting. We went through a lot of thick jungle with "wait-a-minute" vines, bamboo, and big trees. We carried a lot of C-rations in our packs, but my appetite in Vietnam was never very good. I liked the fruit and pound cakes and the beans and wieners, but the rest of it I usually didn't eat; I don't know why. When I went to Vietnam, I weighed 185 pounds; when I came home, I weighed 125. Maybe it was because some of the C-rations were dated 1952—that was Korean War vintage.

In April of 1970, we were doing our usual thing in III Corps, walking through the jungle looking for Charlie, when we got word on the radio that Hueys were coming in to pick us up. All we knew was that we were being flown to a new location. The choppers dropped us off at a huge field covered with other helicopters and tanks. GIs were everywhere. It looked like an invasion army, and in fact, it was. A few minutes after we got there, a colonel started barking orders over a microphone, saying President Nixon had ordered us to go into Cambodia.

"Most of you won't be coming back," the colonel said. Very melodramatic, or at least the colonel wanted it to sound that way. After his little speech, we were told to load up with everything we could carry and get ready to move out about ten a.m. The big Chinook choppers were already loaded with tons of ammo, food, and other supplies.

Most of the Cav troopers were really upset. Some of them were hollering, "My orders say Vietnam. They don't say nothing about Cambodia. I can't go." Lieutenant Smith seemed to consider the whole thing just another job. I don't remember that he gave us a pep talk or really ever said much about going into Cambodia.

Personally, I was extremely uneasy about going over the border. That's where Charlie had his big base camps and staging areas for attacks into Vietnam, but I scrambled into a Huey with six other guys and we went a click or two across the border to set up for the night. The engineer battalion already had some bulldozers there pushing up dirt for a firebase perimeter. Thank God, the night was peaceful.

At about eight a.m. on the second day, my platoon made contact with some NVA. We were walking along the base of a ridgeline when we suddenly heard people talking. As we moved very quietly up the ridge and closer to the voices, we saw five men in NVA uniforms who had women and children with them—their wives and kids, for all I know. They were sitting around a camp in the woods, about thirty feet from us, eating rice. Oddly, I remember thinking they shouldn't be eating breakfast that late in the morning. Maybe that was because we always got moving about six a.m.

Lieutenant Smith told us to form a line so we could fan the whole camp with M-60s, M-16s, M-79s, and hand grenades. At his signal, we cut loose on them—NVA, women, and kids. They screamed and yelled and tried to run for their weapons in the midst of all the noise and explosions. A few of them made straight for the woods and we never saw them again. I don't think a one of the NVA ever got a shot off at us.

It was over in thirty seconds. We walked into what was left of the camp and found five NVA bodies. We also saw the bodies of three or four women dressed in *ao dais* and sandals, as well as the bodies of three kids who were a couple of years old at most. I don't remember what the kids were wearing, but they may have been barefoot. It was hard to remember details in the euphoria that followed a firefight. I do remember, though, that a few women and children got away in all the smoke and confusion.

We gathered up all the weapons we could carry. Then we set fire to everything else in the camp—tents, a small hootch, and a cache of rice. We left the bodies where they were and moved on. I don't think it bothered anybody that women and children were caught up in the firefight. That was just part of the Vietnam War. The way we saw it, they were collaborating with the enemy. The women and kids were in the wrong place at the wrong time. Now, we wouldn't have intentionally killed those kids if they had been there by themselves. They were just in the way. We couldn't distinguish between them and everybody else in the heat of a firefight. In a firefight, you start shooting and keep on shooting until it's over.

The Cav stayed in Cambodia for two months. It was no different from Vietnam so far as my platoon was concerned. We never walked on a trail, we didn't make any unnecessary noise, and we didn't pitch any tents at night or sleep in hammocks. We slept on the ground in camouflaged positions. In other words, we didn't take chances.

When the Cav brought supplies out to us on a Huey, it made sure we had plenty of razors and water. We even had a barber, a black guy out of the stockade on good behavior, who came out once in a while on the resupply chopper. Getting clean clothing was another matter. In fact, during my first three months in the bush, I wore the same boots, the same shirt, the same pair of pants, the same socks. At night, we'd all take off our boots and socks and try to let our feet get dry. That's about all we could do, considering that it rained so much.

I had a bit of trouble with a second lieutenant who replaced Lieutenant Smith. The new LT was fresh out of OCS and he was determined to show us how to fight the war. I had been in the bush for five months by that time, and I knew a few things about combat, too. One day, the lieutenant wanted us to walk down a road while we were on a patrol. I told him I wouldn't do it. Walking down a road was just asking for trouble.

"You go ahead and walk down that road," I said. "I'm going over here about two hundred meters in the woods and walk parallel to the road." He said he would have me court-martialed if I didn't follow his orders. "Do it," I told him. "I'd rather be court-martialed than go down that road and get killed because of your stupidity." To my surprise, he actually listened to me. We moved over to the woods and away from the possibility of an ambush.

We found some huge NVA training areas and arms caches while we were in Cambodia. Some of the training areas even had soccer fields. In big hootches, we sometimes came across full-size bamboo mockups of our tanks and helicopters. The mockups pointed out their weak spots and were used to train gunners, I suppose. I remember finding little medallions at one of these places that depicted an NVA soldier standing in a field and shooting down an American helicopter in flames. Another medallion showed a soldier attacking a tank.

The NVA were always gone when we went into their training bases. When we first went in, we grabbed all the documents we could find and sent them to the rear on a helicopter. Then we combed the place for souvenirs and burned it down. Going through those bases was fascinating, but I could never understand how the NVA managed to live in such primitive conditions.

While I was in Cambodia, I kept seeing guys with less time than I had in the bush get reassigned to the rear. With Nixon still talking about getting the troops out of the war, nobody wanted to be the last one killed over there. Since I had put in more than my share of time in the bush, I started to pull some strings to land a job in the rear. I remembered a buddy back at Bien Hoa, a company clerk that I had gone to NCO school with.

"Don't worry," he said, "I'll get you out of the woods. It might take a couple of weeks, but I'll get you out."

I was going to Taiwan for a week on R&R, so I stopped by to see him when I got to Bien Hoa to catch my flight. He said the liquor manager's job at the Bien Hoa PX had opened up. "Do you think you want it?" he asked me. "Hell, yes, I'll take it," I said. I was ready to take anything to get out of the bush. He called up my battalion commander, a lieutenant colonel, on the radio and started talking to him like he was trading a car. It was hard for me to believe what I was hearing—a deal was being worked out for me. My buddy offered three PFCs for me, but the colonel said, no, Sergeant Spooner is an experienced NCO and very valuable to the reconnaissance platoon. By the time the bargaining was over, I found out I was worth five PFCs and three shake-and-bake NCOs who had just come in-country.

Working at the Bien Hoa PX was great duty. I only worked from ten a.m. until three p.m.; the rest of the time I could do whatever I wanted to. To make it even better, Bien Hoa was an air force base and those people lived better than the army ever did. I even had my own little room in a hootch cleaned every day by a *mamasan*.

I spent two months at Bien Hoa before going home on early release. You could get out of the service three months early if you were going back to school. I had decided to go back to the junior college in St. Pete, so I came back to Oldsmar in December of 1970 and essentially took up where my civilian life had left off. I went back to work at Sears and lived with my parents.

One of the first things I noticed after getting back was that nobody wanted to talk about Vietnam. I did. I really wanted to talk about it, but anytime I brought the war up in a conversation, the other person would usually say, "That's in the past. Don't you want to forget about it?"

I got married in September of 1971, nine months after I got back from Vietnam. The marriage lasted fourteen years and produced two kids, but I think it began to come apart as early as 1975, when we were living in Winter Haven. I was the manager of a couple of gift shops there, but on the day Saigon fell, I was alone at home, watching the news reports on television. What I was seeing was almost too much to bear. I broke down and cried, an unusual emotional response for me. I mean, I just cried my eyes out because the whole war at that very moment seemed such a total, incredible waste to me.

My wife was due home in a few minutes. I washed my face and tried to look like I was all right when she walked through the door. I didn't want her to know that I had been crying. She had never shown much interest in knowing what I had been through in Vietnam; she would pretend to listen when I tried to talk about it. In her own way, she was like everybody else: forget Vietnam.

We later moved to Houma, Louisiana, where I worked for five years for a tugboat company. My dad had worked for the same firm and liked it; I did, too, because I got to travel a lot to Central and South America. Unfortunately, the work was better than my marriage, which was slowly coming apart. My wife and I finally split up in 1982.

I came back to Oldsmar and it seems that a lot of things simply haven't worked out for me. I learned that it's hard enough to get a job when you're forty years old, but when you write "Vietnam veteran" on a job application, that's the end of it. I finally went to the Vet Center in Tampa to ask for help after one particularly bad day about a year and a half ago, a day when I hit rock bottom emotionally. I still go over there every Tuesday night to meet with a group of five veterans.

The Vet Center has made a big difference in my life. I never realized until I started going there that I was treating a job interview as a combat assignment. I didn't have any problems getting dressed in the morning to go to an interview, nor did I have any trouble getting to it. But once I got to a company or office, I'd freeze up—I couldn't even get out of the car. You know, it really was like Vietnam: get your stuff together, take a nice helicopter ride somewhere, but once you land, you get scared.

I think a lot of the other problems that I'm working through go back to the war, too. For a long time, I didn't recognize them—anger, hate, emotional shutdown—as learned responses from combat training. I've come to believe we vets should have undergone some kind of debriefing or deprogramming after we came back from the war. That's where the government really failed Vietnam veterans.

In addition to everything else, I'm trying to deal with my feelings about the Vietnamese. I just can't stand those people. There are a lot of them in the Tampa area but I don't deal with them. They didn't want us in Vietnam—they didn't even want their own country. They wouldn't fight for it, but now they get to come to the United States, where our government helps them live ten times better than they did in Vietnam. I look at them and think that a third of all the homeless people in the country are Vietnam veterans.

I was proud to be a soldier. I'm not ashamed of having been drafted and sent to Vietnam, but the way we were treated when we came back . . . even some of the old-line veterans organizations didn't want to have much to do with us. This country will spend a million dollars to help save a couple of whales in Alaska, but it doesn't seem to want to help the people who fought for it get a decent standard of living and a good place to live.

Garland C. "Pete" Hendricks

Wake Forest, North Carolina

Marine fighter-bomber pilot,

1970–71

•

The sign at the entrance to Pete Hendricks's homestead just outside the Southern Baptist Seminary town of Wake Forest reads, "Welcome to Jenkins Road. Enjoy your visit but please don't stay." Pete and his wife, Robin, live in a twenty-two hundred square-foot, flat-roof barn that he converted into a comfortable, if rustic, home several years ago when he took up housebuilding. Both savor the privacy of country living, but for Pete, being surrounded by the woods has a deeper and more profound attraction. In the solitude of this place he wrote a semi-autobiographical novel, *The Second War*, published by Viking-Penguin in 1990, as his way of coming to terms with the war.

"It's about a young man from a small town in North Carolina who joins the marines, goes to Vietnam, and comes home to deal with 'all of that,'" Pete told me as his two dogs, Sally Jane and Company C, debated whether to make peace with the stranger who had invaded their territory.

If housebuilders who live in the woods and write as a sideline are supposed to resemble Henry David Thoreau, then Pete Hendricks certainly does. Perhaps that was why it was so hard at first for me to imagine him as a marine pilot who flew two hundred bombing missions—a hundred more than he had to—over Vietnam in 1970–71.

Pete's journey to war began when he was an indifferent student at Wake Forest University in the mid-sixties. One day he went to see the navy's Blue Angels put on a show of precision flying at the Winston-Salem airport.

"After the show was over," he said as we relaxed in his kitchen, "I walked through the security line at the airport like I knew what I was doing. I spotted a marine pilot lying against the landing gear of one of the

F-11 Tiger jets that was about to be refueled. So I crawled under the belly of the airplane and asked him what I had to do to be a marine pilot."

In 1965, a recruiter for the navy came to Wake Forest. He offered to give me and several other students an eight-hour test that supposedly would tell the navy whether we had the spatial orientation and brains to fly an airplane. As an inducement to take the test, he said, we would get a ride in a little T-34 trainer. Frankly, I thought the test was a piece of cake. When I went up for my hour-long ride, it consisted mostly of aerobatics, but the pilot let me take the controls for a while and we were both surprised to learn that I could fly the airplane. I mean, I had a natural feel for it. So what eventually drew me into the Marine Corps was not the mystique of the corps itself, but flying.

I had two years left at Wake Forest. By 1966, I still hadn't found anything I was interested in academically and my grades showed it. I looked around at all the professors and the other students and came to the conclusion that none of them had ever done anything. So much was going on in the world at the time—Vietnam, the Civil Rights movement, politics—and I didn't see a soul who had done anything. I finally said, "This ain't for me." I took a job that summer with the U.S. Forest Service out in Arizona to help thin timber and suppress fires. While I was there, I decided I didn't want to go back to Wake Forest in the fall, so I hustled down to the Marine Corps recruiting office in Mesa one Saturday morning and signed up for four years.

It was that simple. When I told the recruiter I wanted to fly jet airplanes, though, he laughed and said the odds were ten thousand to one. Eighteen months later, I showed him my lieutenant's bars and orders to flight school.

I put in for flight training in 1968 while I was in OCS at Quantico Marine Base in Virginia, but the pipeline was full of navy and marine pilot trainees at the time—there was a year-long backlog—and I ended up going to an air force base in Del Rio, Texas. This turned out to be a good deal, because marine pilots trained by the air force were guaranteed to get jets. If you got trained by the navy, you might end up flying helicopters or cargo planes. From Del Rio, I went to Cherry Point Marine Air Station in North Carolina for training in the A-6 Intruder, a two-man, twin-engine jet. It was a subsonic attack bird and one great airplane. I loved it because it had the best mission in the marines, which was low-level interdiction at night and in bad weather.

My orders for Vietnam came through in March of 1970. I had figured ever since joining the marines that I would be going to Vietnam. After all, that's where the flying was; it certainly wasn't in this country. I mean, you could sit down there at Cherry Point and fly training missions every third day for the rest of your life. It was the marines in Vietnam who had the airplanes, the maintenance, the spare parts. I never carried a live bomb until I got to Vietnam. In fact, I had made only one dive bombing run at night, a scary thing to do, but I was still certified as combat-ready. I wanted to get to Vietnam and really learn how to do it.

I was aware of the antiwar feeling in the country at the time, but I didn't pay a lot of attention to it. As I saw it, once I had started identifying with the fighter-pilot mentality, I had gone beyond all the little guys. There's a lot of truth in all the "right stuff" talk that's come out in the last few years about jet airplane drivers. I didn't really care what the war protesters were saying and doing. I realize it's an arrogant thing to say, but I believed they were lesser creatures than I was. That kind of arrogance has to be implanted in a pilot for him to strap an airplane to his back day after day. A pilot has to believe he isn't going to die.

In a way, I was lucky to get posted to Vietnam. A lot of pilots were being sent to the West Coast or Japan in 1970 because the American part of the war was winding down. I got one of the last marine pilot slots at Danang air base, with VMA-225. Since my squadron flew mostly night missions, my navigator and I usually got our target assignments at four o'clock in the afternoon. Sometimes we would draw a hard target, but other times we'd get what was called an armed reconnaissance mission, which meant we could go hunting for targets of opportunity. After the briefing, we would go eat supper, have a couple of drinks, and hit the sack for a few hours of rest before our scheduled takeoff time. It wasn't unusual to take off at one o'clock in the morning.

I dropped bombs in support of the Cambodian invasion on my first missions. I spent a week on that and remember the time frame well, because that's when those kids were shot at Kent State. After Cambodia, most of my flying was over southern Laos and northern South Vietnam, sometimes on missions planned with the help of a computerized monitoring system on the Ho Chi Minh Trail. Sensors planted along the trail by the Igloo White project radioed seismic data to an orbiting aircraft, which then sent the data on to a computer center in Thailand. Igloo White could tell us when and where the North Vietnamese were driving trucks along the trail, at least some of the time, so we could go in with A-6s and pick out individual targets with our radar.

Flying the A-6 was sort of like playing an airborne video game. My navigator and I both had cockpit displays that looked like little television screens. In fact, everything in the A-6 was so computerized that it was just a matter of following the symbols on the screens to achieve precise flying. Even the flight controls required only a soft touch to maneuver the airplane, but it could still be a very exciting ship to fly.

On most of our combat hops, we would leave altitude and make a twelve- to fifteen-mile run in on the trucks, gun emplacements, or whatever the target was. Of course, that's when the NVA liked to send up a barrage of Triple A, usually from 23mm and 37mm guns. These guns fired tracers that were red, white, or yellow, depending on which country they were made in. Just like fireworks, they left a little puff of white smoke in the sky when they exploded. Most of the time, we flew straight through these barrages, which could make the air so turbulent the A-6 would begin to shake. But, really, the flak was more or less a big light show, especially on night missions. Sometimes we would count the rounds coming at us. We knew there were six rounds in a clip, and that each one would get closer to the front of the aircraft than the next one. When the third one barely missed the canopy, I would raise my feet because I figured the fourth one was going to come right through the belly of the airplane.

As we closed in on the target, the radar-directed guns started firing. These were 57mm and 85mm guns, and once in a while big 100mm guns that could reach up to forty-five thousand feet. Radar-directed guns could train on us as soon as we started rolling in on the target. So with guns of all sizes cutting loose as we went in, it wasn't unusual to draw a hundred rounds of Triple A during a night mission. The truth is, we really didn't notice it that much. We were more concerned with hitting the target.

After a while, I got paired with Randy West, a navigator from Sanford, North Carolina. We were both southern grits and that became our call sign. We were the Grit Flight. Randy didn't get to see much of the countryside because he usually had his head down looking at the targets on his display console. Every now and then, I'd say, "Hey, Randy, look outside." He'd take a quick look at all the flak bursting around us and growl, "Don't tell me about that shit." I was the one who had to sit there and look at it.

Probably the worst time we had with flak was near the Ho Chi Minh Trail in Laos. Randy and I had flown over the area several times before without much response from the North Vietnamese. On this hop, though, we must have drawn three or four hundred rounds of Triple A before we even got to the target, and we couldn't figure out why. There wasn't much traffic on the trail that night. We went ahead and unloaded on the target and it blew up for a week, just eating up the whole side of a mountain. We had bombed a huge petroleum storage area.

It was unusual for our aircraft to take a hit because we always came in so fast and low on our way to the target. On top of that, we flew mostly at night and in bad weather. All the NVA gunners could hope for most of the time was a barrage hit unless they had good radar. Of course, we carried some electronic countermeasures gear and aluminum chaff to jinx the radars on the big Triple A guns. It was a bit like hide-and-seek. We tried to fool them into punching holes in the sky in places we weren't.

The only results we ever saw of most of our missions came from the RF-4B reconnaissance birds that went out every morning to photograph the area we had hit during the night. It was unusual to get photos that showed very much destruction, though once in a while we could see five or six trucks burned to hell.

We got very few opportunities to fly into North Vietnam, and certainly never beyond the Red River, which would have taken us within range of the big SAM sites. We only encountered MiGs one time over North Vietnam. I saw them, but they couldn't see us because we were down low on a daytime hop. I called in their location on the guard channel and I'll bet thirty of our fighters pounced on the poor bastards. I mean, marine, navy, and air force fighters were all over the sky.

Some guys didn't come back from the type of missions my squadron flew. It was a game, but a serious one. I always knew there was a possibility it could happen to me. But when somebody did get killed, there really wasn't much of a ripple among the pilots. The first thing that had to be done was taking care of the guy's personal possessions. One of the pilots in the squadron usually accompanied his property home. Not the body, the property. Pilots didn't leave bodies to be picked up and sent back to the states. But my squadron really didn't lose very many people. We had the hottest job and the lowest fatality rate because, as I said, it was so hard to hit us.

We lived well at Danang. Our Quonset huts were air-conditioned because we had to sleep during the day. And the food was great. We used to send a C-130 down to Australia on Saturday to get fresh lobster and steak for Sunday. In addition to all that, Randy and I used to take an airplane over to Ubon Air Base in Thailand every month for three days of unofficial R&R. My squadron kept a crew at Ubon all the time. We flew the ship to Ubon and the crew that was there would take it back to Danang. Three days later, somebody else would bring the airplane back, and we'd fly it home. For the most part, we just took it easy at Ubon, eating, drinking, and swapping war stories with the air force fighter jocks there.

The big deal in Vietnam was to get a hundred missions. I did it in five months. I had heard of guys in other outfits who had racked up two hundred missions, but nobody in my squadron had done that. I started working on two hundred missions just for the hell of it. After I made that decision, I went down to Australia in January of 1971 for my second R&R. But after I got back to Danang, I started to notice that something was changing inside me. My enthusiasm for combat flying was fading, and I think a big marine operation west of Danang had a lot to do with it. This operation called for a lot of suppression bombing before a reinforced battalion of grunts could be flown in on helicopters. My squadron was supposed to hit some NVA hot spots with two-thousand-pound bombs. I remember talking to a couple of other pilots about the insanity of sending the grunts into that area. You see, we all knew the only reason the grunts were going in was so the colonel could get a Legion of Merit with a V device for organizing and executing a successful combat operation. He was risking the lives of fourteen hundred men to make general.

I led the strike. Now, dive bombing during the day wasn't my squadron's forte, but the operation needed people who could drop two-thousand-pound bombs in a high dive. It was very windy that day and even a bomb that weighed a ton wasn't immune to wind. OV-10s marked the target with smoke rockets and I rolled in to drop two bombs. I could see a lot of choppers down below and I knew the colonel was in one of the control ships watching everything that was going on. I missed the target and really didn't care what he or anybody else thought about it.

"Oh, great," I said to myself. "Maybe they'll go home." It was the first time I had thought that way.

I was concerned about the grunts because I had spent some time with them on the ground. The marines had a program that sent pilots out to the ground units and brought ground commanders into the squadron for a few days. These swaps were supposed to help coordinate close air support. I went out to the boonies twice for three-day stints with the guys who called in airstrikes. In my clean green utilities, I must have looked pretty strange to the grunts.

"If you walk out here on a patrol in a green suit, you're going to get in the can before anybody else," one of them told me. "Here, have some mud."

Randy and I never got shot down in Vietnam, but we did have to crash-land an A-6 at Danang in December of 1970. We had been out on a daytime dive-bombing hop. I did a six-G pullout after dropping the bombs and jinxing to get away from some .50-calibers the NVA were firing at us. As I jinxed to avoid the tracers, the airplane started to come apart, or so I thought. I put the nose up and kept our speed below 225 knots to hold down the vibration. I called in battle damage to Danang tower when I discovered I couldn't get the left landing gear down. I dumped all my extra fuel and popped my bomb racks off to make sure the bottom of the aircraft was clean. Danang had sprayed the right lane of the runway with foam and had fire trucks all over the place as I breezed the jet in.

"I sure wish we were rabbit hunting back in North Carolina," Randy said over the intercom.

I let the airspeed bleed as I eased my left wing down onto the runway. There was a lot of noise as we slid along, but no fire or threat of an explosion. In fact, I flew the airplane the next day on a test hop. The shop fixed it overnight. The left landing gear had gotten hung up on the gear doors. It was a simple hydraulic sequencing problem. Somebody told me a gunnery sergeant hit the gear with a sledgehammer and it fell down. So much for all the excitement.

By the time I had two months left in-country, I was getting very tired of flying combat hops. I realized I needed a change, so I moved over to being the squadron test pilot. It was good duty: I took airplanes coming out of the Danang repair shops and flew them over the South China Sea for an hour, just doing aerobatics for the fun of it, to check them out.

I didn't really want to leave Vietnam. I thought so then and I think so now: it was an exciting, dramatic place to fly an airplane. There was a tremendous amount of spirit among the marine airplane drivers that I didn't want to leave. But my whole squadron was ordered home, and there was nothing we could do about it except take twenty-six days to fly across the Pacific. Each time we'd stop somewhere—the Philippines, Guam, Midway, Wake Island, Hawaii—everybody would get drunk. God, we stayed in the Philippines for a week, Guam for a week, Wake three days, Hawaii four days. It was a party, a real party.

We landed at El Toro Marine Air Station in California and actually had a welcome-home ceremony. It was a big deal to have a whole squadron of three hundred enlisted men, twelve airplanes, and twenty-four aircrewmen come in. The people at El Toro had rounded up a bunch of generals to greet us, but I think we were more interested in the garbage cans full of ice-cold beer. Still, it was a very nice thing to do.

The only civilian clothes I had when I got back to the states was what I called my cowboy suit, Levis, shirt, and boots. The first time I tried to go off base in that outfit, the young enlisted marines at the gate started giving me all kinds of grief. My hair was a little too long and I had on Levis. Everything about my appearance was so against the rules that they wouldn't let me off the base. I had to go into a nearby building to see the gunnery sergeant, who promptly asked to see my ID. Of course, when he saw I was a captain, he jumped up and it was "I'm sorry, sir," this and that. But he made it clear that I couldn't go off base in my Levis.

I thought, "Wait a minute. Something's wrong here." The incident at the gate made me realize that I was no longer in a combat situation. That feeling got stronger after I took some leave and rejoined the squadron at Cherry Point to help train new pilots. Now I had to file flight plans, get position reports—the whole structure of flying had changed. I wasn't allowed to get in "belly time," which was flying right over the treetops of eastern North Carolina at five hundred knots. It wasn't fun anymore. There were too many rules. I was used to only one rule: hit the target.

I went down to be the operations officer at Bogue Field, an auxiliary base on the coast near Morehead City, North Carolina. It was a pretty good deal. I rented a little house, got a dog, and bought a pickup truck. I spent my days at the base and went home at night to cook supper for me and my dog. I did that for two years. I still flew once in a while to keep my flight status, but basically I got out of professional flying.

I started coming home to Wake Forest on the weekends in 1972 to build a barn on fifteen acres that I bought with twenty thousand dollars in savings from Vietnam. It was clear to me that I was losing interest in the marines, so I finally decided to get out in October of 1974. I had put in eight years and two days. The truth is, I was ready to get out. I just couldn't handle all the rules. One of my problems—and this is true of any enlisted man who becomes an officer—was my concern for the men who worked for me at Bogue Field. I bent the rules for them, loaned them money and that sort of thing, and my superior officers didn't like that. I had two hundred men working for me, and if any rules came down from above that I didn't think were in the best interest of the men, or that I thought wouldn't work, I ignored them.

Not long before I left the marines, I bought a second place, an eighteen-acre farm, near Wake Forest. It had sixteen thousand laying hens, so I went straight from the marines on a Friday to picking up eggs on the following Monday morning. I was also married by this time. My wife and I remodeled the farm house, and even though I knew very little about carpentry, I didn't consider that a problem. I felt no restraint on my ability to do whatever I set out to do—a holdover from driving airplanes. It was while I was living on the farm, incidentally, that I first got involved in politics. I took it upon myself to shape up the local soil and water conservation group. I hit one brick wall after another trying to do that, but I just moved up to the next level and knocked down what had been in the way. Within five years, I was writing speeches for former governor Bob Scott, who had decided to reenter politics.

And that's when everything started to fall apart. My wife and I split. I had to sell the farm because I had been spending too much time in politics and too little on the farm. Another shock came when Bob Scott didn't win the Democratic nomination for governor. It was then that post-traumatic stress disorder crept into my life. I'd never had any indication of it before. I think my problem was that I had never thought much about Vietnam. The whole time I was out here in Wake Forest farming, I never thought much about being in Vietnam. I didn't even think much about flying. It was just a part of my life that had happened and was over. But suddenly there was PTSD. I came out here to this place and stayed in it a year; I didn't work, I didn't do anything. One of my sisters brought me food. I was depressed for a year and I didn't understand that it had anything to do with Vietnam. I was just content to sit here and stagnate.

I finally realized I had to do something. I went over to the VA hospital in Durham and told them I wanted to talk to somebody. You see, I had never really talked to anybody about the war since I got back from Vietnam, so I really didn't know what I was looking for at the VA. In one of the luckiest breaks of my life, they sent me down to see a psychiatric resident named Don Ross, a young fellow, very sharp. We talked for a while and he asked me to come back a week later. When I did, he took me up to the mental ward. That place was right out of *One Flew Over the Cuckoo's Nest*. I mean, men were sitting around just looking far off in the distance or else concentrating totally on some insignificant detail like examining their fingers. If Ross took me up there as a kind of shock treatment, it worked. I think he somehow knew I could get beyond PTSD without any organized treatment—that if I understood what it was, I could deal with it.

I started to get out and do things again. It didn't stop the depression—that could still go on for days—but it did stop my withdrawal from life. Then in 1981 a sister who lives near Columbia, South Carolina, became concerned enough to sort of take me in. I was thirty-five years old.

Looking around for something worthwhile to do in Columbia, I went over to the University of South Carolina and signed up for a fiction-writing course. I knew something about writing from my work with Bob Scott. To my surprise, the whole process of PTSD started to unravel after

I started work on a semi-autobiographical novel about politics and Vietnam.

I came back up here after several months in South Carolina and built a little one-room shack to live in. I had rented out the house as a way to get some income. About this time I met Robin, and we just fit together perfectly from the first time I saw her. Even after we got married, though, I continued to use the shack as a place to write. I delivered the Raleigh *News and Observer* every morning seven days a week, which kept my nights free to work on the novel. Later, with the help of Peggy Payne, a novelist who lives in Chatham County, and Angela Davis-Gardner, another novelist who lives in Raleigh, I joined a fiction-writing group at Duke.

It didn't take me long to realize that I was going in the wrong direction with the manuscript. I ended up canning the five hundred pages I had written, four whole years of work, and started over from the beginning. So, it's taken me eight years to produce what I have now.

Except for what can't be purged, writing the novel has cleared my soul of most of whatever was in there. I really don't understand the dynamics of what happened to me, but I do have enough understanding now to control it. Maybe a lot of it goes back to coming home after Vietnam. Wake Forest is like any other small town in the South, a very settled place. In my case, at least, all of the confrontations I had about Vietnam were with people I have known all my life, people I went to grade school with. I'm probably the only one in my high school group who went to the war.

I never talked about what I had done in Vietnam after I came back here. Vietnam was a taboo subject and I knew it. But every now and then, an angry stab would come from a lifelong friend during a conversation. I remember one guy in particular who was drafted but somehow managed to get his status changed. He stayed in law school and went to all the protests and that sort of thing.

I came across him one day when he was half-drunk.

"Why the hell did you do all that? Why did you kill all those people?" he asked me.

I thought to myself, "This guy is my friend. He's got a problem and I'll just let him work it out."

I never said anything in reply to him. I never considered that I had to. I began to feel sorry for people like him. I still considered them lesser creatures, and maybe that was the arrogance of a fighter pilot coming back or maybe it was something else. I don't know. But at that point, I began to think that this guy and a lot of others in my generation had failed. They hadn't met their responsibilities to the country. In fact, I felt they had missed the only chance they'd ever have to define themselves as individuals. I took a lot of hits from them, usually very snide and angry remarks. I remember thinking, "God, these poor fellows just didn't make the grade."

I really consider my generation a failure because it didn't accept its responsibility in the Vietnam War. There are only a few of us who did, and it takes more than a few to fight a war. Most of the people in my generation couldn't face their responsibility, couldn't even face themselves. I think my generation was too pampered—you know, the baby boomers. They're too soft, they have no concept of a common goal as a nation, and as a result the whole country stumbled during the 1960s.

Ironically, the strength that's carried me through all this, the one thing that made me survive, came from my Vietnam experience. Flying combat missions was incredibly demanding. Once I could see I was in that downward spiral of depression and PTSD, my strength came from remembering.

"Well," I said to myself at one point, "this is nothing. I've been through stuff a lot harder than this in Vietnam."

Karen K. Johnson

Little Rock, Arkansas

Women's Army Corps officer,

1970–72

●

The road to Fort Roots VA hospital climbs a steep hill on the wooded north bank of the Arkansas River, just a few miles from downtown Little Rock. A beautifully crafted rock wall built during the 1930s by the Works Progress Administration follows the road for part of its length. The hospital itself, like several others in the VA system, began life decades ago as an army post. The manicured parade ground is still there, as are many of the handsome brick homes on Officers' Row and the stolid, rectangular barracks that housed enlisted men.

I talked to Karen, who served in Vietnam as an army information officer from 1970 to 1972, on a Monday. The Friday before, she had resigned her partnership in a successful law practice to take a nine-month stint as a two-hundred-dollar-a-week field representative at the hospital for Vietnam Veterans of America. When we talked, she was still moving photographs and other personal items into her office, a space hardly larger than a walk-in closet. One of the snapshots, its colors fading toward yellow, showed a blonde dressed in jungle fatigues. It was Karen, standing on a beach somewhere in Vietnam.

After a quick lunch in the hospital cafeteria, Karen and I returned to her office to talk most of the afternoon. She told me she was born in Petersburg, Virginia, the daughter of an army officer who lost his life in France.

"I can distinctly remember when the army brought my father's body back from Europe in 1948. I was four years old and it was a very impressionistic event in my life. He was the youngest son of a family that was very patriotic, and I picked up a lot of that as a child."

Although she earned a degree in journalism from Oklahoma State

University in 1964, Karen was uncertain about what she wanted to do. Newspaper work quickly lost its appeal—"I came to the conclusion very fast that I wasn't going to get rich as a journalist"—and she eventually joined the army to become an officer in the old Women's Army Corps.

"On February 2, 1965, I was sworn into the service and went off to Fort McClellan, Alabama, for WAC officer basic training," she said. "It was the proudest day of my life when I put on the uniform of the United States Army. I was gung-ho and I was doing it for my father."

Fort McClellan at the time was known as Squaw Valley or Menopause Manor—take your pick. WAC training was twenty weeks long and it was run entirely by women. Lt. Col. Elizabeth Hoisington, who eventually became the first woman general in the army, ran the place like a women's finishing school. I mean, we could *never* have creases in the seat of our skirts. After class, we rushed back to the barracks and ironed our skirts so they would be full in formation. It was like a women's West Point. We cleaned our barracks and we polished the floors. After they were polished for an inspection, we didn't walk on them: we jumped from bed to bed to get from one end of the barracks to the other.

It was tough. Everything in our locker drawers had to be folded a certain way. It was a high sin to let the raw edges of a towel face the inspecting officer. I still fold my towels that way. My husband will ask, "Why do you always do this?" I tell him some things never change. Overall, though, I think the training at Fort McClellan was a good experience. I had been an only child at home and lived rather like a slob—I liked to sleep until noon—and the army was a big change from all that.

A lot of rumors were always flying around Fort McClellan about the training program being cut short. Supposedly, a lot of us were to be shipped overseas, maybe even to Vietnam. As luck would have it, a Vietnamese woman officer was in my class. We called her Pinkie because her name in English meant Pink Cloud. Her husband was in the South Vietnamese army and she was very concerned about what was happening back home, but I don't think any of us really understood her anxiety at the time.

After I got my commission, I stayed at Fort McClellan for a year as a platoon training officer. I did go overseas in 1966, but it was to West Germany as part of a backfill operation. The trained troops of the Seventh Army were being pulled out for Vietnam and green ones from the states were coming in to replace them. WAC officers didn't normally go overseas for the first two years of their service; the army wanted us to be mature enough to avoid embarrassing it. But the old ways were changing because of Vietnam. I stayed in Germany until May of 1968 as the commanding officer of the WAC Detachment at Frankfurt. Actually, I held sixteen other titles while I was there: dependent schools officer, mess officer—you name it, I got it.

I was a student in the advanced course for women officers back at Fort McClellan in February of 1970 when somebody came into my classroom and told me I had a telephone call. Of course, it wasn't the army way to leave class for telephone calls, so I asked, "Who died?" I was told to go down to the commandant's office to take a call from a Major Foote at the Pentagon personnel office.

"You're being considered for a very prestigious assignment," the voice on the other end of the line said. "There are three people on the list that hold the correct MOS and credentials. You are at the bottom of the list because you have not been back in the states for two years. If you were selected for this assignment, would you waive the two-year period?"

I said I would, figuring the two people ahead of me would certainly jump at a chance to go back overseas, whatever the assignment was. When assignments were posted in May, my name wasn't on the list to talk to a major who had come down from Washington to hand them out. I managed to get up with her between her interviews with the other officers. "You already have your assignment," she said. "What assignment?" I asked her. Nobody had told me anything. She informed me that I was going to Vietnam. Suddenly, the telephone call back in February meant something. "I sure as hell never got a call back telling me I had been selected," I said. "Oh," she replied, "you were."

I really didn't know much about Vietnam. When I was in Germany, the only newspaper I read was the *Stars and Stripes*, and it didn't carry much news about the war. I was twenty-two years old at the time and having a ball. I was skiing, driving a Fiat sports car, touring castles, and dating a guy that I eventually married. I mean, the war was the farthest thing from my mind. It didn't really hit me until 1968, when one of my cousins was killed over there. Jimmy was a chopper pilot with the 101st Airborne Division. He was shot down in a part of the A Shau Valley where his body couldn't be recovered, which only added to the grief in my family.

As it turned out, the Women's Army Corps had only a few slots for women officers in Vietnam and I was selected for one of them because I had a degree in journalism and good grades. WAC desperately wanted women to serve in Vietnam for future promotions, so in a way a ticket was being punched for the Women's Army Corps. After coming back from Germany, I had gone to the Defense Information School in Indiana and from there to Fort Dix, New Jersey, as the officer in charge of the post newspaper. The paper was selected as the outstanding newspaper in First Army, and now I was about to graduate with honors from the WAC Advanced Course. So I guess my credentials looked pretty good to the people at the Pentagon.

I was pulled out of class and taught how to dig a foxhole, field-strip an M-16 rifle, and fire a .45 pistol. I burned my hand when I picked up an M-16 with a hot barrel and almost lost my right thumb cocking the pistol. I could see right then and there that I was not well suited to the mechanical side of the war.

Before I left for Vietnam, I went home to Oklahoma and filed for divorce because I knew my marriage wasn't going to work out. I also wanted to go to Disneyland, so I went out to Los Angeles a week before my departure date. The night before I was to leave the states, I checked into the Mark Hopkins Hotel in San Francisco, determined, as I had promised myself, to experience some of the pleasures of the world before giving one's body for one's country.

I was supposed to be at Travis by two p.m. the next day to catch a flight scheduled to leave at eight p.m. But you know the army: hurry up and wait. I got up to Travis on time and went through some paperwork only to be told, "OK, be back two hours before flight time." With nothing else to do, I wandered over to the officers' club and met three fellows who, it turned out, were going to be on the plane with me. We were there during Happy Hour. Finally, one of the guys looked down at his watch.

"Oh, my God, we're late for our flight!" he yelled.

We shot out of the club and hailed a taxi. It pulled up to the terminal while all the other passengers were boarding the jetliner. At first, an air force sergeant with no sense of humor said we would be manifested on another flight and charged leave time. I had no objection to that; it meant more time in California. But somebody found a way to get us on the plane—dead drunk.

The plane landed in Hawaii at three a.m. We woke up, found an all-night bar, and put down two pineapple drinks, which turned out our lights until we got to Wake Island—one of the stewardesses later said she was worried if we were still alive. At seven a.m., we came into Wake. Of course, the bars weren't open yet, but we remedied that little problem. We found a liquor store, bought a bottle of booze, and started on bourbon and water.

Next stop, Okinawa. There I had to be on top of things. One of my uncles was a full colonel, the commander of a logistical outfit on the island. He was supposed to meet me at the airport for a short visit, which he did. Before I got back on the airplane, though, the guys and I had a few more drinks. One of the movies on the plane was that John Wayne film about the Green Berets—talk about mental agony!

We got to Saigon about ten p.m. That hot, humid air came rushing into the airplane when the crew opened the doors. The smell was awful. A sergeant who came aboard announced that all GS-15s and above could then deplane. Nobody got up. Then he said all field-grade officers and above could deplane. Nobody moved. And then he said, "Everybody else." It suddenly came home to me that a captain in the United States was somebody, but here I was just another piece of meat. As I walked off the plane, I saw Vietnamese workers scrambling into the belly of the airplane like a bunch of ants. They threw our luggage into old wooden handcarts.

Talk about cultural shock—it was as if I had walked out of a spacecraft onto another planet. I waited in the terminal at Tan Son Nhut, which was an open-air place, very French, until a WAC officer, Lt. Col. Ann Smith, finally came up to me. She said she had been trying to figure out what to do with me—nobody knew what my assignment was. So here I was in Vietnam, me and my ninety-three pounds of luggage, and nobody knew what I was supposed to be doing there.

I stayed at a BOQ that night. Precisely at 6:30 a.m. the next day, Colonel Smith picked me up in an air-conditioned Ford sedan and took me to the processing point. I strutted out to the car in my cords, black high-heeled shoes, and little overseas cap. Everybody else at processing was in boots and jungle fatigues. When I went through a long line to pick up equipment, a sergeant issued me olive-drab boxer shorts.

"What am I going to do with these?" I said.

"Polish your shoes with 'em, ma'am," he replied.

I also picked up two pairs of combat boots, three sets of fatigues, some towels, T-shirts, a hat, and a set of dog tags. Weapons issue was around the corner, but I didn't go there because I figured I was a noncombatant. At least, I had been told that. I went over to a bus with all my gear and waited for everybody else to finish drawing equipment.

A few minutes later, a sergeant came around and asked me what I was doing on the bus. I said I was waiting for the men to come back from weapons issue.

"Ma'am," he said, "do you think somebody over here is going to watch out for you? We've got enough trouble taking care of ourselves. This is not tootsie-footsie land. Go draw a weapon." There was a pecking order for weapons in Vietnam: pilots got .38-caliber revolvers, field-grade officers and above got .45 automatic pistols, company-grade officers and below got M-16 rifles. I was an exception, though. I managed to get a .45 and a shoulder holster—it looked better than web gear.

The army in Vietnam carried a steep learning curve. Nobody in the states had really told me what to expect over there. Suddenly, I had to learn about military payment certificates, which looked like Monopoly money, and ration cards that went all the way down to shoe polish and clothing starch. And I was to wear fatigues every day.

At first, I was assigned to the public information office at MACV Headquarters, a huge metal building at Tan Son Nhut that almost everybody called "Pentagon East." The building was two stories high, had five wings, and was a reasonably comfortable place—it had a snack bar, air conditioning, flush toilets, even an American Express office. I went into a lieutenant colonel's slot to run a newspaper called *The MACV Advisor*, and actually got paid my first month there as a light colonel. When I tried to get the overpayment straightened out, one of the guys in the pay section said it was too hard to do because of taxes and Social Security and everything else, and I shouldn't worry about it until I got back to the real world. And if I didn't get back, it was a problem for my estate.

In 1970, MACV was full of officers from all branches of the military. Almost everybody in the States was begging to go to Vietnam to get his ticket punched. People were fighting each other to get a real working job, and there I was, a WAC captain sitting in a light colonel's slot. Of course, everybody was eyeing it, and who came in to take it but my old boss from Fort Dix, Lt. Col. A. J. "Moose" Nealon. I ended up as the command information officer at USARV in Long Binh. I was simply told one morning that I would be going out there that afternoon. I didn't even have time to pick up my belongings at my BOQ; they were brought out in a car.

Long Binh was a big place, barren and desolate compared to Saigon. The place was all dirt and wooden barracks, and it took forever and a day to get from one side to the other. Company-grade officers lived in forty-man barracks and field-grade officers in thirty-two-man barracks, but colonels and generals rated air-conditioned trailers complete with kitchens and hot water. Thanks to the colonel that I went to work for, I got assigned to a room in an air-conditioned VIP hootch.

I got to see how the other half lived one day when my boss, Colonel Mock, asked me to go to lunch with him over at the general officers' compound. As a member of the commanding general's staff, he had privileges at the general officers' mess. I was never so shocked in my whole life. The generals had little cottages in the compound, which had a fence around it with an MP at the gate. The mess was carpeted. When we got there, the generals were passing out cigars and having brandy before lunch. Enlisted men in spotless fatigues were serving them hors d'oeuvres. For lunch, we had delicious crab legs and ice cream. Those fellows ate well.

There were maybe fifty civilian women at Long Binh, some of them secretaries. USARV decided at one point that it had enough of these women to put them in a field-grade barracks, which was in a rather out-of-the-way part of the post. Naturally, the women protested and tried to pull strings to keep from going out there, but that's where most of them ended up. A few of the lucky ones got assigned to the nurses' quarters at the hospital. I felt a bit isolated at Long Binh because I wasn't part of the WAC detachment there. Most enlisted WACs worked at the Twenty-fourth Evacuation Hospital. There were a couple of field-grade WAC officers around, but they didn't socialize with me, presumably because I was only a captain. On the whole, however, it wasn't as bad as it sounds, because I traveled around the country a lot in my job.

One of my responsibilities was overseeing distribution of the *Stars and Stripes* throughout Vietnam. When I first got to USARV, *Stripes* was printing 100,000 copies a day for about 250,000 troops, so nobody had any trouble getting a copy. Then the General Accounting Office in all its wisdom decreed there should be only one free copy printed for every five people in-country. Well, you've never heard such an uproar in all your life. People either weren't getting the crossword puzzle, or somebody had already worked it. The generals were screaming. The MACV general officers' compound wanted fifty copies every morning, and it fell on me to tell them they couldn't have that many. Imagine how that went over. My boss finally had to veto my decision, and we continued to send fifty copies a day over there—which meant some troopers in the field weren't getting *Stripes* because the generals didn't want to pay a dime for their own copy.

Overseeing the distribution of *Stripes* was a mind-boggling job. For one thing, I had to know where the troops were in Vietnam every day. Not just army, but air force, navy, marines, and everybody else. Where they were and how many there were. The military intelligence people often caused as much trouble as anything else. "I can't tell you where that unit is tonight," somebody would say. "In that case," I told him, "you're not getting any papers." Things would clear up after a couple of days.

Whenever a unit moved in Vietnam, it was my job to see that it got the correct number of newspapers. My goal was to get the paper to a unit on the move within forty-eight hours of publication. *Stripes* was printed in Japan and flown into Cam Ranh Bay at four a.m. every day on a World Airways 707 for distribution to units in the Central Highlands. From there, the plane went to Bangkok before making its dropoff in Saigon and going on to Danang and then back to Japan. It always seemed to break down every morning in Bangkok—never in Danang or Cam Ranh or Saigon. This caused enormous problems because the generals wanted to read their papers at breakfast.

My office kept up with all the shifting troop movements and everything else, including six *Stars and Stripes* bookstores in various parts of the country, with pencil and paper. We had no desktop computers in those days. It was a big operation that cost a lot of money. The Defense Department paid World Airways twenty-four thousand dollars a day to deliver *Stars and Stripes* to Vietnam and Thailand.

There always seemed to be a foulup in the distribution of the paper or in the management of the bookstores, and I usually was the one who had to go work on it. On one such venture to investigate shortages of *Playboy* and *Penthouse* in the bookstores, I rode up Highway 1 from Nha Trang to Chu Lai in a black Ford van driven by a Korean civilian who worked for me. Since my blond hair and freckles didn't exactly mark me as a Vietnamese, I sat in the back in a folding chair, my .45 drawn and ready. Mr. Kim kept up a running commentary on the trip, including a graphic description of how Korean men stay virile by eating dog testicles every August, when male dogs are supposed to be at their peak—I got the message. So did he.

USARV had its own publications like the *Army Reporter*, which was a twelve-page weekly newspaper, and a magazine called *Uptight*. That was a good name, because we were all uptight over there. We also published a weekly post newspaper for Long Binh, which had thirty thousand troops, and a mimeograph news bulletin delivered every day at six a.m. and five p.m. to the mess halls—Long Binh had sixteen of them, as I remember. The bulletin was only a paste-up of wire service stories, but it eventually became very popular throughout the III Corps area. We earned a good reputation for what we were doing and how much we cared about the grunts.

In 1971, *Uptight* magazine was named the outstanding military publication for the army. I flew back to Washington, D.C., in March to accept a big award on behalf of USARV at the State Department. What a shock: one day I was in Saigon and the next I was on the eighth floor of the State Department, mingling with all these officers in their fancy uniforms. One of the perks that came with the award was a two-week internship with the old *National Observer* newspaper. I was given a press pass and sent to the Senate to cover the end-the-war debates. I discovered that I had very mixed emotions about it. I was thinking, "End the war? What will we do?" You know, the war was—that was my job. I think now I should have gone in there and yelled, "Hell, yes!"

But at the time it was mind-boggling to me that anybody would want to end the war. It seemed almost sacrilegious. I mean, we needed to stay there and win it, and now I was watching all these senators arguing back and forth about ending it. What good was it to end the war when so many people were dead? I really couldn't understand what they were doing. I understood what *I* was doing because I was so busy in Vietnam. I had made it my mission in life to see that not only the troops got their copies of *Stars and Stripes*, but that they got them within forty-eight hours of publication. It had become a very important game, a challenge, for me to see how well I could do. I never wanted to be just somebody; I wanted to be the best. Now these people in Washington wanted to shut down my game and my challenge, and I didn't understand why. I thought wars were supposed to end themselves: you win, the other side surrenders, and they break their swords over their knees. The war wasn't supposed to end back here. It was my first exposure to the antiwar movement, and it left me hurting and in turmoil.

The people at the *National Observer* left me alone. They just ignored me, didn't talk to me. I thought some of them would want to know what it was like being a military correspondent in Vietnam or how I liked the internship, but everybody seemed too busy to talk. I felt like an intruder, that I was in their way, so I spent most of my two weeks in the Senate gallery, gathering material for the one article that I had to write as part of the internship.

I went back to Vietnam in April, near the end of my first tour. I was still unsure about what was going on in the states. Everybody in Vietnam talked about going back to the "real world," but the part of it I had just seen didn't make much sense to me. Vietnam was much more organized, much more exciting. It was a place where we worked twelve hours a day, seven days a week, with a little time for relaxation at the officers' club. Although I didn't realize it at the time, Vietnam had become my world.

Forty-three enlisted men worked in the USARV Information Office. At any given time, most of them were out in the bush covering the war. One of these young men was an exceptional reporter. Steve really cared about what was going on in Vietnam. I noticed after a while that our photo supplies were always short, and it turned out that Steve was taking pictures of the grunts in the bush and sending copies to them and their parents. He believed strongly that those of us in the rear owed something to the guys in the line units. Maybe he felt some guilt because he was working out of a big headquarters, where very little happened.

When Lam Son 719, the Vietnamese army's invasion of Laos, got underway in February of 1971, the army moved fifty thousand American troops north to support it. Steve went out for a week to cover that part of the operation. When he came back to Long Binh to drop off his film and write his stories, he asked to go back, even though he was only a week away from DEROS. No one wanted him to go back to Lam Son 719, but he insisted. A day after Steve went north again, the colonel called me in. He said there was a body at the Danang mortuary, and it might be Steve's. I took Steve's dental records to Danang so that the body could be identified. I learned that he had been sitting on top of an APC that hit a mine; the blast came up and blew away the upper part of his body. Graves Registration had tried to find enough pieces to put into a body bag for shipment back to the states.

Steve's death was a low blow for me and everybody else. My office hadn't lost anybody before, and it made all of us feel very mortal. We held a memorial service for Steve at the Long Binh Chapel and took up money for a scholarship fund. For the rest of my tour, I realized that not only could it happen, it did happen, and it didn't make any difference who you were or where you were assigned.

In July of 1971, I agreed to stay for a second tour in Vietnam when the army promised me that I would be at the top of the drop list. In other words, I signed up for another year, but I served only eight months of it. I decided to stay on because I knew how our record-keeping system worked. We still had three filing cabinets full of unit assignments that we had to keep track of for *Stars and Stripes* and the other publications.

With Vietnamization in full swing in 1971, we were winding down the American side of the war. Late that year, when we were about to pull out of the Central Highlands, John Paul Vann, the famous American adviser, called my commanding general and growled about the newspapers not getting to Pleiku—again. The general said he was sick and tired of Vann's complaints and that we would have to figure out what was going wrong.

I caught a plane to Cam Ranh Bay, and then to Nha Trang, checking on the delivery people and other aspects of the system. Then I went on to Pleiku to find out what was going on there. My room was next to John Paul Vann's. In person, I found him to be very nice; he had stocked a small refrigerator in my room with wine and beer. Outside Vann's room, though, there was always an aide or an ARVN guard, and his personal helicopter was never more than a few yards away from the hootch.

As it turned out, I was in Pleiku on a Saturday night, the last night the officers' club was to be open. I thought, "How sad. Think of the people who have been through here, the history of it all." The Fourth Division had been at Pleiku for years. It had fought and bled for all that land, and now we were giving it back. About twenty of us gathered at the club and decided to drink all the booze to mark the occasion. John Paul Vann dropped by for a short while at eight p.m., then went back to his room to work. The rest of us wanted to play. We brought out the dice: whoever won had to put away a drink. At one point, I had twelve drinks stacked up in front of me. Knowing I couldn't handle that much alcohol, I started trying for double or nothing so other people would have to drink my booty. About three o'clock in the morning, when few of us could stand up straight, we discovered that we were all hungry. Somehow we trooped over to the chaplain's hootch to devour some cheese and crackers that his wife had sent him, as well as anything else we could find to eat.

I got back to my hootch about six a.m. A few minutes later, the VC hit Pleiku and all bloody hell broke loose—mortars, rockets, small arms fire. I jumped out of bed, put a flak jacket over my yellow pajamas, plopped a helmet on my head, and grabbed my .45 pistol. I had one boot on and was wrestling with the other one when I said the hell with it. When I got to the door of my hootch, loose boot and pistol in my hands, the chaplain ran by and suggested that we go back to the officers' club and get under the pool table because it had a slate top. I thought that was an excellent idea. Then I saw another officer run by on his way to the bunker. This one didn't have any clothes on. A few moments later, he came running back. It seems an all-girl Korean band was already in the bunker when he rushed into it. This guy ran back through live fire to put his pants on.

I later told him, "Gee, you've got five kids at home. You almost made them orphans by doing that."

John Paul Vann went up in his chopper to direct the perimeter defense during the attack. By seven a.m. we were all in the mess hall having breakfast. Vann toasted us with coffee for a job well done, but he couldn't resist poking fun at the naked major. Other than that, very little was said about the attack. It was almost as if nothing had happened. The attack apparently came about because Charlie had learned that several generals were scheduled to have a pow-wow at Pleiku later that day. They were going to confer about pulling out of the highlands, but the meeting was cancelled and the generals were flown out to reduce the chance of another attack. Maybe it was a good idea. The Caribou transport that I flew out on that morning drew sniper fire on takeoff.

I came back from Vietnam on March 3, 1972, after twenty months in-country. I had applied for law school while I was in Vietnam, but the army said that was not in the best interest of the service, so it sent me to the Army Recruiting Command in Hampton, Virginia. The command later moved to Fort Sheridan, in Chicago, which made all the travel involved in my job even more tiring. Fortunately, I got away from all that in the winter of 1974, when I went to the Command and General Staff College for a couple of weeks to fulfill the residency phase of a correspondence course that I had started in Vietnam. One of the people I got to know at the staff college was Rep. Sonny Montgomery of Mississippi, who was an officer in the National Guard. A wonderful gentleman and a great dancer.

In the summer of 1974, I enrolled at the University of Oklahoma to earn a master's degree in journalism. By 1976, I had the degree, a promotion to major—and a very real emptiness inside. I think I adopted Winona, who was an abused foster child, because of that, and also to make up for some of the abject poverty I had seen in Vietnam.

The late 1970s was a difficult, depressing time. There were several deaths from cancer in my family, including my mother, during those years. I was back in Hampton, Virginia, a long way from home, and I was facing another European tour, which I didn't really want. The best thing that happened to me during this period was meeting Michael, who was an air force communications officer stationed nearby. We became constant companions and decided to marry after Winona finished high school in 1979.

I decided to leave the army in 1980 for several reasons, but chief among them had to be the pettiness of the peacetime military. I know now that I missed the intensity of Vietnam. It's really true that once you've seen war, everything else is anticlimactic.

Since Michael is from Arkansas, he wrangled an assignment before leaving the air force that allowed us to come here, close to both our families. It also allowed me to start law school at the University of Arkansas at Little Rock in the fall of 1980. Very much on the schedule Mike and I had set for ourselves, I went into private practice in 1983 and worked a lot of long days to build up a good-sized firm.

I thought I had put Vietnam behind me. I hadn't even read any books on the war. When one of the Little Rock newspapers interviewed me in 1987 for an article on Veterans' Day, the reporter asked me how I felt about the war. "Well," I said, "I've never thought about it very much." And that was the truth. The paper ran the story on the front page on Veterans' Day. I was asked to give a television interview that night, just because I was a woman veteran. I now think both of those interviews helped me see that a major event—Vietnam—had happened right in front of my face and I hadn't realized it. It's taken me almost twenty years to see the war for what it was.

You know, I wasn't in the states while a lot of the opposition to the war was going on. When I got back in 1972, the draft had been abolished, things were calming down, and I really had formed no opinions on the war. I didn't have any moral outrage about it. The army had said, "It's a fine war, so go kill people, count bodies, and if you don't take your malaria pill, we're going to court-martial you." Nothing seemed wrong to me.

In the last few months, I've become deeply involved in the Vietnam Women's Memorial Project. Senator Dale Bumpers's subcommittee held hearings on the Women's Memorial bill in February of 1988, and I went up to Washington to testify in favor of it. Something had snapped inside of me when J. Carter Brown, the director of the National Gallery of Art, said the next thing somebody would want on the Capitol Mall was a memorial for the canine corps. I had put up with being ostracized for being a Vietnam veteran and having people ask me, "What are you wearing your husband's Bronze Star for?" or "Oh, you must have been a nurse in Vietnam." To speak my piece, I went on television and said all the opposition against the Vietnam Women's Memorial was a disgrace and that women veterans had kept silent long enough.

Going public brought me in contact with other women who had served in Vietnam. I was fascinated to hear about their experiences. They opened up with their feelings. The more they talked about what they had seen, the more sadness I felt about Vietnam. My overall view of it began to change from "it was a fine war for Regular Army officers" to a realization that it was a very sad chapter in the nation's history.

A couple of months ago, I was thinking about all the demands of my law practice, the workdays of sixteen or seventeen hours, as well as everything I wanted to do for the Women's Memorial and Vietnam Veterans of America. I began to feel that practicing law was an infringement on my time, that what I really wanted to do was help Vietnam veterans and learn more about the war. I found that I couldn't say to Diane Evans at the Women's Memorial Project, "Call me back in five years. It will be more convenient then for me to help you." I'm sure a lot of what I have decided to do comes from the suicide of a Vietnam veteran in July of 1988. Carl was a member of our VVA Chapter 184. He was a good organizer who spent a lot of his time traveling around Arkansas, getting other VVA chapters started. He had fought with the First Cav in Vietnam. Carl was the type of man we all looked up to: he was calm and you could talk to him. He had a wife, two teenage kids, a business, and a house on the lake. When I found out what he had done, I was in a state of shock and disbelief.

You know, I sometimes think Vietnam is like a Contac capsule secretly implanted in veterans. It has little beads that explode every so often. And for some of us, they didn't start exploding until much later in life. More than sixty thousand Vietnam veterans have killed themselves since the end of the war, more than the number who died in the war itself. I will tell you that it took a lot of guts for me to go down to the Little Rock Vet Center and talk to Angie Brewi, one of the counselors there. The first two or three visits, I would pretend that I was talking to her about normal things. What I really wanted to say was, "I need to talk to you," but that would have been an admission that something was wrong, and I wasn't about to do that.

Finally, I went to see Angie one day and just said, "Please make me an appointment." We talked for three hours the next day and again for an hour a couple of weeks later. I think talking to her straight, as well as to Michael and some fellow veterans, has helped me get Vietnam in focus.

When I went to my law office last Friday, I told my partners that I had made up my mind to leave the practice. I told them I would sign a quitclaim deed leaving them almost everything except my personal items. I left there at one-thirty p.m. and came over here to the VA hospital to pick up the key to this office. People say, "You gave up a law practice for two hundred dollars a week to work on Vietnam veterans' issues while you have a husband in law school?" Yes, and it's left me feeling better than I have in a long time.

Paul L. Lieberman

Return to Vietnam,

1988

•

Despite the many difficulties involved in traveling to a country that does not enjoy diplomatic recognition by the United States, veterans are beginning to return to Vietnam. Southerners are among them. For some, going back is a way of confronting and perhaps exorcising the ghosts of the war; others are helping to build health clinics and orphanages through groups such as the California-based Veterans Vietnam Restoration Project, which is under the leadership of Fredy Champagne, an Arkansas veteran. Paul Lieberman, whose story was told near the end of this book, was among the first Vietnam veterans to go back. He returned in June 1988 for nine days with Ed Henry and Bob Dalton, both former marines who live in northern Virginia.

The return to Vietnam, Paul said, was an experience that "kept me tripping between past and present."

The flight from Bangkok to Hanoi only lasted ninety minutes. Ed, Bob, and I talked about everything *but* Vietnam. I was very nervous going through customs at the Hanoi airport until one of the agents smiled and said, "Welcome back."

I wanted to see what Vietnam was like after the war, without the American presence. But there was more. In a way, I think I needed to go back to find a part of myself I had left there.

On our second day in Hanoi, I went to the ruins of an old temple at Co Loa Citadel, which dates from the third century A.D. A Vietnamese man about thirty years old who was giving a talk about the place to a group of visitors suddenly stopped in mid-breath and stared at us. It seemed like a minute before he began to speak again.

"My mother and father were killed in the bombings of Hanoi," he said through our interpreter. I could see that he was missing all the fingers on his left hand.

"I don't blame you Americans," he said. "The war is over. It's time for our two countries to reconcile with each other. We must learn to live in peace with each other."

As far as I was concerned, that was absolution for me. His words took away all the guilt, all the feelings that Vietnam had somehow been my fault.

From Hanoi, we flew down to Tan Son Nhut airfield at Saigon, or Ho Chi Minh City, as it's now called. I knew right where I was all the time. We stayed at the Rex Hotel, which had been used by American officers during the war, and we walked over to the Caravelle, where the press used to stay. When we went out on the streets, a lot of Vietnamese crowded around and tried to touch us. I think one of the saddest sights was all the Amerasian kids on the streets. Those are our kids who are still over there. When we abandoned Saigon, we abandoned them, too.

On a day-long side trip to Vung Tau to see the places I had known there, Ed and I drove by Long Binh. All that was left was a huge empty field and two big buildings on a hill, the old USARV headquarters. It really brought me out of the past. Long Binh was gone. It was funny in a way, but the thoughts I had that day were of the good times and the friends that I had known in Vietnam.

And yet, it was almost as if we had never been there.

Glossary

•

AIT. Advanced Individual Training, the next level beyond basic training.

AK-47. Soviet-designed automatic rifle, counterpart of the U.S. M-16 rifle.

APC. Armored personnel carrier.

Article 15. Nonjudicial military punishment, usually administered by a company commander.

ARVN. Army of the Republic of Vietnam.

BAR. Browning Automatic Rifle.

BOQ. Bachelor officers' quarters.

Bouncing Betties. Spring-loaded antipersonnel mines.

Chicom. Chinese Communist.

CIB. Combat Infantryman Badge.

CINCPAC. Commander-in-Chief Pacific, the next command level above MACV.

Claymore. U.S. antipersonnel mine that fired seven hundred steel balls in a fan-shaped pattern.

Composition 4. A military high explosive.

COMUSMACV. Commander, United States Military Assistance Command Vietnam.

DEROS. Date of estimated return from overseas service.

DI. Drill instructor.

EM. Enlisted man.

FADAC. Early computer for artillery fire direction.

Game Warden. U.S. interdiction program on South Vietnamese rivers and other inland waterways.

General Giap. Senior General Vo Nguyen Giap, primary architect of North Vietnamese strategy.

HEAT. High explosive antitank.

Huey. UH-1 transport and medical evacuation helicopter.

Laager. Military vehicles arranged in a circle for protection against attack.

LAW. M-72 Light Antitank Weapon.

M-79. Shotgun-like 40mm grenade launcher.

MAAG. Military Assistance Advisory Group, predecessor of MACV.

MACV. Military Assistance Command Vietnam.

Market Time. Counterpart of Game Warden in coastal waters.

Medevac. Medical evacuation.

Montagnards. Non-Vietnamese tribes in the Central Highlands.

MOS. Military occupational specialty.

Napalm. Jellied gasoline bombs dropped by aircraft.

NCO. Noncommissioned officer.

Ngo Dinh Diem. President of South Vietnam, overthrown and killed during a military coup in November 1963.

NVA. North Vietnamese Army.

Peter pilot. Inexperienced helicopter pilot.

Prick-25. PRC-25 portable radio.

PTSD. Post-traumatic stress disorder.

Reefer. Refrigerator.

RPG. Rocket-propelled grenade.

RTO. Radio-telephone operator.

Sapper. Viet Cong or North Vietnamese demolition specialist.

SOG. Studies and Observation Group, the covert action section of MACV.

SR-71 Blackbird. Fastest and highest-flying reconnaissance aircraft in the world.

USARV. United States Army Vietnam, administrative and logistical headquarters reporting to MACV.

Note: South Vietnam was divided into four military regions: I Corps, the northern tier of provinces; II Corps, the broad middle part of the country; III Corps, the area dominated by Saigon and rubber plantations; and IV Corps, the Mekong Delta.

When the U.S. Army discarded the regimental system in the late 1950s, it tried to continue unit lineage by giving its combat battalions a regimental "parent," such as the First Battalion, Sixteenth Infantry (Regiment). Two to four battalions constituted an army brigade. The marines still had regiments, but did not use the term. The Fourth Marines, for example, were known only by that name, not as the Fourth Marine Regiment.

Index

•

James Wilson is a journalist, editor, and teacher. For sixteen months in 1966 and 1967, he was an army staff officer in Vietnam, where he served with the forward headquarters of the First Cavalry Division in Binh Dinh Province, the Third Brigade of the Fourth Infantry Division in War Zone C, and U.S. Army Vietnam Headquarters in Saigon. He lives in Chapel Hill, North Carolina.

Library of Congress Cataloging-in-Publication Data
Wilson, James Robert 1942–
Landing zones : southern veterans remember Vietnam / by James R. Wilson.
ISBN 0-8223-1041-4
1. Vietnamese Conflict, 1961–1975—Personal narratives, American. 2. Veterans—Southern States—Interviews. I. Title.
DS559.5W57   1990
959.704'38—dc20   90-31859 CIP

DUE DATE